Best, Gary Dean.

To free a people

DATE DUE

_____TO FREE A PEOPLE

Recent titles in
Contributions in American History

Series Editor: Jon L. Wakelyn

The Southern Common People: Studies in Nineteenth-Century
Social History
Edward Magdol and Jon L. Wakelyn

Northern Schools, Southern Blacks, and Reconstruction:
Freedman's Education, 1862-1875
Ronald E. Butchart

John Eliot's Indian Dialogues: A Study in Cultural Interaction
Henry W. Bowden and James P. Ronda

The XYZ Affair
William Stinchcombe

American Foreign Relations: A Historiographical Review
Gerald K. Haines and J. Samuel Walker

Communism, Anticommunism, and the CIO
Harvey A. Levenstein

Fellow Workers ands Friends: I.W.W. Free-Speech Fights as
Told by Participants
Philip S. Foner

From the Old South to the New: Essays on
the Transitional South
Walter J. Fraser, Jr. and Winfred B. Moore, Jr.

American Political Trials
Michal R. Belknap

The Evolution of American Electoral Systems
*Paul Kleppner, Walter Dean Burnham, Ronald P. Formisano,
Samuel P. Hays, Richard Jensen, and William G. Shade*

Class, Conflict, and Consensus: Antebellum Southern
Community Studies
Orville Vernon Burton and Robert C. McMath, Jr.

Toward A New South? Studies in Post-Civil War
Southern Communities
Orville Vernon Burton and Robert C. McMath, Jr.

TO FREE A PEOPLE

American Jewish Leaders and The Jewish Problem in Eastern Europe, 1890-1914

Gary Dean Best

Contributions in American History, Number 98

GREENWOOD PRESS
Westport, Connecticut • London, England

Library of Congress Cataloging in Publication Data

Best, Gary Dean.
    To free a people.

    (Contributions in American history ; no. 98, ISSN
0084-9219)
    Bibliography: p.
    Includes index.
    1. Jews—United States—Politics and government.
2. Jews—Soviet Union—Persecutions. 3. Jews—Romania—
Persecutions. 4. United States—Foreign relations—
Soviet Union. 5. Soviet Union—Foreign relations—
United States. I. Title. II. Series.

E184.J5B524   973'.04924   81-4265
ISBN 0-313-22532-X (lib. bdg.)   AACR2

Library of Congress Catalog Card Number: 81-4265
ISBN: 0-313-22532-X
ISSN: 0084-9219

First published in 1982

Greenwood Press
A division of Congressional Information Service, Inc.
88 Post Road West
Westport, Connecticut 06881

Printed in the United States of America

10 9 8 7 6 5 4 3 2 1

For
Professor Herbert F. Margulies,
mentor and friend

Contents

Preface

What follows is neither a study of the disabilities and atrocities suffered by Jews in eastern Europe, nor solely a description of American diplomatic initiatives on behalf of oppressed Jewry in that part of the world. Both of these subjects have been dealt with in other works. But whereas the lobbying efforts of American Jews after the formation of the American Jewish Committee in 1906 have been well described by other authors, lobbying efforts before the formation of that committee have not been considered in any other study. These can only be gleaned from the memoirs and biographies of American Jewish leaders of the period. Yet east European Jews did suffer repression before 1906, and the United States government did occasionally respond sympathetically to their plight. The two were linked by the lobbying efforts of American Jewish leaders like Oscar Straus, Jacob Schiff, Simon Wolf, Mayer Sulzberger, and Adolf Kraus, and by the mobilization of Jewish public opinion by other leaders like Philip Cowen of the *American Hebrew*. Their efforts began long before the formation of the American Jewish Committee in 1906, and the influence of these men continued to be most important in Jewish lobbying efforts for years after that committee was formed.

This work describes the efforts of American Jewish leaders

to ameliorate the conditions of Russian and Rumanian Jews during the years 1890-1914. It is not concerned with the motives of those within the successive administrations in Washington, D.C. who responded to the Jewish lobbying efforts, but rather with the attempts to influence those administrations. The study focuses on two aspects of those attempts: the effort to make the American people and their government into champions of human rights internationally, centering on the Jewish question in eastern Europe, and the effort to preserve the United States as a haven for oppressed peoples who sought to immigrate to this country. These were efforts that looked to the United States as the solution to the Jewish problem in eastern Europe. There is, of course, another aspect of American Jewish activity not dealt with in this study—the efforts of American Zionists, in league with Zionists in Europe, who sought the solution to the Jewish problem through the reestablishment of a Jewish nation in Palestine. Their efforts have not been included since, as Melvin I. Urofsky pointed out in *American Zionism from Herzl to the Holocaust*, American Zionism did not begin its transformation from "a moribund fringe group" into a dynamic movement until 1914, which is the terminal year considered here.

    Research for this study began originally with a grant from the American Jewish Historical Society in 1970 to study the activities of Jacob H. Schiff in assisting Japan to finance its war with Russia, 1904-1905. It was resumed with a grant from the National Endowment for the Humanities for the summer of 1976. Without the first grant my interest in American Jewish history probably would never have been stimulated. Without the second the research would have been nearly impossible to accomplish. During the summers of 1976, 1977, and 1978 I visited the Library of Congress Manuscript Reading Room and the National Archives in Washington, D.C., the Princeton University Library, the extensive holdings of the American Jewish Historical Society Library at Brandeis University, and the valuable collections in the American Jewish Archives at Hebrew Union College. I also utilized the periodical collections in Klau Library at Hebrew Union College, and those of the American Jewish Periodical Center there. I received magnificent cooperation at most repositories I visited, but special thanks must be extended to Bernard Wax and Nathan Kaganoff of the American Jewish Historical Society, and to Jacob Marcus and Abraham Peck of the American Jewish Archives, as well as to the other kind staff members of both the society and the archives for their unfailing helpfulness. I am indebted to John Schiff for permission to use the Jacob H. Schiff Papers, to the late Gilbert W. Kahn for permission to use the Otto M. Kahn Papers, and to James Marshall for permission to use the Louis Marshall Papers.

I am grateful also to the American Jewish Archives and the American Jewish Historical Society for their permission to quote from the following articles upon which chapters 2, 4, and 6 are based: "The Jewish 'Center of Gravity' and Secretary Hay's Roumanian Notes," *American Jewish Archives* 32 (April 1980): 23-34; "Financing a Foreign War: Jacob H. Schiff and Japan, 1904-05," *American Jewish Historical Quarterly* 61 (June 1972): 313-24; "Jacob Schiff's Galveston Movement: An Experiment in Immigrant Deflection, 1907-1914," *American Jewish Archives* 30 (April 1978): 43-79.

I am indebted to Moses Rischin, Melvin Urofsky, and Arthur P. Dudden, as well as Zosa Szajkowski, for their encouragement and for the inspiration furnished by their own work in American Jewish history. Walter Johnson and Herbert Margulies of the University of Hawaii at Manoa were kind enough to read the manuscript in an early draft and to make suggestions for improving both the content and the writing.

Finally, I owe a special debt of gratitude to Kenneth Herrick, director of the University of Hawaii at Hilo Library, and his splendid staff, especially Sherie Gusukuma and a pair of student helpers, Sharon Kaya and Nora Takaki, for their heroic work in obtaining interlibrary loans for this project.

_____TO FREE
A PEOPLE

Introduction

The case for the United States as a humanitarian nation in the late nineteenth and early twentieth centuries is a difficult one to make. Both in the private actions of its citizens and in governmental actions and policies, the United States presented a sorry picture to the world. The massacres of Chinese in the American West in the 1870s and 1880s which, in the words of one historian, "became such a commonplace occurrence that the newspapers seldom bothered to print the stories," and in which the authorities "winked at the attacks, and politicians all but incited more of the same," are some of the most vivid examples.[1] The discriminatory legislation against Chinese immigration, which began with the Chinese Exclusion Act of 1882, and similar movements against the Japanese in the early twentieth century, singled out Oriental people for discriminatory treatment by the United States government. Another group singled out, especially in the southern states, were American blacks. As John Hope Franklin has pointed out, there were more than 2,500 lynchings in the last sixteen years of the nineteenth century and another 1,100 in the twentieth century up to the outbreak of World War I.[2] In these atrocities, too, local authorities were frequently culpable.

But the sorry record of the United States is not complete

without consideration also of the brutal suppression of Filipino insurgents by the United States Army at the turn of the century. A nation that had just waged war against the Spanish in the name of humanity, now duplicated in the Philippines the same savage tactics the Spanish had used in Cuba. The use of dumdum (expanding) bullets, the practice of water torture, the reprisals against innocent civilians for the deaths of American soldiers, the burning of villages, and other atrocities were tactics hardly in accordance with America's image of itself as a humanitarian nation and offering little basis for American protests against the inhumanity of other nations.[3] Yet the United States did protest against the mistreatment of the Jewish subjects of Rumania and Russia, even though American policymakers were aware of the gap between this nation's own record and its protests to others, and despite the fact that Russian officials, in particular, seized gleefully upon the contradiction. The fact that the United States protested, despite its own unenviable record, can be attributed to the influence of American Jewish leaders in developing a powerful lobby in behalf of Jewish concerns.

On February 27, 1905, Cyrus Adler, president of the American Jewish Historical Society, addressed the thirteenth annual meeting of the society on the topic "Jews in the Diplomatic Correspondence of the United States." In 1905 American Jews already had seen frequent diplomatic initiatives by President Theodore Roosevelt and his Secretary of State John Hay. Dr. Adler told his audience that the diplomatic correspondence of the United States

> shows that the humanitarian diplomacy of President Theodore Roosevelt and Secretary John Hay is a legitimate descendant [*sic*] of the position taken by John Forsyth and General Wallace in Turkey; of the attitude of Lewis Cass and President Buchanan in dealings with Switzerland; of the position of Mr. Evarts and Mr. Blaine in representations made to Morocco. When John A. Kasson, Minister to Austria, proposed in 1878, that this government should take steps toward securing the

rights of the Jews in Roumania, none other than sentiments of humanity actuated him, since there were no
American interests involved and the rights of no American citizens were being abridged. . . . In our correspondence with Russia from 1880 on, William M. Evarts,
John W. Foster, James G. Blaine, A. A. Adee, Frederick
T. Frelinghuysen and again President Roosevelt and
Mr. Hay have reiterated the right of this government to
approach Russia, not only in behalf of American citizens
of the Jewish faith but to use their good offices to
ameliorate the conditions of the persecuted subjects
of the Czar of Russia. This statement does not take into
account the sentiments of our country as represented
in party platforms or even in the more solemn expression employed by Harrison and other Presidents in their
messages to Congress, nor the almost unanimous voice
of the American people as expressed in public meetings
in 1882 and 1891, or more recently after the Kishineff
massacre.[4]

Here was a clear statement of the historical record of American
humanitarian diplomacy. Yet it would be wrong to conclude that
such humanitarian initiatives emanated from purely altruistic
motives. If governments closer to the democratic end of the
political spectrum champion humanitarian causes in international relations more frequently than those farther removed from
the liberal end of the spectrum, it does not necessarily follow
that they are more innately humane in the formulation of their
policies, but rather that they are more subject to the demands
of domestic interest groups. When a specific policy is humanitarian, it carries the dual benefit of placing a nation on a high
moral plane which all can appreciate, while at the same time
serving the interests of the administration in securing the approbation of the electorate.

The history of American humanitarian diplomacy in behalf
of Jewish rights in eastern Europe is incomplete, then, if it
does not include the story of the efforts of American Jewish
leaders to influence that diplomacy in a humanitarian direc-

tion. Senator J. William Fulbright, for many years chairman of the Senate Foreign Relations Committee, has described the American Jewish lobby as "the most powerful and efficient foreign policy lobby in American politics."[5] The origins of that lobby—of Jewish concern expressed through pressure for specific American foreign policies—extends well back into American history. The quarter century between 1890 and 1914 was a seminal one in the development of that lobby, a time when America's emergence as a major world power was accompanied by the rise of American Jewry to a position of preeminence in the international Jewish community. During this period the major focus of the American Jews was the disabilities and atrocities to which Jews frequently were subjected in eastern Europe—especially Rumania and Russia—and with their own disabilities to travel to the latter country.

American Jewish concern with the treatment of Jews in Rumania began, however, well before 1890. As early as June 14, 1867 the Board of Delegates of American Israelites asked the United States government to initiate action in behalf of the persecuted Jews of Rumania. Secretary of State William H. Seward instructed the U.S. minister to Turkey, Edward J. Morris, to ascertain the facts in the matter. Morris met with the agent of the Danubian principalities (Rumania did not exist yet as a nation) and informed him that the United States would lose confidence in his government if it did not cease its repression of Jews.[6] A renewal of Rumanian persecution of its Jewish population in 1870 led to new appeals for international diplomatic good offices, and Simon Wolf, representing the Union of American Hebrew Congregations began in May of that year to press for a resolution of Congress protesting the situation in that country.[7] In the following month, President Ulysses S. Grant appointed a prominent American Jew, Grand Master of B'nai B'rith Benjamin F. Peixotto, as U.S. consul at Bucharest, Rumania. At a meeting with Peixotto and Wolf, the president told them:

> The story of the sufferings of the Hebrews of Roumania profoundly touches every sensibility of our nature. It

is one long series of outrage and wrong, and even if there
be exaggeration in the accounts which have reached us,
enough is evident to prove the imperative duty of all
civilized nations to extend their moral aid in behalf of
a people so unhappy. Prince Charles and his ministers
and the public men of that country may be brought to
see that the future of their nation lies in a direction
totally opposite to these laws, and persecutions,
whether great or petty, which have hitherto so invidi-
ously marked its character. . . . I have no doubt your
presence and influence, together with the efforts of
your colleagues of the great powers with whom, in this
matter, you will always be prompt to act, will result
in mitigating the evils complained of and end in termin-
ating them. The United States, knowing no difference
between her citizens on account of religion or nativity,
naturally believes in a civilization the world over which
will secure the same universal views.[8]

Further outrages were committed against the Jews in Rumania
in 1872, however, leading to a renewed request by Wolf for
action by the U.S. State Department. Resolutions were introduced in Congress, and the State Department expressed through
consul Peixotto the displeasure of the United States with the
course of events in Rumania.[9] On April 18, 1872, Peixotto
joined with the consuls of Germany, Austria-Hungary, France,
Great Britain, Greece, and Italy in a collective note to the
Rumanian government protesting the actions of the government in its investigation and conduct with respect to these
latest anti-Semitic outrages. Peixotto's action was approved by
Secretary of State Hamilton Fish.[10] In July, at Peixotto's suggestion, Secretary of State Fish addressed notes to the American
diplomatic representatives in Austria-Hungary, France, Germany,
Great Britain, Italy, Russia, and Turkey—all of them signatories
to the Treaty of Paris of 1858—asking them to request those
governments to intervene with Rumania in behalf of the Jews.
The notes, however, had only slight effect, generating support
only from the British government, which had already made its
own protest to the Rumanians over the events of 1872.[11]

Russia's victory over Turkey in 1877 led to the convening in Berlin of a new European congress to consider the Balkan question. Jews in Europe demanded that the congress should take up the question of Jewish rights in Rumania. The United States did not participate in the Congress of Berlin, but the government exerted its influence in behalf of Rumanian Jews whenever the opportunity arose. This assembly resulted in the Treaty of Berlin of 1878, which provided for the independence of Rumania and contained terms providing that "the difference of religious creeds and confessions shall not be alleged against any person as a ground for exclusion or incapacity in matters relating to the enjoyment of civil and political rights, admissions to public employments, functions, and honors, to the exercise of the various professions and industries in any locality whatsoever."[12] Rumania, however, made it clear from the outset that it had no strong commitment to the terms of the treaty guaranteeing the rights of Jews, and the stage was set for further disabilities in that country.

In Russia, the disabilities and outrages inflicted upon those of the Jewish faith exceeded even those in Rumania. In the 1860s and 1870s the United States government expressed interest in, and concern with, the status of Jews in Russia.[13] In 1872, upon learning of pogroms in Russia, Simon Wolf saw to it that resolutions of protest were introduced in both houses of Congress and asked President Grant to use his good offices in behalf of the Jews of Russia. According to Wolf's memoirs, the President promptly convened a special meeting of the cabinet, with Wolf in attendance, and it was unanimously agreed that a cable should be sent to the American legation in St. Petersburg. According to Wolf, the U.S. minister to Russia "promptly acted, and successfully." The legation was also requested to furnish the State Department with a full statement of the facts concerning the condition of the Jews in Russia "so that our government could act intelligently."[14] Again in 1880 Simon Wolf, together with Adolphus S. Solomons, responded to news of further repression of Russian Jews by asking the United States government to instruct the minister in St. Petersburg to "make such representations to the Czar's Government, in the interest of religious freedom and suffering humanity, as will best accord with the most emphasized liberal sentiments of the American people." Even Wolf and Solomons, however, recognized the "impropriety of one nation interfering with the internal affairs of another in matters of a purely local character."[15] Here, of course, was the dilemma continually posed for American Jews and for the United States government in seeking to ameliorate the condition of Jews in Russia or elsewhere. The United States had no grounds in international diplomatic practice for protesting internal matters in other countries unless those matters could be demonstrated clearly to conflict with the interests of the United States or its citizens. Such abstract concerns as "human rights" were attractive to public opinion, but had only slight currency in the relations between nations.

In a dispatch of April 14, 1880, Secretary of State William M. Evarts notified Minister John W. Foster in St. Petersburg of the concern expressed by American Jewish leaders, but fell short of asking Foster to take action along the lines requested by Wolf and Solomons. In his ambiguously worded message, Evarts noted that it would, "of course, be inadmissible for the Government of the United States to approach the government of Russia in criticism of its laws and regulations, except so far as such laws and regulations may injuriously affect citizens of this country," and no such action was requested of Foster. Rather, the American minister was informed that if "any pertinent occasion may arise," he should keep in mind the attitude of his own government, which "must always be in complete harmony with the principle of extending all rights and privileges, without distinction on account of creed," when he transacted any business or negotiations with the Russian government.[16] The apparent intent of the dispatch, then, was to acquaint Foster with the views of his government, but not to press him to take any action based on those views. Predictably, Foster took no action.

In subsequent months American Jews in Russia ran afoul of Russian laws restricting Jews in that country. These difficulties involving American citizens furnished the occasion for an instruction from Evarts that Foster take up the question of Russian discrimination against American Jews with the Russian

Foreign Ministry.[17] When Foster argued that the moment was inexpedient, the State Department contradicted him and ordered an immediate expression to the Russian government of American outrage over the discrimination against American Jews.[18] In December Foster finally reported to the State Department on a round of conversations he had held with the minister of foreign affairs, the minister of the interior, and the minister of worship. Since the problem was one of American Jews in Russia being subjected to the same discriminatory regulations that restricted Russian Jews, the question inevitably reduced itself to the disabilities under which Russian Jews were required to live. Elaborate rationales for the Russian policies against the Jews were presented to Foster. The Jews were almost all Polish and were "a bad class of society, largely engaged in smuggling and illegal transactions." Recently they had "been active participants in revolutionary conspiracies and plots against the life of the Emperor, and had shown a restless and disloyal inclination." Foster told the minister of foreign affairs that, while his interview was for the purpose of obtaining "proper recognition of the rights of American Jews, my Government [takes] a deep interest in the amelioration of the Jewish race in other nations." He was gratified, he told the foreign minister, to learn that a commission had been established to study the Jewish question in Russia, including "the question of the modification in a liberal sense of the Russian laws regarding the Jews," since the experience of the United States had "amply shown the wisdom of removing all discriminations against them in the laws and of placing this race upon an equal footing with all other citizens." The validity of the American experience as a guide for Russian policies was, however, questioned by the Russian Minister of the Interior Ignatiev, who pointed out that the number of Jews in the United States was relatively small, while there were 6 million within Russia. In a subsequent meeting with the foreign minister, the Russian brought to Foster's attention what he thought was a better analogy between American and Russian behavior in the restrictive policies of the United States toward Chinese immigrants.[19]

In July of 1881 the continued Russian discrimination against

American Jews visiting that country pushed official American
concern with the Russian Jewish problem even farther into the
background. In a long dispatch to be communicated to the
Russian foreign minister, Secretary of State James G. Blaine
reviewed for Minister Foster the genesis of this sensitive issue
between the two countries. Not before 1860, Blaine told
Foster, had the Russians discriminated against American Jews
traveling in Russia. Only since that year had they begun to
discriminate in violation of the American interpretation of the
1832 treaty between the two nations. As Blaine wrote: "From
the time when the treaty of 1832 was signed down to within
a very recent period, there had been nothing in our relations
with Russia to lead to the supposition that our flag did not
carry with it equal protection to every American within the
dominions of the Empire." While American discussions with
the Russians over the question frequently had been linked
with this country's concern over Russia's treatment of its own
Jewish subjects, the secretary of state now sought to separate
the two issues:

> I have observed that in your conferences on this sub-
> ject heretofore with the Minister for Foreign Affairs,
> as reported in your despatches, that you have on some
> occasions, given discreet expression to the feelings of
> sympathy and gratification with which this govern-
> ment and people regard any steps taken in foreign
> countries in the direction of a liberal tolerance anal-
> ogous to that which forms the fundamental principle
> of our national existence. Such expressions were
> natural on your part, and reflected a sentiment which
> we all feel. But in making the President's views known
> to the Minister, I desire that you will carefully sub-
> ordinate such sentiments to the simple consideration
> of what is conscientiously believed to be due to our
> citizens in foreign parts. You will distinctly impress
> upon him that, regardful of the sovereignty in Russia,
> we do not submit any suggestions touching the laws
> and customs of the Empire, except where those laws

and customs conflict with and destroy the rights of
American citizens as secured by treaty obligations.[20]

Blaine's dispatch was forwarded by the Russian foreign minister
to the commission that had been appointed by the minister of
the interior to examine the Jewish question.[21]

The assassination of Czar Alexander II in early 1881, in the
words of one historian, fell "upon the Jews as a national calamity."[22] The new regime in Russia reversed the relatively liberal
course of Alexander II, and not only revived existing anti-
Semitic laws, but also enacted the notorious May Laws in 1882
which further constricted the movement and economic livelihood of Jews in Russia, even within the Pale of Settlement, and
resulted, in their application, in the massive expulsion of Jews
from villages to towns within the Pale of Settlement and of
Jews from outside the Pale into it.[23] Secretary of State Blaine
responded to rumors of even more stringent Russian laws to
check the "injurious activity" of Jews in commerce by suggesting in November 1881 that the United States and Great
Britain might undertake "similar or concerted representations"
in behalf of the Jews in Russia.[24] As Blaine wrote to James
Russell Lowell, U.S. minister in London, referring to President
Garfield:

> It was perfectly clear to the late President that an
> amelioration of the treatment of American Israelites
> in Russia could only result from a very decided better-
> ment of the condition of the native Hebrews—that any
> steps taken toward the relief of one would necessarily
> result in favor of the other—and that, under all the
> peculiar and abnormal aspects of the case, it is com-
> petent and proper to urge upon Russia action in con-
> sonance with the spirit of the age.

Blaine told Lowell that Garfield's successor, President Chester
A. Arthur, was equally convinced that the two issues were
intertwined.[25] Thus, to obtain proper treatment for American
Jews in Russia it was required that the Russians modify their

policies toward their own Jewish subjects. Apprised of these activities in Washington and London, Wickham Hoffman, the U.S. chargé in St. Petersburg, took up the question with the British ambassador there only to be told that there was little likelihood the British government would join with the United States in any such action.[26] As predicted, the British government failed to take any cooperative action with the United States, being more concerned with maintaining friendly relations with Russia than with the rights of Jews in that country.[27]

Evidence of Congressional concern over the treatment of Russian Jews, as expressed through resolutions introduced by Congressman S. S. Cox of New York, led Secretary of State Frederick T. Frelinghuysen to write the U.S. legation in St. Petersburg on April 15, 1882 that the American people had heard "with great regret, the stories of the sufferings of the Jews in Russia." Despite the absence of any apparent injury to American interests, the chargé was instructed:

> Should you be of the opinion that a more vigorous effort might be put forth for the prevention of this great wrong, you will, if a favorable opportunity offers, state with all proper deference that the feeling of friendship which the United States entertains for Russia prompts this Government to express the hope that the Imperial Government will find means to cause the persecution of these unfortunate fellow beings to cease.[28]

While it was not communicated officially to the Russian government, Frelinghuysen's note was released to the public. In June, Minister of the Interior Ignatiev resigned and was replaced by the more liberal Count Tolstoy. A less repressive policy toward the Jews followed Tolstoy's appointment. Chargé Hoffman opined that the publication of Frelinghuysen's note of April 15, "thus bringing unofficially to the knowledge of the Russian Government the strong feeling of the President and People of the United States upon this subject, was not without its influence" in bringing about a more liberal Russian policy toward the Jews.[29]

Although the enforcement of the May Laws was now muted under Count Tolstoy, the repressive policies of 1881 and 1882 had set off a sizable emigration of Jews from Russia and many entered the United States. That the result of the repression of east European Jewry would be their immigration in large numbers to the United States was now clear. This presented a number of problems for the established Jewish community in the United States. As Sheldon Neuringer has pointed out, American Jews were striving for greater acceptance in American society and regarded the Russian immigrants as a possible threat to their aspirations because of their "strange Yiddish jargon, their outlandish appearance, and their bewildering modes of religious expression." Moreover, the Russian immigrants showed a "low capacity for becoming quickly self-dependent," which was likely to make them dependent upon Jewish charities and result in enormous financial burdens upon the American Jewish community. While established American Jews sympathized deeply with the plight of their Russian coreligionists and sought to expand the amount of financial assistance by creating such agencies as the Hebrew Emigrant Aid Society, it is apparent that the German leaders of the American Jewish community preferred the problems of Russian Jewry to be solved in their native land so that massive immigration to the United States would be unnecessary.[30] Sympathy for the plight of Russian Jews was now joined by the desire to make their immigration unnecessary, which provided American Jewish leaders with dual motives to intervene with the United States government on behalf of east European Jewry.

In their efforts before 1890 to alleviate conditions for Jews in eastern Europe, the American Jewish leadership found Simon Wolf to be its most consistent and effective spokesman for Jewish interests with the successive administrations in Washington, D.C. Born in Germany in 1836, Wolf immigrated to the United States in 1848, studied law, and was admitted to the Ohio bar in 1861. After a year of law practice in Ohio, Wolf moved to Washington, D.C. where he began the careful cultivation of political figures which was to stand his coreligionists in such good stead. His relations with American presidents dated from a call he paid on James Buchanan, while his first intercession on behalf of a Jewish cause was with Abraham Lincoln. Throughout his years in Washington, D.C. as representative of the Union of American Hebrew Congregations and the Independent Order of B'nai B'rith, Wolf carefully built bridges to office-holders, including presidents and prospective presidents. His method included thoughtful notes on appropriate occasions. Active as a campaigner for Republican candidates, Wolf nevertheless managed to remain on good terms with Democrats. During the Grant administration he was rewarded with appointment as recorder of deeds for the District of Columbia, and he served President James A. Garfield as U.S. consul general and agent diplomatique to Egypt from 1881 to 1882.[31]

Jacob H. Schiff and Oscar S. Straus did not take active roles as spokesmen for the Jews in diplomatic questions until the 1890s. Born in Germany in 1847, Schiff immigrated to the United States in 1865, entered banking, and formed the investment firm of Budge, Schiff and Company in 1867. During the five years this firm operated, Schiff spent most of his time in Germany and Holland marketing American railroad bonds among investors there, and after the firm was dissolved he briefly took a position with a German banking firm. Returning to the United States in 1874, Schiff joined Kuhn, Loeb and Company on January 1, 1875, and a few months later married the oldest daughter of Solomon Loeb. Before long Schiff was taking the leading role in the firm, and when Loeb, the last of the original partners, virtually retired in 1885, Schiff was, at thirty-eight, in the words of his biographer, "the undisputed head of the firm."[32] According to the same source: "The relations of the Czarist Government of Russia to its Jewish subjects from 1880 onward loomed very large in engaging Schiff's mind, heart and energy, and affected to some extent even his business career." Yet Schiff apparently made no attempt to influence American policy toward eastern Europe before 1890.[33]

Oscar Straus also was born in Germany, in 1850. His father Lazarus immigrated to the United States in 1852, and after a short time the family followed. The firm of L. Straus and Sons dealt in crockery in New York City in the late 1860s and early 1870s and then opened a china and glassware department in the R. H. Macy and Company department store. Eventually the ownership of Macy's was taken over by the Straus family. At Columbia, Straus was elected to Phi Beta Kappa and graduated in 1871. Two years later he completed Columbia Law School, but after a brief law practice he entered the family firm in 1880. He remained active, however, in New York reform politics. His services to the Grover Cleveland campaign in 1884 led to his appointment in March of 1887 as U.S. minister to Turkey. In this position Straus's energies were largely absorbed by his responsibilities as a diplomat. In the presidential election of 1888 Cleveland failed in his bid for a second term, and in February of 1889 Straus submitted his resignation and rejoined the family business.[34]

By 1890, then, these three American Jewish leaders were well positioned to exert an influence on American foreign policymakers. Simon Wolf, at fifty-four, possessed years of experience and a wealth of contacts among public officials of both political parties, but especially among Republicans. Oscar Straus, at forty, had behind him a distinguished record of diplomatic service and a record of usefulness to the Democratic party. Jacob Schiff, forty-three, was a distinguished financier with a record of municipal service in the city of New York and to the Republican Party. These three would delegate themselves as representatives of the Jewish community in the United States for nearly two decades and would render yeoman service to the cause of Jewish human rights in eastern Europe for a quarter of a century.

While Wolf, Schiff, and Straus were the major figures, they were not without able assistance in advancing the cause they represented. The list of distinguished American Jews who aided in the formulation of a humanitarian American foreign policy concerning the Jews of eastern Europe is too long to mention here. Some of those names will appear in the pages which follow. Five, however, deserve special note: Leo N. Levi, Jesse Seligman, Adolf Kraus, Philip Cowen, and Louis Marshall.

Levi was born in the United States, earned a law degree at the University of Virginia, and practiced law in Texas until he moved to New York City in 1899. From 1900 until his death in 1904, Levi was head of the Independent Order of B'nai B'rith.[35] Jesse Seligman was born in Germany in 1827 and joined his brothers' firm in the United States in 1841. After a career in the drygoods business he joined with them in forming the banking firm of J. & W. Seligman and Company in 1862 and headed the firm after 1880.[36] Adolf Kraus was born in Bohemia in 1850, immigrated to the United States in 1865, and began the practice of law in 1877. He served as president of B'nai B'rith from 1905 until his death in 1928.[37] Philip Cowen was born in the United States in 1853 and cofounded the *American Hebrew* in 1879, serving as its editor and publisher for twenty-seven years before joining the U.S. Immigration Service in 1905. Cowen made the *American Hebrew* a vigorous journalistic supporter of the lobbying efforts of the American Jewish leadership.[38] Louis Marshall also was born in the United States in 1856 and after graduation from Columbia Law School was admitted to the bar in 1878. From 1894 onward he was a member of the law firm of Guggenheim, Untermyer and Marshall.[39]

These American Jewish leaders frequently disagreed among themselves over the best course to follow in response to a particular crisis, and their conduct and their actions were frequently criticized by others who sought to speak for the American Jewish community. The growing number of east European Jews in the United States especially bridled at the assumption of leadership by German Jewish leaders whom they regarded as distant, cold, and basically less than sympathetic to their interests and to those of their brethren still in eastern Europe. Thus, the east European Jews sometimes opposed the ends sought by German Jewish leaders and more frequently the means by which they sought to attain their ends. While the older "assimilationist" leaders sought to influence the administrations in Washington through quiet intervention with the president and other top officials, the east Europeans preferred public protests which were embarrassing to the American

Jewish leadership. In the twentieth century east European Jews in the United States became increasingly active as their numbers grew and as the standing of individual members of the community increased. By the time of the Kishinev massacre (1903), in particular, they had begun to exert an influence of their own.

However, in the quarter century between 1890 and 1914 the American Jewish leaders forged the foundation for a strong American Jewish lobby which significantly influenced American foreign policy toward eastern Europe between those years and served as the basis for the powerful present-day American Jewish lobby.

NOTES

1. Betty L. Sung, *The Story of the Chinese in America* (New York, 1967), pp. 43-46.

2. John Hope Franklin, *From Slavery to Freedom* (New York, 1967), p. 439.

3. For one account of the atrocities in the Philippines, see Leon Wolff, *Little Brown Brother* (Garden City, N.Y., 1961), pp. 305-12.

4. Cyrus Adler, "Jews in the Diplomatic Correspondence of the United States," *Publications of the American Jewish Historical Society* 15 (1906): v-vi.

5. J. William Fulbright, *The Crippled Giant* (New York, 1972), p. 109.

6. Cyrus Adler and Aaron M. Margalith, *American Intercession on Behalf of the Jews in the Diplomatic Correspondence of the United States, 1840-1938* (New York, 1943), p. 100; Max J. Kohler and Simon Wolf, *Jewish Disabilities in the Balkan States* (Baltimore, 1916), pp. 2-3.

7. Simon Wolf, *The Presidents I Have Known* (Washington, D.C., 1918), p. 76.

8. Ibid., pp. 74-75.

9. Cyrus Adler and Aaron M. Margalith, *With Firmness in the Right* (New York, 1946), pp. 74-75.

10. Ibid., pp. 106-7.

11. Ibid., pp. 108-9.

12. Ibid., pp. 112-15.

13. Ibid., pp. 173-75.

14. Wolf, *Presidents*, pp. 86-87.

15. Adler and Margalith, *Firmness*, pp. 177-78.

16. Evarts to Foster, April 14, 1880, in *Diplomatic Instructions of the Department of State, 1806-1906, Russia*, National Archives Microfilm Publication M77, reel 138 (hereafter cited as DS M77/138).

17. Evarts to Foster, June 28, 1880, DS M77/138.

18. Evarts to Foster, September 4, 1880, DS M77/138.

19. Foster to Evarts, December 30, 1880, *Despatches from United States Ministers to Russia, 1801-1906*, National Archives Microfilm Publication M35, reel 36 (hereafter cited as DS M35/35).

20. Blaine to Foster, July 29, 1881, DS M77/138.

21. Hoffman to Secretary of State, October 8, 1881, DS M35/36.

22. S. M. Dubnow, *History of the Jews in Russia and Poland*, 3 vols. (Philadelphia, 1918), 2: 293.

23. Samuel Joseph, *Jewish Immigration to the United States From 1881 to 1910* (New York, 1914), p. 58.

24. Blaine to Hoffman, November 23, 1881, DS M77/138.

25. Blaine to Lowell, November 22, 1881, quoted in Aryeh Yodfat, "The Jewish Question in American-Russian Relations (1875-1917)," (Ph.D. diss., American University, 1963), p. 38.

26. Hoffman to Blaine, December 13, 1881, DS M35/36.

27. Yodfat, "The Jewish Question," pp. 38-39.

28. Ibid.; Frelinghuysen to Hoffman, April 15, 1882, DS M77/138.

29. Hoffman to Frelinghuysen, July 1, 1882, DS M35/36.

30. Sheldon M. Neuringer, "American Jewry and United States Immigration Policy, 1881-1953" (Ph.D. diss., University of Wisconsin, 1969), pp. 1-13.

31. *Dictionary of American Biography* (1936), 20: 449; Wolf, *Presidents*.

32. Cyrus M. Adler, *Jacob H. Schiff: His Life and Letters*, 2 vols. (Garden City, N.Y., 1928), 1: 1-14.

33. Ibid., p. 14.

34. Naomi Cohen, *A Dual Heritage* (Philadelphia, 1969), pp. 1-38.

35. *Universal Jewish Encyclopedia* (New York, 1969), 9: 468.

36. Ibid., 6: 464.

37. *Who Was Who in America* (Chicago, 1943), 1: 692.

38. *Encyclopedia Judaica* (Jerusalem, 1972), 5: 1023.

39. Norton Rosenstock, *Louis Marshall: Defender of Jewish Rights* (Detroit, 1965).

CHAPTER 1

Russia, 1890-1895

The period 1882-1900 saw the beginning of one of the greatest migrations of human beings in history. The onset of both official and unofficial repression of Russia's Jewish subjects during this period set in motion an exodus of Russian Jews to the shores of the United States. Between 1882 and 1890 the numbers were substantial, rising from 3,125 in 1881 to nearly 21,000 in 1890 and topping the 20,000 figure in both 1887 and 1888. In 1891, however, the number soared to over 43,000—more than in the previous two years combined—and in 1892 the immigration of Russian Jews to the United States totaled 64,253, a number which was not exceeded until 1904. Between 1891 and 1900 the total number of Russian Jews immigrating to the United States has been estimated at well over a quarter of a million.[1] But the story of the relation of the United States to the tragedy of this decade is not confined solely to its growing role as a place of refuge for these Russian Jews. Throughout the 1890s the United States government took an active interest in the human rights of Jews in Russia. American diplomatic intercession came at the urging of Jews already in the United States who sought to ameliorate the condition of their coreligionists in Russia.

The condition of Jews in Russia had somewhat improved in 1882 after Count Dimitrij Tolstoy replaced Count Ignatiev as minister of the interior. While an arch-reactionary in other ways, Tolstoy pursued a somewhat more humane policy toward the Jews than had his predecessor.[2] Tolstoy died in 1889, however, and in the late summer of 1890 U.S. attention was drawn by news that the May Laws of 1882 were now to be enforced in Russia.[3] Questions were raised in the British Parliament, and a resolution was introduced in the U.S. House of Representatives protesting "in the name of humanity, against such inhuman and barbarous acts as the enforcement by Russia of the edicts of 1882 against the Jews, and requesting the President to transmit, through our representatives in Russia, this protest to the Russian Government."[4] An inquiry of the American legation in St. Petersburg by the State Department brought the reply that "instead of new measures of oppression being threatened, there is some prospect of an amelioration taking place in the condition of the Israelite subjects of the Tsar."[5]

The inquiry by the State Department resulted from the initiative of Oscar Straus. Upon receiving information of the Russian actions from Sir Julian Goldsmid in London via banker Jesse Seligman, Straus wrote to the Department of State. The optimistic response from the American chargé in St. Petersburg, however, was contradicted by private information Straus received from London that the British ambassador in St. Petersburg had confirmed the rumors of new actions against the Jews. This additional information was submitted by Straus to President Harrison and his cabinet. In the meantime, Secretary of State Blaine passed through New York and visited there with Jesse Seligman, who pressed the matter upon him. According to Straus, the unwillingness of the British to act meant that American Jews must "have our government take this initiative step so that France and the other enlightened governments of Europe will act in a similar manner."[6] European Jews, then, had failed to evoke action from their governments in response to this new outburst of official anti-Semitism in Russia, and American Jewish leaders saw it as their duty to bring about action by those governments through the example of the United States taking the initiative.

Despite the continued rumors of anti-Semitic actions by the

Russian government, however, George W. Wurts, the chargé in St. Petersburg, was adamant in denying that Russian Jews had anything to fear. When the State Department, acting on information furnished by American Jews, specifically queried if the Russian government contemplated enforcing the May Laws of 1882 against its Jewish subjects, Wurts responded that the charge had been denied "on the highest authority."[7] The arrival of Charles Emory Smith as the new U.S. minister to Russia brought similar assurances from the Russian government that the rumors so agitating European and American Jewish leaders concerning new anti-Semitic policies there were without foundation.[8] Straus, however, continually pressed upon the State Department the contrary evidence which he was receiving from other sources and questioned the accuracy of the reports coming to the State Department.[9]

Philip Cowen's *American Hebrew* concluded that American statesmen had "something yet to learn in the way of duplicity from Russian government officials," and hoped Secretary of State Blaine would "not permit himself to be deceived by verbal quibbles." The United States, the *American Hebrew* urged, should ascertain the facts in the matter, not just for humanitarian reasons but because "enforcement of these edicts implies a vast immigration from Russia and the bulk of it will tend in this direction." It was, therefore, a "serious question whether this government should be content to sit idly by while thousands are flocking to our shores at the instance of the government wherein they dwell."[10] Here was an expression of the concern of the American Jewish community over the prospect of a sizable Russian Jewish immigration to the United States, translated into a justification for American protest to the Russian government.

Meanwhile, Straus pressed English Jewish leaders for further proof of anti-Semitic actions in Russia which might be presented to the State Department to controvert the reports it was receiving from the U.S. minister in Russia, Charles Emory Smith. Suggestions arose from Europe that a mass meeting should be held in the United States to protest the Russian actions, but Straus argued against it, explaining the subject was "too foreign and too far distant to arouse a general public interest." The State Department, he insisted, was in full sympathy with the cause of Russian Jews and could be counted upon to act promptly and with concern once it possessed the requisite information. A public meeting, he argued, "instead of being an assistance to our cause might have the contrary effect. A direct representation and protest through our diplomatic representatives, I assume, will have more effect than any indirect method through the medium of public meetings."[11] Here was stated the position of American Jewish leaders where protest meetings were concerned. If the goal was diplomatic protest, then American Jewish leaders, confident of the willingness of the American government to respond to their entreaties, viewed public protests as useless or even counterproductive. English Jewish leaders, less effective in moving their government to action, could resort only to such public protests to display their concern. Thus, while a great protest meeting was held in London with considerable publicity, no such rally was held in the United States.[12]

The opposition of American Jewish leaders to following the English course of action was strengthened when five of them, including Straus and Jacob Schiff, met with the secretary of state on December 18, 1890, to protest the inaccurate information emanating from the legation in St. Petersburg. According to Schiff's account of the visit, Secretary of State Blaine assured the Jewish leaders that he knew full well the reports being submitted from St. Petersburg were incorrect and that the minister had allowed himself to be deceived. Blaine told the Jewish leaders that he had wired Smith to this effect and had instructed him to do everything possible "to exercise a friendly influence upon the Russian Government in favor of its Jewish subjects." As Schiff recounted, Blaine assured him he was "ready to help us in every way and that he would continue to instruct our ministers to act energetically." The secretary of state, however, was opposed to any public meetings of protest since such actions only made his relations with the Russian government the more difficult by making it appear that his initiatives had been forced upon him by such pressures rather than emanating from a sincere concern on the part of the United States government. As Schiff put it, the secretary's position was "in accord with our own views, for while mass meetings always adopt resolutions and achieve nothing, such proceedings only irritate the Russian Government, and our unfortunate co-religionists have to suffer for it."[13]

Schiff and Straus were thus confirmed in their opposition to a mass meeting, and Straus moved to head off such a demonstration being organized in Washington, D.C. by Simon Wolf. As Straus wrote Mayer Sulzberger, the other Jewish leaders were convinced that such a meeting would hurt rather than aid their cause. He asked that Sulzberger, if he had any influence with Wolf, "advise him to abstain from such a move as this," since the kind of diplomatic protest which Blaine had assured them he was preparing would have "infinitely more effect than a hundred public meetings."[14] Straus also counseled that American Jewish leaders should insure that when Charles Emory Smith was replaced as minister to Russia, his successor would be someone who was not only "sympathetic" to the cause of Russian Jews but who would also "have his eyes open to protest in as vigorous a manner as possible the interest that lies so near to our hearts." There was "no doubt" in Straus's mind that "we can easily bring this about should at any time Mr. Smith resign or another minister be appointed."[15] Meanwhile, Schiff had busied himself with "trying to win over the daily press . . . and the other periodicals which have great influence upon the thinking public."[16]

Through January and February of 1891 American Jewish leaders continued to press for U.S. diplomatic action to aid Russian Jews in the face of the enforcement of the 1882 edicts. In mid-January Straus again journeyed to Washington with Jesse Seligman for an interview with the secretary of state. The amount of effort involved in assembling arguments to be presented at the meeting was "very great," but Straus looked forward to a "favorable result."[17] As additional evidence reached him from his European sources concerning Russian persecutions, the evidence was forwarded quickly to the State Department.[18] To his close friend in England, Jewish banker Ernest Cassel, Jacob Schiff wrote that he and the other American Jewish leaders were "working very effectively here through the press and the Department of State to exert wholesome influence in St. Petersburg," and that they had been assured the Secretary of State would "make representations to the Russian Government on behalf of our oppressed Russian coreligionists."[19]

American Jews were wrong to conclude that Charles Emory Smith in St. Petersburg was unsympathetic with their cause or easily misled by the Russian government. In September of 1890, responding to a story in the London *Times* that five or six hundred Jewish families had been ordered expelled from Odessa, Smith had communicated with the British embassy in St. Petersburg and had learned that inquiries of the British consul at Odessa had proved the story wrong.[20] In February of 1891 Smith had what he described as "an extended, interesting and suggestive conversation with the Imperial Minister of Foreign Affairs, Mr. de Giers, concerning the attitude and policy of Russia in respect to the Jewish subjects of the Empire." The topic came up on the initiative of the Russian foreign minister and caught Smith without any specific instructions from the Department of State as to what position he should take in such a conversation. Smith, therefore, limited himself "chiefly to eliciting information and to reserve representations deemed expedient or obligatory until another occasion, after communicating with the Department." He did, however, point out to de Giers that:

> while we recognize the treatment of the people within its own borders as a question of domestic concern which belongs primarily to Russia, except so far as it may affect the rights of American citizens, we hold, and in any reference to the subject the representative of the United States must hold, the attitude which is in harmony with the theory and practice of our government, which makes no distinction on account of creed.

The American people, he told the Russian foreign minister, "would witness with satisfaction movements toward the amelioration of the condition of the Jews; at the same time in any utterance on the question we desired to approach it in a fair and friendly spirit, and with a just sense of the peculiar situation of Russia."[21]

Prior to receipt of this long dispatch from Smith, Secretary of State Blaine addressed to him on February 18, 1891 a message to be read to the Russian minister of foreign affairs. That message first reviewed the Jewish problem in Russia and then observed that "oppressive measures" on the part of the Russian government were compelling large numbers of Jews to leave that country, as was demonstrated by the great increase in the immigration of destitute Russian Jews to the United States. The numbers of such immigrants, and their indigent condition, offered the prospect that American charitable resources would be sorely taxed. The American people and their government could not, therefore, "avoid a feeling of concern at the enforcement of measures which threaten to frustrate their efforts to minister to the wants and improve the condition of those who are driven to seek a livelihood within their borders." The United States was mindful of "the ties of good relationship that have long subsisted between the United States and Russia, and of the friendly acts of Russia towards our country in the past," and the United States sought to preserve those friendly ties. America did not "assume to dictate the internal policy of other nations," but each government had the mutual duty to "use its power with a due regard for the other and for the results which its exercise produces on the rest of the world." For this reason, the United States felt constrained to bring to Russia's attention the effects on this country, "upon whose shores are cast daily evidences of the suffering and destitution wrought by the enforcement of the edicts against this unhappy people." Secretary of State Blaine was "persuaded that His Imperial Majesty the Emperor of Russia and his councilors can feel no sympathy with measures which are forced upon other nations by such deplorable consequences."[22]

Thus, as Cowen's *American Hebrew* had suggested, the

United States government had taken the issue of immigration
as grounds for a protest to the Russian government over its
treatment of its Jewish subjects. America could now point to
a way in which its national interest was damaged by Russian
repression of its Jews. It was a weak argument, it is true, since
the United States was clearly able to regulate its own immigration and thus protect itself from any such consequences of
Russia's action. Moreover, it could be argued that the American case was weakened by recourse to such tenuous reasoning
rather than continuing to make the appeal on the moral grounds
of human rights. But for government officials chary about protesting the purely domestic policies of another nation on such
abstract grounds as human rights, particularly where the American record was so spotty in this regard, even such a weak basis
for protest as the immigration issue must have seemed preferable.

As this dispatch was en route to St. Petersburg, Smith was
seeking on his own initiative to ascertain the true situation in
Russia regarding current and contemplated actions against the
Jews. He had sent circular letters to the U.S. consuls at Warsaw,
Odessa, and Riga, all located in areas where Jews were to be
found in considerable numbers, inquiring as to the state of
Russian policies toward the Jews in those regions. All consuls
reported that there was "no evidence of the application and enforcement of new measures against the Hebrews." But those
consuls on the western frontier of the empire detected signs
"of the more stringent execution of old laws which have heretofore been so loosely and lightly observed as practically to be
inoperative." Smith also found that Russian policy was "inducing some withdrawal" of the Jews from the cities of
Moscow and St. Petersburg.[23] Thus armed with the results of
his own inquiry, which substantiated many of the charges
being made by European and American Jews concerning the
state of affairs in Russia, Smith met with the Russian minister
of foreign affairs once again on March 11, 1891 to communicate to him the dispatch of February 18 from Blaine. Smith
presented de Giers with a copy of Blaine's letter and then gave
him a verbal summary of its contents, touching on the concern
raised in the United States over "the more vigorous enforce-

ment of old laws whose severity had not been understood so
long as they had not been applied." According to Smith's
account of the conversation, he told de Giers:

> That the Jews in Russia were subjected to coercive
> and oppressive measures which compelled them to quit
> their homes was shown by the number of unfortunate
> and indigent Russian Jews who were now arriving in the
> United States. You [Blaine] had been informed on ex-
> cellent authority that within a period of ten years this
> immigration amounted to 200,000. Most of these im-
> migrants had been well provided for, but a further
> influx of destitute persons entirely unprepared for the
> conditions and requirements of American life would be
> a very serious burden upon the American people. It was
> in this aspect of the results forced upon our country
> that the condition of the Jews in Russia under existing
> measures presented itself to the attention of our Govern-
> ment and people and, in view of the mutual duties of
> nations, constrained this expression of their sentiment.

After some questions and observations, de Giers had "concluded
by saying that the dispatch would be received in the same
friendly spirit in which it was sent; that he would submit it to
the Emperor, and that if it was determined to make reply either
verbally or in writing, it would be duly communicated."[24]

Despairing of action by their own government, British Jews
had appealed to American Jewish leaders to bring about some
diplomatic initiative by the United States government. Told by
the British Foreign Office that the British government could
not interfere with the Czar's treatment of his Jewish subjects,
British Jews had turned to public protests which proved of no
avail.[25] The Russian government had declared it would not
even consent to receive the resolution adopted by the London
mass meeting.[26] American Jewish leaders, however, had been
more successful in bringing about action on the part of their
government. Working closely with Secretary of State Blaine,
American Jewish leaders—including Jesse Seligman, Jacob
Schiff, and Oscar Straus—were successful in their lobbying

efforts to get from their government the application of diplomatic pressure upon the government of the Czar. As a result, after 1890 the Jews of Europe would turn more and more to their coreligionists in the United States for leadership in such crises.

The situation in Russia seemed somewhat improved in March of 1891, when Schiff could observe late in the month that he was "particularly happy to hear that somewhat better reports are coming in about the situation in Russia," although Jewish families there continued to be uprooted under the 1882 May Laws.[27] Then on March 28, 1891, twenty thousand Jews, most of them artisans, were ordered to leave Moscow. On April 20, Charles Emory Smith reported to the State Department that similar expulsion orders were expected for St. Petersburg.[28] Consequently the Jewish emigration from Russia did not abate but rather increased, and the press of Jewish immigrants from Russia upon the resources of the American Jewish community was unrelenting. The confirmation of the new abominations was proof of the futility of the Blaine initiative in February, and the State Department was silent on the new reports, only acknowledging the dispatches received from the legation in St. Petersburg.

Meanwhile the increase of immigration as a result of the new repression in Russia had led to renewed demands for a more restrictive immigration policy in the United States. Concern that the new immigrants would become wards of public charity, and suspicions that some of the new arrivals were being assisted financially in making the passage to the United States, led to the passage in 1891 of a new immigration act which excluded those deemed likely to become a "public charge" and provided for the detention of those whose passage had been paid for by individuals or organizations abroad. The law, however, permitted a great deal of discretion in the employment of its provisions, and Simon Wolf pressed the administration in Washington, D.C. for a lenient application of the law, promising that Jewish immigrants would be provided for by the American Jewish community and would not become public charges. Secretary of the Treasury Charles Foster responded favorably in August 1891, promising to apply the 1891 immi-

gration law leniently on the condition that American Jewry
undertake to disperse Jewish immigrants to points other than
the crowded eastern industrial centers. This initiative by
Simon Wolf, Sheldon Neuringer points out, marked "the first
time that American Jews had ever tried to move United States
immigration policy in a more liberal direction" and represented
a new confidence on the part of the Jewish community in
their ability to handle the new immigrants. This new confidence
arose, in part, because of the assistance furnished by the $2.4
million provided for that purpose by the Baron Maurice De
Hirsch in 1889 and also because of the resources offered by
Russian Jewish immigrants already in the United States.[29]

Though now committed to a liberal immigration policy for
Russian Jews, the American Jewish leaders recognized that
immigration was of no assistance to the millions of Jews who
remained behind in Russia, and in June of 1891 they began to
cast about for other methods by which international public
opinion might be aroused concerning Russia's treatment of
her Jewish subjects. Straus suggested that an international
congress of Jews be held in England or in France "to consider
this question with the view of making an official and concerted
protest to their respective governments to take action in the
matter." In Straus's view, such a congress would also have the
effect "of bringing officially before the nations of such respective delegates an authenticated statement or report of the nature
and extent of the persecutions" which would doubtless arouse
the sympathy of the people of those nations and bring pressure
for some form of concerted action.

> The time has arrived when it has become incumbent
> upon us to take an aggressive stand and to take action
> to lay before the enlightened people of the world a true
> statement of this most terrible and inhuman persecution,
> as cruel in many respects as the Spanish Inquisition was,
> and of more consequence because a far greater number
> are affected by it.[30]

In effect, Straus was seeking to internationalize the protest
since appeals from the United States government alone seemed

to have no effect. Jacob Schiff agreed. In response to a suggestion from Jesse Seligman that American Jews should organize a commission to go to Russia to investigate conditions there, Schiff wrote that the Russian government would doubtless snub the United States government if it, alone, asked the Czar to receive such a commission. Schiff suggested, instead, an international commission composed of Jews from the United States, Great Britain, France, Germany, and Austria, which would ask the Russian government to receive "and to discuss and, if possible, agree with it upon some plan under which the expatriation of the Jews will be divided over a number of years." If such a commission could be formed, upon the initiative of the United States government, "it would not only give an enormous moral strength to this government and to the present administration, but the Russian Government can hardly decline to receive and negotiate with an international commission thus appointed and organized." Seligman was to meet with the president in a few days, and Schiff suggested that he take up the idea with Harrison.[31]

Seligman and Oscar Straus met with President Harrison on July 1, 1891 and "explained to him fully the condition of affairs and in which he has taken a most sympathetic interest." Whether Straus's proposed international congress or Schiff's commission was discussed is not recorded, but Harrison informed the two Jewish leaders of his resolve to investigate the Russian situation thoroughly. As a result of the interview, Harrison instructed an immigration commission headed by Colonel John B. Weber, which was to study immigration matters in Europe, to proceed also to Russia and to do a detailed study of conditions there. As Straus understood Harrison's purposes, "it is the President's intention upon the receipt of this report, to take such action as the circumstances will admit of." Straus was encouraged by the president's action and particularly by his choice of Weber to head the mission, since he regarded Weber as "entirely in sympathy with us, and we could have no better man if we had our selection than he is, as he is fully impressed with the humanitarian side of this question." Seligman and Straus interviewed Weber before his departure and furnished him with letters of recommendation "so that he will fall in proper hands in Russia and be able to learn the true state of affairs and not be blinded by the official side which the Russian Government is so skillful in presenting."[32] Schiff also wrote letters of recommendation for Weber.[33]

On November 5, 1891, President Harrison informed Straus that the Weber mission had returned and was preparing its report. The president wrote that, "from his talk with me I conclude that it will contain some important information as to the expulsion of the Jews from Russia."[34] Straus responded that he was confident Weber's report would "portray the true condition without fear or favor."[35] Based on the information furnished by the Weber mission, Harrison included a reference to the Russian Jewish situation in his third annual message to Congress on December 9, 1891. In that message the president informed the Congress that his administration had expressed its concern to the Russian government over "the harsh measures now being enforced against the Hebrews in Russia." Those measures, he noted, had led great numbers of Jews to leave Russia in a destitute condition, with many of them immigrating to the United States since so many other countries were closed to them, making it difficult to find homes and jobs for them all in this country. Harrison observed:

> The banishment, whether by direct decrees or by not less certain indirect methods, of so large a number of men and women is not a local question. A decree to leave one country is in the nature of things an order to enter another—some other. This consideration, as well as the suggestion of humanity, furnishes ample ground for the remonstrances which we have presented to Russia, while our historic friendship for that Government can not fail to give the assurance that our representations are those of a sincere wellwisher.[36]

Here, then, was another expression of the immigration issue as the basis for legitimate remonstrance by the United States. Oscar Straus had a hand in the phrasing of this portion of the president's message.[37]

The report of the Weber mission was released in February of 1892, and Russia received more attention in it than any other country. While the immigration from other countries was deemed from "normal causes," the report said the exodus from Russia was "incited by causes within the control of the authorities," and there was "a propulsive force behind it which can be stopped by an imperial edict or by an intimation to cease the persecutions" against the Jews. The report drew heavily on interviews with Jews both within and outside the Pale of Settlement and indicted the Russian government in the "simple language in which they were described" by the sufferers, with corroboration supplied by the observations of the commissioners themselves. The commissioners regarded the Russian chapter of the report as "a convincing history of the terrible conditions which heretofore have been but partially described and largely disbelieved because of their incredible character." The report on Russia concluded:

> While the principle of non-intervention in the regulation and management of the domestic affairs of foreign countries is recognized and generally observed by all nations, especially by the United States, it can not in respect of the Russian Government be regarded as a friendly act to strip these persons of their substance and force them to our land impoverished in means and crushed in spirit. Neither should it be regarded as a violation of this principle to protest against a continuance of such measures in view of their effect upon our affairs, even if the question of humanity be eliminated from consideration. To push these people upon us in a condition which makes our duty of self-protection war against the spirit of our institutions and the ordinary instincts of humanity calls for a protest so emphatic that it will be both heard and heeded.[38]

Thus the report came down firmly on the side of the immigration issue as a basis for American protest. Jacob Schiff greeted the report as "a powerful document which is sure . . . to call forth the condemnation by every right-thinking American of

Russia, and we expect that the effect which the report will have upon public opinion will go far towards bringing about an exertion of the influence of the United States Government with the Russian Government in favor of our persecuted brethren."[39]

Meantime, Schiff was exerting himself in other ways to aid both those Russian Jews immigrating to the United States and those remaining behind in Russia. The Weber report contributed to the development of a sentiment favorable to the Russian Jewish immigration in America, but its influence was soon offset by newspaper stories that fifty-seven Jewish immigrants on one liner had been found with typhus. This led to some cries for stricter enforcement of the immigration laws and caused Schiff to urge President Harrison to use his influence against those who were seeking to close the gates only "because of an unfortunate and largely magnified outbreak of an illness among a single shipload of immigrants."[40] As a member of the executive committee of the American Committee for the Amelioration of the Conditions of the Russian Refugees, Schiff also helped to raise funds for the care of the immigrants.[41]

In 1890, influenced in part by the writings of George Kennan on the situation in Russia which were appearing in *Century Magazine*, a group in England formed the English Society of Friends of Russian Freedom. The society began the publication of a journal, *Free Russia*, in August for the purpose of "wide dissemination, from time to time, of accurate information upon the political position of Russia in domestic affairs, the condition of the people, the treatment of political exiles, and all the actions of the authorities in suppressing all aspirations for freedom."[42] Although the concerns of the group were broader than the issue simply of Jewish repression in Russia, its aim of greater freedom in Russia was eagerly supported by American Jewish leaders. The following month a Free Russia Publishing Association was formed in the United States, with the financial support of Jacob Schiff, Oscar Straus, and other wealthy American Jews, to publish *Free Russia* in the United States.[43] Early in 1891 a separate American Society of Friends of Russian Freedom was formed.[44] Among those involved in establishing the American organization were such prominent figures as Mark Twain, William Lloyd Garrison, the Reverend Edward Everett Hale, Julia Ward Howe, James Russell Lowell, John Greenleaf Whittier, Lyman Abbott (editor of *Outlook* magazine), and George Kennan. Of the latter it has been said: "No one person did more to cause the people of the United States to turn against their presumed benefactor [Russia] of yesteryear."[45] The "benefactor" reference, of course, is to the popular impression that Russia had demonstrated her support of the Union cause in the American Civil War. After the June-July issue of 1894, however, the American edition of *Free Russia* ceased publication for lack of financial support, and the English edition of the journal was again distributed in the United States. In that year the American Society also disbanded. During its brief lifetime, nonetheless, the organization brought to the attention of Americans the situation of Jews and others suffering under Russian tyranny and fought unsuccessfully against ratification in 1893 of an extradition treaty with Russia.[46] The American Society would reappear after the Kishinev massacre in 1903.

In 1892 American Jewish leaders drew hope from the appointment of a new minister to Russia. The selection of Andrew D. White as minister was greeted with enthusiasm by both Oscar Straus and Jacob Schiff.[47] Schiff wrote White that American Jews had always been concerned that the United States should be represented in St. Petersburg "by a man of enlightened views who should not permit himself to be influenced by the atmosphere often prevailing in court circles." No other choice for minister "could have given us greater pleasure," Schiff told him. White's "love of liberty" and his "ardent sympathy for those oppressed for conscience's sake" meant that Russian Jews would "realize the full measure of benefit attending the presence in St. Petersburg of the envoy from our republic, the only nation in the world which has practically manifested sentiments of humanity towards the subjects of the tsar in their recent terrible suffering." American Jewish leaders expected White to be a good influence on the Russian government in illustrating for the Russians "the advantages that would accrue to Russia were the discriminations against Hebrews removed."[48]

In November of that same year Benjamin Harrison was defeated in his bid for reelection, despite the efforts of American Jewish leaders like Simon Wolf in his behalf.[49] The inauguration of President Grover Cleveland for the second time brought to the State Department Walter Q. Gresham as secretary of state. The new administration scarcely had settled into office before fresh reports of anti-Jewish edicts in Russia brought new requests from American Jewish leaders for action by the United States government. Straus quickly arranged an interview with the secretary of state for himself, Jesse Seligman, Jacob Schiff, and Mayer Isaacs.[50] To Andrew White Straus wrote: "It seems to me, to put it mildly, the moral influence of our government ought to have some weight in averting this catastrophe, especially with you in St. Petersburg and Mr. Cleveland in Washington, and I am in hopes that action on the part of other countries will be taken in the same direction."[51]

The conference was held in mid-May, with not only Gresham but also President Cleveland in attendance. During the meeting, held in the White House, the American Jewish leaders went over the entire subject of Russian anti-Semitic edicts and their enforcement, as well as the large immigration to the United States which was resulting. Straus, after dealing with the humane basis for a protest by the United States, hit hard on the theme that the Russian actions were forcing Jews to immigrate to this country, and that this "minor consideration afforded a good ground for remonstrance—it was contrary to the comity of nations for any nation to put such a pressure upon a portion of its population as to force them in an impoverished condition to seek refuge in other lands." The president expressed agreement with Straus's position, and it was decided that instructions should be sent to Minister White to ascertain the actual condition of affairs and to do whatever could be done to ameliorate the situation of Russian Jews. The president also intimated that the governments of England and France might be consulted to see whether some joint action might not be taken to put a stop to the persecutions.[52]

On May 17, 1893, Secretary of State Gresham cabled White about representations made in Washington "that the Russian Government is about to enforce [an] edict against Jews which will result in a large emigration of destitute people of that class to the United States." White was instructed to inquire whether there was any foundation for the rumors.[53] The minister responded that it was again only a case of the Russian government "enforcing old edicts, regulations and restrictions with apparently even increased severity," and he promised a dispatch with greater information.[54] The promised note was not mailed until six weeks later on July 6, 1893 but was many pages in length and dealt extensively with the disabilities under which Russian Jews were forced to live. Early in the report White told Gresham that upon his arrival in St. Petersburg the rumors were that the treatment of the Jews was to improve

> but the hopes based on this rumor have grown less and less, and it is now clear that the tendency is all in the direction not only of excluding Israelites more rigorously than ever from parts of the Empire where they were formerly allowed on sufferance, but to make life more and more difficult for them in those parts of the Empire where they have been allowed to live for many generations. . . . In the vast jungle of the laws of this Empire [there are] more than one thousand (1000) decrees and statutes relating to them, besides innumerable circulars, open or secret, regulations, restrictions, extensions and temporary arrangements, general, special and local, forming such a tangle of growth that probably no human being can say what the law as a whole is, least of all can a Jew in any province have any certain knowledge of his rights.

Referring to the Weber report, White confessed that when he had first read it the "statements seemed to be exaggerated, or at least over-colored; but it is with very great regret that I say that this is no longer my opinion." The policy of the Russian government was "driving them out of the country in great

masses."[55] In sum, White's report was what one source has referred to as "a classical document" which "deserves to be read
in full by every student of the Jewish question and by the
student of the Jew in Russia in particular."[56] But while refut-
ing virtually every charge which had been made in Russia
against the Jews, and outlining their accomplishments, White
offered no suggestion as to possible action by the United
States government to improve the situation.

Secretary of State Gresham wrote White again concerning
the matter in late December and also called to his attention
a news story from London which reported that destitute Jewish
emigrants were being assisted with funds to immigrate to
America. White, however, found the report to be inaccurate.[57]
Rumors continued to agitate the legation in St. Petersburg and
Jews in the United States of further expulsions of Jews from
St. Petersburg, Moscow, and other restricted areas. The dead-
line for the expulsions, however, was continually extended,
and gradually the sense of crisis diminished.[58] As a result,
immigration to the United States dropped from the high levels
of the early 1890s. The State Department now resumed its
pressure on the Russian government to drop restrictions
against American Jews wishing to travel to Russia. In June of
1893 the chargé in St. Petersburg took the matter up with the
Russian Foreign Ministry, calling attention to the influence of
Jews in the United States and the importance of that influence in a democratic system of government.[59] The legation in
St. Petersburg, however, showed an unwillingness to press the
passport matter with the Russian government, an attitude
which aroused considerable displeasure in the State Department and sharp rebukes from Acting Secretary of State Adee
in July and August of 1895. Russian intransigence, however,
combined with the unwillingness of the legation to press the
matter actively, meant the passport issue between the two nations could not be resolved.[60] The reduction in immigration
and the decline in anti-Jewish incidents in Russia left American Jews with little to concern themselves in Russia. Not until
1903 would Russia again capture the attention of American
Jewish leaders as it had during the early 1890s.

NOTES

1. Samuel Joseph, *Jewish Immigration to the United States from 1881 to 1910* (New York, 1941), p. 93.

2. Mark Wischnitzer, *To Dwell in Safety* (Philadelphia, 1948), p. 48.

3. *American Hebrew*, August 1, 1890; *New York Times*, July 21 and 31, and August 1, 1890.

4. *New York Times*, August 2 and 6, 1890.

5. George W. Wurtz to Acting Secretary of State Wharton, August 1, 1890, Department of State *Despatches from United States Ministers to Russia, 1808-1906*, National Archives Microfilm Publication M35, reel 41 (hereafter cited as DS M35/41).

6. Straus to Baron de Hirsch, August 8, 1890, Oscar S. Straus Papers, Library of Congress.

7. Wharton to Wurtz, August 7, 1890, *Diplomatic Instructions of the Department of State, 1801-1906, Russia*, National Archives Microfilm Publication M77, reel 138 (hereafter cited as DS M77/138); Wurtz to Wharton, August 9, 1890, DS M35/41.

8. Smith to Blaine, September 25, 1890, DS M35/41.

9. Straus to Adee, October 23, 1890, Straus Papers.

10. *American Hebrew*, October 31, 1890.

11. Straus to Goldsmid, December 2, 1890, Straus Papers.

12. *American Hebrew*, December 12 and 19, 1890.

13. Schiff to Loeb, December 20, 1890, Jacob H. Schiff Papers, American Jewish Archives.

14. Straus to Sulzberger, December 23, 1890, Straus Papers.

15. Ibid.

16. Schiff to Loeb, December 20, 1890, Schiff Papers.

17. Straus to Jacob Straus, January 15, 1891, Straus Papers.

18. Straus to Joseph, February 7, 1891, Straus Papers.

19. Schiff to Cassel, January 20, 1891, Schiff Papers.

20. Smith to Blaine, September 25, 1890, DS M35/41.

21. Smith to Blaine, February 10, 1891, DS M35/42.

22. Printed in U.S. Department of State, *Papers Relating to the Foreign Relations of the United States, 1891*, p. 740.

23. Smith to Blaine, February 28, 1891, DS M35/42.

24. Smith to Blaine, March 12, 1891, DS M35/42.

25. *New York Times*, August 6, 1890.

26. *American Hebrew*, December 26, 1890.

27. Schiff to Loeb, March 25, 1891, Schiff Papers; Cyrus M. Adler

and Aaron W. Margalith, *With Firmness in the Right* (New York, 1946), p. 225.

28. Smith to Blaine, April 20, 1891, DS M35/42.

29. Sheldon M. Neuringer, "American Jewry and United States Immigration Policy, 1881-1953" (Ph.D. diss., University of Wisconsin, 1969), pp. 20-25.

30. Straus to Baron de Hirsch, June 5, 1891, Straus Papers.

31. Schiff to Seligman, June 29, 1891, Schiff Papers.

32. Straus to Baron de Hirsch, July 7, 1891, Straus Papers.

33. Schiff to Philip Schiff, July 8, 1891, Schiff Papers.

34. Harrison to Straus, November 5, 1891, Benjamin H. Harrison Papers, Library of Congress.

35. Straus to Harrison, November 11, 1891, Straus Papers.

36. James D. Richardson, ed., *A Compilation of the Messages and Papers of the Presidents* (New York, 1897), vol. 13: 5623.

37. Max J. Kohler to Simon Wolf, November 23, 1916, Max J. Kohler Papers, American Jewish Historical Society Library.

38. *Letter from the Secretary of the Treasury Transmitting a Report of the Commissioners of the Immigration Upon the Causes Which Incite Immigration to the United States*, 52nd Congress, 1st Session, House Executive Document 235 (Washington, D.C., 1892), vol. 1: 100.

39. Schiff to Simon Borg, May 9, 1892, Schiff Papers.

40. Quoted in Neuringer, "American Jewry," p. 29.

41. See, for example, *American Hebrew*, February 12, 1892.

42. *Free Russia*, August 1890.

43. Ibid., September 1890 and April 1906.

44. Ibid., May 1891.

45. Ibid., June 1891; Thomas A. Bailey, *America Faces Russia* (Ithaca, N.Y., 1950), p. 126.

46. *Free Russia*, April 1906.

47. Straus to White, July 2, 1892, and July 22, 1892, Straus Papers.

48. Schiff to White, August 1, 1892, Schiff Papers.

49. See Wolf to Halford, October 15, 1892, Harrison Papers.

50. Straus to Walter Gresham, May 10, 1893, Straus Papers.

51. Straus to White, May 13, 1893, Straus Papers.

52. Straus to White, June 6, 1893, Straus Papers.

53. Gresham to White, May 17, 1893, DS M77/139.

54. White to Gresham, May 18, 1893, DS M35/44.

55. White to Gresham, July 6, 1893, DS M35/45.

56. Adler and Margalith, *Firmness*, p. 238.

57. Aryeh Yodfat, "The Jewish Question in American-Russian Relations, 1875-1917" (Ph.D. diss., American University, 1963), pp. 67-68.

58. See Creighton Webb to Gresham, August 28 and September 3, 1893, White to Gresham, December 15, 1893, and Webb to Gresham, December 31, 1893, all in DS M35/45.

59. Yodfat, "The Jewish Question," p. 71.

60. Ibid., pp. 73-74.

CHAPTER 2

Rumania, 1900-1903

On June 14, 1900, Jacob Schiff wrote to the Jewish Colonization Association (ICA):

> If, upon the assumption that Roumanian authorities are discriminating against Jewish subjects in violation of the Berlin and other treaties, it should become desirable and necessary to ask the cooperation of the United States Government, acting in unison with the European powers, we shall be very willing to use every influence we possess to induce action on the part of our government. Moreover, as you are aware, the Union of American Hebrew Congregations has a special standing committee on "civil and religious rights" of which the honorable Simon Wolf of Washington is chairman, and which likewise will no doubt, when requisite, make an appeal to the Secretary of State of the United States if such should appear judicious.[1]

Early in 1900 the conditions of Jews in Rumania had worsened as new disabilities were imposed upon them by the government which rendered their livelihood even more difficult. European Jews proposed a conference of international Jewry to consider the Rumanian Jewish problem. Schiff, however, was opposed to American participation in any such conference since American Jews, in his view, had all they could cope with simply in caring for those Rumanian Jews who immigrated to the United States.[2] The immigration of Rumanian Jews had increased sizably in 1900, and only through the intervention of American Jewish leaders with the immigration authorities were they permitted into the United States.[3]

The increased immigration of Jews from Rumania, coupled with reports of repressive measures in that country, led the United States government to send Robert Watchorn, an immigration inspector, to survey conditions in that country.[4] Watchorn's report, which was published in two issues of the *American Hebrew* in October of 1900, described the disabilities under which Rumanian Jews were forced to live. He found that in education and in almost every other aspect of life the Jews were forced to live under severe restrictions. "His choice of calling," wrote Watchorn, "is so harshly restricted that it is a great wonder that he finds himself able to meet the ordinary burdens imposed by the State, and much more, that he assumes gratuitously other burdens, such as the school burden." Watchorn described the many occupations from which Jews were barred, the limitations of towns in which Jews were permitted to live, and the requirement on employers to employ two Christians for every Jew that they hired. Watchorn concluded that "the conditions surrounding the Jews in Roumania are harsh, unrelentingly harsh—and that the desire to emigrate will live contemporary with these fettering regulations, and will manifest itself with feverish anxiety, whenever its hopes are kindled by extraneous offers of aid."[5]

The *American Hebrew* concluded from the report that Rumania felt confident in defying the world in its violation of the provisions regarding the Jews in the Treaty of Berlin, since the country felt sure "that no Power will undertake to resent its conduct or compel it to stand by the treaty of Berlin." The journal noted the difference between the Jewish problem as it existed in Rumania and in Russia—in the latter it was largely a religious question, while in the former it was "purely an economic one." The Watchorn report, the journal concluded, had shown American Jews where their duty lay, and they would not shirk from it.[6]

After 1881 scarcely a year had passed in Rumania without the addition of some new restriction of the educational and economic opportunities of the Jews of that kingdom. Through the 1880s and 1890s the attention of international Jewry had been absorbed mainly with the periodic repression of Jews in Russia, but by 1900 the increase in the immigration of Rumanian Jews to the United States, combined with the tales of increased Jewish disabilities in that country, led American Jewish leaders to seek ways of ameliorating conditions there. As Schiff's letter to the ICA indicates, American Jewish leaders by 1900 had great confidence in their ability to evoke from the United States government a response to any appeals for diplomatic intercession in behalf of the Jews in Rumania, based on their success in the early 1890s where Russia had been concerned. Moreover, the influence of the United States in world affairs could be presumed to be stronger in 1900 than in the early 1890s. The naval buildup and industrial growth of that decade had made the United States a nation to be reckoned with. The American victory over Spain in 1898 had led to the acquisition of an overseas empire which rivaled those of the European powers. If there had been any doubt before, there was none any longer that the United States was a world power. As a result, some American Jewish leaders suggested that the "center of gravity" of international Jewry was clearly shifting to the United States.[7]

In defiance of the condemnation which its behavior was engendering, the Rumanian government further constricted the opportunities for the livelihood of Jews in that country by additional restrictions in 1901. The most notorious was the Trades Law of March 1901, the effect of which was virtually to prohibit the employment of Jewish workers in any trade.[8] European Jewish leaders warned their counterparts in the United States that the effect of such legislation would be to deprive some sixty thousand Rumanian Jews of employment, compelling many of them to leave the country.[9] Most of them presumably would be forced to immigrate to the United States, a prospect that was not greeted with enthusiasm by some American Jewish leaders. According to Sheldon Neuringer, American Jews were concerned that the Rumanian immigration contained a number of Hebraic scholars and unskilled persons with unlikely prospects of self-dependence in the United States. This situation led the United Hebrew Charities to protest to the London Jewish Board of Guardians over their sending immigrants "not adapted to life in America."[10]

In London Jewish leaders like Lord Rothschild sought action, with slight success, from the British government.[11] The Rumanian situation, however, seemed especially appropriate for a diplomatic situation. Rumanian Jews had been endowed with legal rights by international treaties, even though those rights were being ignored by their government. As previously noted, Rumania was a creation of the Treaty of Berlin of 1878, one article of which provided that:

> The difference of religious creeds and confessions shall not be alleged against any persons as a ground for exclusion or incapacity in matters relating to the enjoyment of civil and political rights, admission to public employments, functions and honors, or the exercise of various professions and industries in any locality whatever.[12]

The question was whether the European powers who were parties to the Treaty of Berlin could be induced to force Rumanian adherence to the terms of the treaty.

In April of 1902 Jacob Schiff, widely regarded as the leading figure in the American Jewish community and one of the two foremost investment bankers in the United States, had a great deal on his mind. Not many months had elapsed since he and E. H. Harriman of the Union Pacific Railway had been locked in a great financial contest with banker J. P. Morgan and railroad tycoon James J. Hill, the outcome of which had been the formation of the Northern Securities Company, a holding company designed to protect the interests of both sides. Now in April of 1902 the Northern Securities Company was itself under attack, challenged in the federal courts by the administration of Theodore Roosevelt.[13] Early in the month Schiff had the opportunity to travel to Washington to press his views on the situation in person to the president.[14] Schiff resolved to take advantage of the opportunity also to take up with Roosevelt the desirability of some action on the part of the government in behalf of the human rights of the Jews of Rumania. Before leaving for Washington, Schiff met with Oscar Straus. Straus knew from his European contacts that there was little likelihood any European government would intercede in behalf of Rumanian Jewry, and that European Jews, with little justification, looked to American Jewish leaders to exert influence on the United States government to take the lead in applying pressure on the Rumanian government.[15] Schiff, who had advocated joint action with the European powers two years earlier, now wrote in April concerning the Rumanian situation that he was:

> thoroughly alive to the necessity of our moving so that, if possible, a better state of affairs may be brought about. The President has asked me to go to Washington on another matter and I expect to be there on Thursday, and hope when I talk to the President I shall have an opportunity to unofficially interrogate him as to what can be done by his administration towards an effectual relief of the horrible situation which exists.[16]

On April 1 Schiff met with Straus and was briefed on the latter's understanding of the Rumanian situation. The next day Straus sent to Schiff a memorandum to be presented to Roosevelt "regarding the inhuman treatment of the Jews by the Roumanian Government." Straus wrote:

> Following the conversation I had with you yesterday regarding the terrible persecutions of our coreligionists by the Roumanian Government, and as you informed me that you intended going to Washington tomorrow

> and have a conversation with the President respecting
> some other matters, I trust that you will lay before
> him a statement regarding the inhuman treatment of
> the Jews by the Roumanian Government.
>
> If the matter were of concern to the government and
> people of the United States, and especially to the Jews
> of our country, from only a humanitarian standpoint,
> I would not have the President's noble heart disturbed
> with its recital, but as it is one of practically interna-
> tional bearing, I think it but proper and just that we
> should get the President's advice on the subject.

Straus then recited for Schiff the provisions of the Treaty of
Berlin bearing upon the Jewish question. He added:

> Notwithstanding this express provision of the treaty,
> the Jews are excluded from civil rights, excepting that
> they are compelled to serve in the army, but not per-
> mitted to become officers therein.
>
> They are subject to exceptional taxes, they are practi-
> cally excluded from all professions and from owning
> and cultivating land, and new laws are being promul-
> gated, practically shutting them out from every avenue
> of self-support. They are not permitted to become
> citizens, excepting in rare instances. Now what is the
> result?

The result, of course, was mass exodus of Jews from Rumania,
with a high proportion of that emigration coming to the shores
of the United States. Using what was by now the stock argument of American Jewish leaders as grounds for American protest, Straus suggested the forcing of large numbers of a country's subjects to immigrate to the United States, many of them
in a pauperized condition, constituted an unfriendly act toward
this nation which gave the United States the right "not only
to protest but to remonstrate against such inhuman laws that
discredit the age in which we are living."[17]

In his letter to Schiff, Straus also pointed to the strong position the United States had taken under President Ulysses S. Grant in the face of such action by Rumania in 1872 and the moderating effect such action had apparently exerted on the government there, and argued that similar action by the United States was now called for and would be equally effective. He suggested a strong resolution by both houses of Congress "expressive of sympathy and protesting against the inhuman treatment on the part of Roumania of unoffending people, who are driven by the hand of persecution to seek refuge in our country." Straus also urged that a minister or special commissioner should be sent to Rumania to "remonstrate against this action" by the government there. Such actions, he believed, would not only have an immediate impact on Rumania, but would also awaken other enlightened European nations to take an interest in the situation.[18]

After consulting also with Leo N. Levi, head of B'nai B'rith, on the Rumanian problem Schiff met with President Roosevelt on April 4, 1902.[19] The conservative banker was quite a contrast to the impetuous and progressive Roosevelt, but in fact their ties were close. Like the president, Schiff was a New Yorker and a Republican and his own relations with progressive reformers in that city were substantial. There were, of course, other reasons why Roosevelt was well advised to listen carefully when Schiff offered counsel relating to Jewish concerns. The Jewish vote was growing more substantial daily, especially in the Eastern cities, and sizable campaign donations flowed into Republican coffers from Jewish businessmen like Schiff. Since Roosevelt had antagonized Schiff through his actions in the Northern Securities matter, he could well exhibit sympathy in the Rumanian affair. Schiff found the president uninformed about the persecutions in Rumania. Roosevelt called in Secretary of State John Hay who pointed out the difficulties in the way of bringing any diplomatic pressure to bear on the Rumanian government, but the president assured Schiff of sympathy and promised to find some method of taking action.[20] As a result of Schiff's visit with the president, Oscar Straus was summoned to Washington for a confer-

ence on the subject with Roosevelt and Hay. At that meeting
Straus pressed for action by the United States government and
presented Roosevelt with a statement concerning the persecution of Rumanian Jews and the resultant immigration of large
numbers of them to the United States. The president referred
the statement to Hay and the secretary of state sought additional information from Straus.[21] It seemed that the United
States was moving to intercede with Rumania.

The apparent sympathy of the Roosevelt administration
toward the cause was encouraging because all signs pointed to
the likelihood that the European powers signatory to the
Berlin treaty were unwilling to take any action on their own
initiative. In March Straus learned that Lord Rothschild had
sought action from the British government without success.
The British, he was told, were "perfectly well inclined, but
will not act alone, and France is still less likely." The news
that Roosevelt seemed disposed to act on behalf of the
Rumanian Jews cheered English Jewish leaders who were confident that if the United States took the lead in the matter the
British government would follow. It was then "highly probable
that the other leading states of Europe would follow so good
an example."[22]

Weeks passed, however, and in mid-May the Roosevelt administration had not yet acted. For Schiff and Straus, who had
trumpeted their successful conference with the administration
to European Jewish leaders, the lack of movement by the
government was an embarrassment. Schiff wrote to Straus suggesting that he communicate once again with the secretary of
state to impress upon him "that we do not mean to let this
matter sleep, and that the eyes of the world are upon us." For
his part, Schiff was working to "induce some of our important
newspapers to reprint the articles on the Roumanian situation
which fill the European, and especially German press. . . . Such
publications in our own press will serve both the purpose of
bringing pressure upon our State Department as well as having
its influence in Europe."[23]

Instead of writing to Hay, Straus wrote directly to President
Roosevelt pointing out that the condition of Jews in Rumania

had only worsened further since his interview with the president. Reviewing once again for Roosevelt the terms of the Berlin treaty, and citing precedents in past American protests over Rumanian persecution of the Jews, Straus concluded:

> The remonstrances of our government in behalf of oppressed humanity, which time and again had so much effect in the past, cannot fail to have great influence at this present crisis impending over the Jews of Roumania. The government of no country has a better right to make such a remonstrance than the United States, which will in all probability receive the largest number of these oppressed people, who are forced by these restrictive and repressive laws to seek a refuge in foreign lands.[24]

Upon receiving a copy of the letter from Straus, Schiff wrote the former that he was "entirely in accord" with its contents. He was, however, "afraid Mr. Hay does not feel very much like taking any action. . . . Where there is a will there is a way, but I fear there is little will in this instance."[25]

Schiff and Straus continued to work quietly, however, and avoided participation in the meetings called in major American cities to protest Rumanian persecution of the Jews. By early June Straus was hopeful that action would be taken soon. He had been told the question was to have been taken up at a cabinet meeting only a few days earlier, but had been postponed for a few days. He was hopeful that the government would make direct diplomatic remonstrances not only to the Rumanian government, but also "through our diplomatic representatives at several of the European courts."[26] A few days later Straus learned from Congressman Lucius N. Littauer—a Republican from upstate New York, a German Jew, and a close friend of the president—that Roosevelt had advised him of his determination to take action in the Rumanian matter. The problem was now to be brought before the cabinet at its June 10 meeting, after which a protest would be brought to the attention of the Rumanian government and also of the governments signa-

tory to the Berlin treaty.[27] Matters seemed to be developing
as Straus desired.

Roosevelt's desire to act, however, was delayed by Hay's ill
health and by the concern of the secretary with finding a proper
diplomatic vehicle for such a protest.[28] Throughout the month
of June rumors circulated that the matter was to be taken up
by a cabinet meeting that month, while public protests against
Rumania continued to be held despite attempts by American
Jewish leaders to discourage such protests in favor of the direct
pressure on the government which they felt was succeeding.[29]
Congressman Littauer pressed Roosevelt for news on the
progress of the diplomatic protests and was told by the president on June 20 that Hay was "working as rapidly as possible"
and that Littauer could expect to receive a copy of the protest
"in a few days." The protest, however, was not forthcoming
in the promised time and on July 10 Littauer pressed Roosevelt
again for action, arguing the likelihood that other governments
would follow the lead of the United States if it acted promptly.[30]
By the middle of July Schiff had grown concerned, querying
Straus about the lack of progress and expressing the fear that if
nothing were done before the president left Washington for the
summer it was unlikely that the protest would be formulated
before the fall season.[31]

In fact, the president did not act before he left Washington,
but he did ask Littauer to visit him at his home at Oyster Bay
to discuss further the Rumanian matter. Littauer promised
Straus he would "insist that this long delay in connection with
this protest must come to an end, for in view of the persecution
going on, I cannot appreciate why this delay should continue."[32]
On July 17 Secretary of State Hay at last forwarded to Roosevelt
the proposed Rumanian note, writing: "You will see in reading
it that it has not been easy to handle, but I have availed myself
of what seems our only excuse, the pending naturalization
treaty with Roumania, to read them a pretty drastic letter on
their duty to the Jews."[33] The president found the draft "ad-
mirable" and made sure that Congressman Littauer informed
Straus and Schiff of its contents.[34]

Hay's protest took the form of a confidential instruction to the American chargé d'affaires in Athens, who was responsible for representing the United States with the Rumanian government. As Hay pointed out to the president, the instruction was with reference to a proposed naturalization treaty between the United States and Rumania. A tentative draft of such a treaty had been submitted previously to the Rumanians, which followed the lines of one submitted to the Serbian government. The proposed treaty was not the prime motivation behind Hay's note, and this point was made clear by his explanation to the president and by the correspondence between American Jewish leaders and the administration in which outrage over Rumania's persecution of its Jewish subjects dominated. It is also inconceivable that the United States would have dispatched copies of the note to the signatories of the Treaty of Berlin if the focus of the affair had been the pending naturalization treaty. Rather, Hay used the pending naturalization treaty as a vehicle for furnishing the chargé, Charles Wilson, with the opportunity to take up the American position with the Rumanians on their treatment of the Jews. After discussing the American naturalization of Rumanian immigrants, Hay moved quickly in the note to an examination of Rumanian immigration to the United States. He reviewed for Wilson (and, through Wilson, for the Rumanians) the treaty rights guaranteed to Jews in Rumania, then wrote:

> With the lapse of time these just prescriptions have been rendered nugatory in great part, as regards the native Jews, by the legislation and municipal regulations of Roumania. Starting from the arbitrary and controvertible premise that the native Jews of Roumania domiciled there for centuries are "aliens not subject to foreign protection," the ability of the Jew to earn even the scanty means of existence that suffices for a frugal race has been constricted by degrees, until nearly every opportunity to win a livelihood is denied; and until the helpless poverty of the Jew has constrained an exodus of such proportions as to cause general concern.[35]

Such persecution, Hay observed, could lead to only one of two results—submission or flight. The United States was a haven for the oppressed of the world, but "its sympathy with them in nowise impairs its just liberty and right to weigh the acts of the oppressor in the light of their effects upon this country, and to judge accordingly." The fact that the Jews of Rumania were being forced to emigrate by virtue of the persecution in their home country, that the United States was virtually the only refuge open to them, and that they arrived in this country in such an abject state so as to need public charity from the time of their arrival, meant "the right of remonstrance against the acts of the Roumanian Government is clearly established in favor of this Government." Rumania was forcing its Jewish subjects "upon the charity of the United States," and the United States government could not be "a tacit party to such an international wrong." Hay concluded:

> It is constrained to protest against the treatment to which the Jews of Roumania are subjected, not alone because it has unimpeachable ground to remonstrate against the resultant injury to itself, but in the name of humanity. The United States may not authoritatively appeal to the stipulations of the treaty of Berlin, to which it was not and can not become signatory, but it does earnestly appeal to the principles consigned therein, because they are principles of international law and eternal justice, advocating the broad toleration which that solemn compact enjoins and standing ready to lend its moral support to the fulfillment thereof by its cosignatories, for the act of Roumania itself has effectively joined the United States to them as an interested party in this regard.[36]

The intent of Hay's note, however, seems to have been lost on the American chargé d'affaires. The subtleties of the note were apparently too profound for Wilson, who took up the note with the Rumanian minister to Greece primarily with

reference to the pending naturalization treaty. The topic of the
Rumanian Jews apparently was brought up only by the Rumanian minister as an argument against the negotiation of such
a naturalization treaty. The real purpose of Hay's communication, to criticize Rumania's treatment of its Jews, was apparently lost on Wilson.[37] In subsequent correspondence, however, Assistant Secretary of State Alvey A. Adee made the real
purpose of the dispatch clear even to Wilson.[38] From the beginning Adee, draftsman of the note for Hay, had intended
that it should be followed by "the next logical step, namely
an appeal to the Berlin signatories to see that the provisions of
article forty-four are carried out in Roumania in purpose and
spirit as the framers meant it." Adee suggested that the United
States should either sound out Great Britain, urging that nation
"to take the initiative as a signatory in calling upon the co-
signatories" to enforce the terms of the treaty, with the United
States simultaneously addressing an appeal to the others, or
that the United States should itself take the initiative by sending identical notes to each of the seven signatory powers "using
as much of the Roumanian instruction as will fit the case."[39]

Like Straus earlier, Littauer, Schiff, and Simon Wolf all suggested that the Hay note on Rumania should itself be sent to
the signatory powers of the Treaty of Berlin. As Schiff wrote
Littauer, he had seen the U.S. protest to Rumania and considered it "a masterful presentation of the conditions which
justify our Government to make a remonstrance and protest."
He had written to both the president and the secretary of
state thanking them and suggesting, as had Littauer, that copies
of the note should be sent to the treaty signatories. Schiff did
not believe that the impression of the American note on the
Rumanian government would be effective "except if, at the
same time, the Roumanian Government becomes aware that
the Great Powers have been notified by our Government of the
position it has assumed."[40] From this it appears that Schiff
was crediting the assurances that he had received from European Jewish leaders that once the United States took the
initiative Great Britain, at the least, would not be far behind.

Secretary of State Hay agreed to send the note on to the

treaty powers and on August 11, 1902, the United States addressed identical notes to its diplomatic representatives to the British, French, German, Italian, Russian, Turkish, and Austro-Hungarian governments, referring to the July 17 dispatch to Wilson on the subject of Rumania. The note added:

> It has seemed to the President that these considerations, relating as they do to the obligations entered into by the signatories of the treaty of Berlin of July 13, 1878, should be brought to the attention of the Governments concerned and commended to their consideration in the hope that, if they are so fortunate as to meet the approval of the several powers, such measures as to them may seem wise may be taken to persuade the Government of Roumania to reconsider the subject of the grievance in question.

The substance of the July 17 note followed concerning the repression of Jews in Rumania, and the resultant immigration to the United States, but without reference to the proposed naturalization treaty which had been the professed purpose of the original note.[41]

The signatories of the Treaty of Berlin, however, evinced little or no interest in the American initiative. Only the British responded with any degree of concern. According to Ambassador Joseph Choate, the British replied to the American note by joining the United States in "deploring the depressed condition of the Roumanian Jews and in regarding with apprehension the results of their enforced emigration," and reported that the British government would communicate with the signatories of the Berlin Treaty "with a view to a joint presentation to the Roumanian Government on the subject."[42] However, the British found no sentiment among the continental powers for such a joint presentation and the matter was dropped.[43] French Jewish leaders sought to stir the governments of France and Italy to action by their entreaties but failed.[44]

American Jewish leaders nevertheless reacted favorably to the notes to Rumania and the treaty powers. Schiff's response

that it was "a masterful presentation" has already been noted.
Simon Wolf expressed himself as "thoroughly satisfied" with
"the splendid letter of Mr. Hay, which is record making and
bound to be of great service to our people at home and abroad."[45]
Leo N. Levi, president of B'nai B'rith, likewise felt "assured
that a valuable step has been taken in the right direction on
this side by the reiteration of the traditional policy of the
Republic."[46] Oscar Straus addressed complimentary letters to
both Roosevelt and Hay. To the latter he wrote:

> You have formulated as no one has done before you,
> the high ethical principles and humanitarian considera-
> tions that lie at the basis of international relations in
> directing the attention of the great powers of Europe
> to the persecutions of Roumania in violation of human
> rights and of the express provisions of the Berlin Treaty.
> The hearts of a suffering people pulsate with gratitude
> for this forceful display and humanitarian remonstrance
> in their behalf.[47]

American Jewish leaders also were gratified by the release to
the Jewish press of the circular note to the treaty powers in
advance of its release to the wire services, thus enabling the
Jewish newspapers of the country to "scoop" the rest of the
media.[48]

European Jewish leaders, unable to evoke actions from their
own governments to protest the happenings in Rumania, had
appealed to American Jewish leaders in 1900 and 1901 to seek
such a protest from the United States government, suggesting
that if the United States took the initiative at least some of
the European powers would cooperate. American Jewish leaders like Oscar Straus had doubted the likelihood that any action
could be obtained from the United States government, but made
a determined effort.[49] Those efforts were rewarded by the Hay
notes. Prominent American Jews had demonstrated that they
could and would act effectively in mobilizing the United States
government to act in behalf of Jewish human rights in eastern
Europe.

Despite his own efforts in behalf of the Rumanian protest,

Jacob Schiff had little faith that it would have much effect. He was convinced that any protest from the United States would be without result unless it were accompanied by expressions of concern from the signatories of the Berlin treaty. It was for that reason that he had suggested the dispatch of the circular note to those powers outlining the American position. When the European powers failed to act as European Jews had suggested they would, Schiff was not surprised. Nor was he very sanguine that the Rumanian government would react to diplomatic efforts from any source. In his view the Jewish problem in Rumania would not be solved by diplomacy, but rather by the press of financial necessities upon the Rumanian government.[50] Financial pressure, however, could be applied only by the great banking houses of Europe, since American bankers were not active in such financial activities. Thereafter, Schiff exerted every effort among European bankers to thwart Rumania's attempts to obtain foreign loans unless the Rumanian government made concessions where the treatment of its Jewish subjects was concerned. Oscar Straus, however, was optimistic that the diplomatic pressure alone would be effective. Writing to Congressman Littauer to thank him for his assistance, Straus confided:

> Our friends here who knew something about what was being attempted felt perfectly confident that we would not be able to get our government to act. All has been done and in the very best form which we possibly could have a right to ask, and I know enough about European matters to feel quite certain the effect will be material and the precedent will be one that will be invoked long after you and I have passed away.[51]

Whether from diplomatic or financial pressure or a combination of both, the Rumanian government did, in fact, begin to show a more conciliatory attitude toward its Jewish subjects in the months following the Hay notes.

American Jewish leaders continued to interest themselves in the treatment of Jews in Rumania after the Hay notes were sent. In March of 1903 Congressman Littauer reported to Straus

on steps he had taken to keep the Department of State abreast
of Rumanian matters. He had found little response to further
appeals for action, but he had insisted with President Roosevelt
that the U.S. minister to Greece should make a fact-finding
trip to Rumania to ascertain the status of Jews there and to
determine whether there had been any practical effect obtained
from the Hay note and the letters to the treaty powers. The
president had agreed, and the American minister had been instructed to make the trip.[52] In his instructions to the minister
Hay cited the circular notes he had sent to the signatories of
the Berlin treaty and informed him that it was "the President's
desire" that he should "discreetly and cautiously endeavor to
learn whether the considerations so presented to them have resulted in any representations to the Roumanian Government by
the powers" for amelioration of the conditions of Jews in that
country in conformity to the terms of the Berlin treaty. "The
matter," Hay wrote, "is one in which the President has deep
interest," and the minister was instructed to furnish all the
information he could gather.[53] The American minister found
no evidence in Rumania that any such representations by the
powers had been made, nor did he form any strong sympathy
for the Jewish position based on his own observations and conversations with government figures in that country.[54] As "proof"
that Rumanian Jews were better off than others in eastern Europe, he cited evidence that as fast as Rumanian Jews emigrated
they were replaced by Jewish immigrants from elsewhere in
eastern Europe.

The fact that Rumanian Jews were at least better off than
those in Russia was made dramatically clear by the Kishinev
pogrom during April of 1903. Rumanian Jews might struggle
for a livelihood, but Russian Jews were being massacred and
their property destroyed. The attention and energies of American Jewish leaders were quickly distracted from Rumania to
Russia by this outrage. New pressures were launched upon the
Roosevelt administration for action toward Russia, in part at
least because the precedents had been established for official
concern in the early 1890s and in 1902.

Attempts have been made to denigrate the role of Secretary
of State Hay in the Rumanian matter. One historian has de-

scribed Hay's note to Wilson as "a strange document, full of interesting *non sequiturs*," in analyzing the argument upon which the State Department rested its remonstrance.[55] The statement, while accurate as far as it goes, ignores the fact that the "non sequiturs" of the Hay note had firm precedent in the American remonstrance to Russia in Blaine's note of February 18, 1891 and in other precedents, including Harrison's message to Congress of December 9, 1891. The same historian writes that the Hay note "was not a note to the Rumanian Government; it was only a confidential instruction about a naturalization treaty to the American Chargé."[56] This, too, is true as far as it goes, but it was clearly Hay's intention in phrasing the note, in his own words, to "read them a pretty drastic letter on their duty to the Jews." A number of historians have pointed out that the note itself was not drafted by Hay, but by Alvey A. Adee, and have suggested that the motivation of Hay and Roosevelt was primarily political.[57] The fact that a secretary of state did not personally pen the first draft of a dispatch which went out over his name is something so commonplace that it hardly deserves mention. Nor is it particularly noteworthy that diplomatic actions are taken with an eye to their domestic political consequences. As a matter of fact, Theodore Roosevelt might well have been looking far ahead to 1904, but the only election on the horizon in 1902 was the congressional race of that year, and the number of congressional races which could be affected by such a move on the part of the Roosevelt administration was small indeed. To the suggestion from a European coreligionist that Roosevelt and Hay were politically motivated in their willingness to take up the Rumanian problem, Jacob Schiff responded with fervor:

> President Roosevelt in his procedure was not at all influenced by the possible advantages which his position towards Roumania might bring him from American voters. The whole character of the man and also of Secretary of State, Mr. John Hay, conflict with any such supposition. . . . Ordinary fairness towards President Roosevelt and his spotless character compels me to disabuse you of this impression, which you have

apparently been holding, although I do not know where you receive it.[58]

Hay himself did not overestimate the effect of his notes on the Rumanian situation even in his correspondence with Jewish leaders. To Oscar Straus he wrote that he hoped "that some good may result from what we have done, even if for the moment Roumania seems obdurate and some of the Great Powers indifferent to the moral question involved."[59]

Not all American Jews felt that sending the Hay notes was a wise course of action in the Rumanian matter. Some hailed Hay's action, but expressed concern that the basis of the American protest—the Rumanian immigration to the United States—might lead to steps for the restriction of immigration. The *American Israelite* editorialized:

> The communication by the Hon. Simon Wolf, in which he explains how the Hay note was brought about, makes it clear that a strong pressure was exercised upon our State Department by Jewish organizations, mostly from New York. The Roumanian government was directly appealed·to without satisfactory result, before our Secretary of State proceeded to arraign its course by appealing to the signatory powers. It is all, then, the direct outcome of a feeling on the part of New York and other Jews that they were unable to cope with the emergency. Whether they have taken the proper steps in moving the tremendous levers of government aid and demonstrating their influence to the world is fairly subject to doubt; whether they have tried every other expedient before resorting to this desperate one may also, in good conscience, be questioned. . . . The historian will some day weigh the whole situation and judge these measures; it may then be found that the Roumanian Jew has been officially branded as "a diseased growth," the last open door brought nearer to closing, simply because our leaders were not strong enough to grasp the situation manfully and firmly.[60]

This, of course, was a continual risk when using the immigration argument as a basis for diplomatic action. The impression could easily gain currency that it was the immigration and not the human rights issue which was the principal problem, and if this problem could not be solved through diplomatic remonstrance it could be through a restrictive immigration policy. Fortunately, the fears of the *American Israelite* were unfounded in 1902.

NOTES

1. Schiff to the ICA, June 14, 1900, Jacob H. Schiff Papers.
2. Schiff to Kahn, June 20, 1900, Schiff Papers.
3. Schiff to Cowen, July 2 and 6, 1900, Philip H. Cowen Papers, American Jewish Historical Society Library.
4. Schiff to Cowen, July 27, 1900, Cowen Papers.
5. *American Hebrew*, October 26, 1900.
6. Ibid.
7. Schiff and Goldman to Hallgarten and Plotke, November 12, 1901, Schiff Papers.
8. *American Hebrew*, October 10, 1902.
9. Mocatta to Straus, February 11, 1902, Oscar S. Straus Papers.
10. Sheldon M. Neuringer, "American Jewry and United States Immigration Policy, 1881-1953" (Ph.D. diss., University of Wisconsin, 1969), p. 52.
11. Mocatta to Straus, March 31, 1902, Straus Papers.
12. Quoted in Max J. Kohler, "Jewish Rights at International Congresses," *American Jewish Yearbook* (1917-1918), pp. 151-52.
13. A recent description of the Northern Securities issue is in Albro Martin, *James J. Hill and the Opening of the Northwest* (New York, 1976), pp. 508-19.
14. Cyrus M. Adler, *Jacob H. Schiff: His Life and Letters*, 2 vols. (Garden City, N.Y., 1928), 1: 411-12.
15. Mocatta to Straus, February 11 and March 31, 1902, Straus Papers. For a brief discussion of Straus's role in the American protest to Rumania see Naomi W. Cohen, *A Dual Heritage* (Philadelphia, 1969), pp. 124-26.
16. Schiff to the ICA, June 14, 1900, and Schiff to Isaacs, April 1, 1902, Schiff Papers.
17. Straus to Schiff, April 2, 1902, Straus Papers.
18. Ibid.

19. Schiff to Levi, April 2, 1902, Schiff Papers.

20. Schiff to Ochs, May 14, 1902, in Adler, *Schiff*, 2: 153.

21. Straus to Mocatta, April 14, 1902, Straus Papers.

22. Mocatta to Straus, May 1, 1902, Straus Papers.

23. Schiff to Straus, May 14, 1902, Straus Papers.

24. Straus to Roosevelt, May 15, 1902, Straus Papers.

25. Schiff to Straus, May 19, 1902, Schiff Papers.

26. Straus to Mocatta, June 6, 1902, Straus Papers.

27. Littauer to Straus, June 9, 1902, Straus Papers.

28. Straus to Mocatta, July 18, 1902, Straus Papers; Hay to Roosevelt, July 17, 1902, Roosevelt Papers, Library of Congress.

29. Straus to Mocatta, June 6, 1902, and Littauer to Straus, June 9, 1902, Straus Papers; *American Hebrew*, June 6, 1902; Straus to Littauer, (mid-June) 1902, Straus Papers.

30. Littauer to Straus, July 10, 1902, Straus Papers.

31. Schiff to Straus, July 14, 1902, Straus Papers.

32. Littauer to Straus, July 14, 1902, Straus Papers.

33. Hay to Roosevelt, July 17, 1902, Roosevelt Papers.

34. Roosevelt to Hay, July 18, 1902, and Hay to Roosevelt, July 21, 1902, Roosevelt Papers.

35. Hay to Wilson, July 17, 1902, in Department of State, *Papers Relating to the Foreign Relations of the United States, 1902*, pp. 910-14.

36. Ibid.

37. Wilson to Hay, August 8, 1902, *Foreign Relations, 1902*, pp. 914-15.

38. Adee to Wilson, August 22, 1902, *Foreign Relations, 1902*, p. 915.

39. Adee to Hay, July 29, 1902, Hay Papers, Library of Congress.

40. Hay to Roosevelt, July 28, 1902, Roosevelt Papers; Adee to Hay, July 29, 1902, Hay Papers; Schiff to Littauer, July 28, 1902, in Adler, *Schiff*, 2: 153-54.

41. Hay to Roosevelt, July 28, 1902, Roosevelt Papers. A copy of the note is printed as Hay to McCormick, August 11, 1902, in *Foreign Relations, 1902*, pp. 42-45.

42. Choate to Hay, September 3, 1902, in *Foreign Relations, 1902*, pp. 549-50.

43. Jackson to Hay, March 21 and April 18, 1903, *Foreign Relations, 1903*, pp. 702-3; see also Lucien Wolf, *Notes on the Diplomatic History of the Jewish Question* (London, 1919), pp. 37-38.

44. *American Hebrew*, November 14, 1902.

45. Wolf to Cowen, September 19, 1902, Cowen Papers.

46. Levi to Wolf, September 10, 1902, Wolf Papers, American Jewish Historical Society Library.

47. Straus to Hay, September 30, 1902, and Straus to Roosevelt, October 1, 1902, Straus Papers.

48. Wolf to Cowen, September 12, 1902, Cowen Papers.

49. Straus to Littauer, September 24, 1902, Straus Papers.

50. Schiff to Nathan, October 10, 1902, Schiff Papers.

51. Straus to Littauer, September 24, 1902, Straus Papers.

52. Littauer to Straus, March 11, 1903, ibid.

53. Hay to Jackson, March 5, 1903, *Foreign Relations, 1903*, p. 704.

54. Jackson to Hay, March 21, 1903, *Foreign Relations, 1903*, p. 704.

55. Tyler Dennett, *John Hay* (New York, 1934), p. 396.

56. Ibid.

57. Ibid.; Kenton J. Clymer, *John Hay* (Ann Arbor, Mich., 1975), p. 77.

58. Schiff to Nathan, October 10, 1902, Schiff Papers.

59. Hay to Straus, October 4, 1902, Straus Papers.

60. *American Israelite*, October 9, 1902.

CHAPTER 3

Russia, 1903

As 1903 began American Jewish leaders had reason to be satisfied with their influence on American policy toward Russia and Rumania. Not only had they been successful in bringing about action by the United States government on behalf of their east European coreligionists, but those actions seemed to have calmed the situation. Nearly a decade of relative tranquility had resulted in Russia after the expressions of official American concern in the early 1890s, and the situation in Rumania seemed likewise to have improved. Certainly there was little cause for feeling that their response to any future emergencies would be any less effective. Moreover, a definite basis for the expression of official American concern had been laid and now rested upon the sound precedents established by the American protests to Russia in the early 1890s and to Rumania in 1902. This, of course, was the alleged damage inflicted upon the United States by the immigration which resulted from repressive policies in those countries. American protests did not need to rest any longer upon humanitarian appeals alone. The fact that the immigration argument presented risks was disturbing to some American Jews, and that it detracted from the idealism of appeals based solely upon humanitarian considerations bothered others, but for those of a legalistic bent the immigration aspect offered a powerful argument which could be used in moving Washington to take action.

The Kishinev massacre and the American response were not without their ironies in 1903. The Russian Empire had initiated the first peace conference at The Hague in 1899, which established rules of warfare and a permanent court of international arbitration, yet the same nation permitted—even encouraged—the anti-Semitism that culminated in such pogroms as that at Kishinev in April 1903. American Jews protested the events in Russia at a time when the United States was, itself, passing through a period of violence against blacks and had just completed a brutally inhumane war of suppression in the Philippines.[1] The Kishinev affair also intruded into Russian-American relations at a time when those relations were already strained over apparent Russian designs on Manchuria to the likely detriment of American economic interests there.[2]

From April 19 through 21, an obviously prearranged and carefully planned pogrom was carried out by Russian mobs against the Jewish population of Kishinev which resulted in the deaths of forty-seven Jews, injury to over four hundred others, and damage to property amounting to an estimated 2.5 million rubles. Appeals from Jewish leaders of the city went unanswered by the authorities until the end of the second day, by which time the greater share of the damage had been done already.[3] News of the outrage was not long in reaching the United States, and American Jewish leaders responded promptly to the reports. The first reaction was to organize relief for the sufferers of the massacre. A wire was sent to Jacob Schiff from the Alliance Universelle Israelite requesting American Jews to organize a committee for fund raising, and Schiff immediately called a meeting of leading American Jews to begin such an effort.[4] Meanwhile, Simon Wolf pressed the State Department to learn from the Russians if assistance might be delivered to the survivors. On April 29, Secretary of State Hay wired Ambassador Robert McCormick to inquire "if financial aid and supplies would be permitted to reach the sufferers" at Kishinev and asked him to ascertain this "without discussing political phase of the situation."[5] A week later the State Department still had received no reply from St. Petersburg.[6]

Meanwhile, Simon Wolf wrote to Leo N. Levi of the B'nai

B'rith to ask the assistance of that organization, with its many
branches across the United States, in raising funds for the relief
of the Kishinev victims. Levi, however, was concerned that the
resources of the American Jewish community should be allo-
cated instead to the care of the inevitable flood of Russian
immigrants, which must be expected as a result of the new
persecutions in Russia, and argued that the relief of the
Kishinev victims was the responsibility of European Jews. European Jews, by calling for financial aid from the United States,
were in Levi's view attempting to "saddle" American Jews
"with the burdens that they should properly bear themselves,"
and it would set "a dangerous precedent to apply for financial
relief in this country whenever such events occurred." He proposed to discourage all efforts to raise money in the B'nai B'rith.[7]
The *American Hebrew* and other Jewish organs, however, followed Schiff and others in urging that American Jews let their
"purse strings open quickly to aid the distress in Russia."[8]

The demands of American Jewish leaders for diplomatic
intercession by the United States government with Russia in the
early 1890s and with Rumania in 1902 had come about in response to policies by those two governments directed at their
Jewish subjects. The Kishinev massacre was not an action of the
Russian government and did not lend itself well to the same
type of diplomatic protest. Awareness of the distinction led
Schiff to abandon the opposition to public protests that he
had displayed in the early 1890s and in 1902 and to assist actively in recruiting major figures for such a mass protest meeting
by non-Jews in New York City. Persuasively he wrote to New
York Mayor Seth Low:

> Upon a call of citizens of New York of the non-Jewish
> faith, a mass meeting will be held on the evening of
> Wednesday, May 27th, at Carnegie Hall to give expres-
> sion to the abhorrence and indignation at the outrages
> which have been committed against the Jews of
> Kishineff, Russia. Men of prominence have been asked
> to address the meeting, and it is hoped that, like other
> communities, New York's expression will be made in

no uncertain voice so that even a government constituted as the Russian Government is, will be made to understand that the civilized world holds it responsible for the outrages it has permitted to be practiced upon innocent and defenseless subjects. It is hoped that you, as chief magistrate of this community, will consent to preside at the mass meeting which has been called, and we doubt not that you will welcome the opportunity as a leader of public opinion to give practical evidence of your desire to cooperate effectively with those who have taken charge of this movement.[9]

In explaining his shift in tactics from diplomatic protest to the arousal of public opinion, Schiff wrote a coreligionist:

As to intervention or remonstrance by the United States, I feel satisfied this is not practicable and would amount to little even if our government would be willing to repeat its proceedings in the Roumanian Jewish question (which I feel satisfied it would not). In the first place, the Russian Government would at once deny its responsibility and give assurances that it has taken measures to prevent recurrences. We all know what these assurances mean, but our government could not but accept them.[10]

Schiff, then, clearly perceived that diplomatic intervention was not appropriate to a situation in which the government concerned could deny all responsibility. Thus, rather than pressing the Roosevelt administration for action toward Russia, Schiff poured his own influential efforts into collecting funds for the relief of the victims at Kishinev and into arousing public opinion.

The State Department, however, was feeling the heat of protests from other Jews and non-Jews alike over the Kishinev affair. The mass meetings held across the country adopted protest resolutions, which were invariably sent to the State Department, along with similar resolutions received from various organizations.[11] When Ambassador McCormick finally reported from St. Petersburg on May 9 that the Russian government denied any atrocities had been committed at Kishinev and that relief was, therefore, not needed, the State Department was deluged with copies of newspaper stories describing the butchery which had taken place there, along with personal accounts of the tragedy which had been written to Jews in Europe and the United States.[12]

Ambassador McCormick's parrotting of the official Russian view to his superiors in Washington, without gathering more accurate information on his own, was unacceptable to American Jewish leaders. An irate Jacob Schiff wrote to Secretary of State Hay that, while he did not wish to urge upon the United States government "any action which on your own accord you do not consider proper to take on the part of our government" in response to the Kishinev situation, he did wish to voice his disgust and disappointment with McCormick's reply to the State Department inquiry. Schiff concluded that the American ambassador had "permitted himself to be made the messenger of the Russian Government for its official denials, which he must have known were misleading, if not actually untrue." The Russian government, he concluded, could not have done better if the dispatch from McCormick had been written for him by Russian officials.[13]

Hay responded that Schiff and others who had written to him in a similar vein had entirely misunderstood McCormick's action. McCormick, Hay pointed out, had "conveyed to the Russian Government the question which I asked him to put, and telegraphed to me the answer which the Russian Government made to him." McCormick had not been asked for an opinion whether the Russian government's response was accurate or not. Then Hay responded to the criticism that the Roosevelt administration had been receiving for its lack of action over the Kishinev matter:

> In regard to the criticisms to which I have been sub-
> jected in the last few days for not taking a more
> aggressive attitude towards the Russian Government,

in view of the horrible outrages reported from
Bessarabia, you can readily see that my position is a
most delicate one, especially in the absence of the
President from Washington. I cannot go into the newspapers and explain the reasons of the action or the
nonaction of the State Department. I might feel pre-
cisely as you do in regard to it, but you are free to
express your feelings and I am not. Any slight indiscre-
tion of speech on my part might commit this government to a course of action for which there would be
no justification either in the law or facts of the case.
There could be only two motives which would induce
this government to take any positive action in such a
case; one is some advantage to itself, and the other is
some advantage to the oppressed and persecuted and
outraged Jews of Russia. What possible advantage
would it be to the United States, and what possible
advantage to the Jews of Russia, if we should make a
protest against these fiendish cruelties and be told that
it was none of our business? What would we do if the
government of Russia should protest against mob
violence in this country, of which you can hardly open
a newspaper without seeing examples? I readily admit
that nothing so bad as these Kisheneff horrors has ever
taken place in America; but the case would not be un-
like them in principle.

Hay marked his reply "Private and Confidential" but indicated
that it could be shown to Straus "or any friend who may
inquire."[14]

Schiff, who understood the limitations upon the government
and had not criticized the secretary of state, nevertheless sought
to explain to Hay the reasons for the criticism which had been
leveled against him by others. He asked the secretary of state
to place himself, "for a moment, in the place of my coreligionists in this country, who for two decades at least have had
quietly to stand by and see how members of their race were
being brutally persecuted by Russia, ending now in this grand

finale—if a finale it is—of something resembling a Bartholomew
night." He doubted if Hay would, under such circumstances,
"become irritated at those who, groping in the dark to find a
way for deliverance of their unfortunate race-brethren, ask you
to take measures which, I well understand, it is, as between
nation and nation, not possible to take." Schiff reminded the
secretary of state that he had not written his earlier letter to
suggest that any action be taken toward Russia, but rather to
express his "mortification" at the action of Ambassador
McCormick. He now understood the reason for McCormick's
action, he told Hay, but confessed that he was "not enough of
a diplomat to fathom the justification for such a position."
Schiff assured Hay that his own criticism was not directed at
the secretary of state, since he realized that Hay was "at all
times very willing to go as far as you can, and possibly a little
further, in bringing the moral influence of this Government
as far as it can be utilized, to lighten the hard lot of the persecuted, be they of the Semitic or any other race, in any of the
countries where, unfortunately, race hatred does yet find
brutal expression."[15]

One difficulty which American Jewish leaders faced in seeking to mobilize public opinion against Russia, was the tradition
of Russian-American friendship dating back, especially, to the
visit of the Russian fleet to northern ports during the American
Civil War—an action considered, wrongly, to have been a demonstration of Russian support for the Union cause. Oscar
Straus, especially, set for himself the task of correcting what
he regarded as an erroneous attitude toward Russia in the
United States. In an interview with the *New York Times* published on May 20, 1903, Straus attacked the Russians for the
massacre at Kishinev, as well as their repression of Finns and
non-Orthodox Christians, and the Russian expansion into
Manchuria, which was becoming a source of concern for those
Americans with interests in East Asia. He then attacked as
fallacious the idea of a tradition of friendship between the
United States and Russia.[16] Straus sent a copy of the interview to Secretary of State Hay.[17] The American Jewish leader
wrote to Lucien Wolf in England that he had "endeavored to
explode the bubble" of the tradition of U.S.-Russian friend-

ship, and he asked Wolf to seek material in the British Foreign
Office archives which would further contribute to that end.[18]
Hay responded to the Straus interview by writing him that it
concerned "a matter which I am unable to discuss from reasons
you will well appreciate." He then referred Straus to the letter
he had sent to Schiff and added that he knew he could "trust
not only your friendship, but your sound judgment in such a
case."[19] Meanwhile, Hay had contributed to the fund for the
relief of the Kishinev victims.[20] President Roosevelt was also
inclined to contribute but did not do so, apparently under
advice from Elihu Root.[21] Hay also advised Roosevelt against
saying anything publicly about the Kishinev massacre.[22]

On May 27 the great protest rally over the Kishinev massacre
was held in the Carnegie Music Hall in New York City. Mayor
Seth Low presided and former president Grover Cleveland was
among the speakers. According to the *New York Times:* "Mr.
Cleveland held that, although the people of the United States
ought to voice an emphatic protest against the anti-Semitic
outrages in Russia, they should be moderate in their demands
as to what action the Government at Washington should take.
The resolutions adopted by the gathering reflected this sentiment."[23] Straus reported to Secretary of State Hay that the
hall had been "packed from pit to dome with a representative
audience to protest against the Kishineff massacres," and that
a reference to Hay had been "greeted with tremendous applause
which shook the house and lasted for several minutes."[24] Hay
responded that he was "very grateful for such manifestations
of confidence and hope I may do nothing unworthy of them."[25]
Reporting on the meeting and the relief efforts in the United
States, Schiff wrote to a European friend that 200,000 francs
had already been sent to France by the relief fund, and that
the Russian Jewish population of the United States had also
sent approximately 100,000 rubles directly to Russia. "In addition," he reported, "a great 'indignation and protest' meeting
has been held at New York at our instigation, but at a call
signed exclusively by Christian fellow citizens. We hope this
meeting will not fail to make an impression upon the Russian
Government."[26]

In late May the B'nai B'rith became more active as the facts

of the Kishinev incident became clearer, and it quickly took
the lead in formulating the principal expression of American
protest over the affair. On May 29 Simon Wolf and Adolphus
S. Solomons met with Secretary of State Hay, at which time
Hay agreed to meet with the executive committee of the
B'nai B'rith in mid-June. In his talk with the two Jewish leaders,
Hay expressed himself as "very much pleased" by the actions
of Leo N. Levi (president of B'nai B'rith) and Wolf in the
Kishinev matter. According to Wolf's letter to Levi, Hay had
told them that "as long as sensible and reasonable men like
Mr. Straus and Mr. Schiff, with whom he is in constant correspondence, and Mr. Levi and myself, act in concern with the
government and its officers, there can be no doubt as to the
ultimate outcome."[27] Clearly Hay was seeking to moderate
the Jewish leadership. The meeting with the executive committee was scheduled to be held with Roosevelt in the White
House.[28]

After a preliminary meeting among themselves in Washington on June 14, the B'nai B'rith committee met with Hay and
Roosevelt at the White House the following day. The committee presented the administration with a memorandum setting
forth their position on the Kishinev matter. That position was
very different from Schiff's position. The memorandum began
by stating: "The United States should officially protest to
Russia as it did recently to Roumania. The precedent is invoked
and the government charged with timidity in this case, because
Russia is a great power, while Roumania is weak." However,
the memorandum hastened to point out, "there may be diplomatic reasons why the Roumanian precedent should not be
followed just now." Nevertheless, something must be done because the American people were "irritated, excited, and im-
patient; they want something done." It was "highly desirable"
that action be taken not only to satisfy the American people
that something was being done, but also to calm the fears of
"the Jews in Russia and thus stem the rush to this country,"
and also to "convert the hostility to Russia on the part of
American citizens, Jews and Gentiles, into friendliness, and
thus insure the traditional amity." The memorandum suggested

that one of two methods might be followed: either a petition
to the czar of Russia, or the convening of an international congress by the United States to consider persecutions and oppres-
sions resulting from racial and religious prejudice and hatred.
The memorandum included a proposed petition to the czar.[29]
According to Leo N. Levi's account of the conference, printed
in the *American Hebrew:*

> As a result of careful consideration . . . it was deter-
> mined, upon the suggestions of the President himself,
> that the official account of the conference should be
> given out to the press by the President, and should
> consist of the memorandum and draft of a petition to
> the Czar, which was submitted on behalf of the com-
> mittee, the official responses of the President and the
> Secretary, and that the whole should serve for the
> present as the definition of the official attitude of the
> President. Every line of what was given out was care-
> fully edited. On my own responsibility, I say that, in
> my opinion, the President intended what he gave out
> as a heart-to-heart talk with the Emperor of Russia.
> I think, further, that the Russian Ambassador so under-
> stands it and expected it. I was informed, not by any
> official of our government, of course, that Count
> Cassini's departure for Europe was postponed until
> after the conference on Monday and the publication
> of the views of the government. We did not ask the
> President to make a direct representation to Russia. . . .
> The President believes, as we do, that he should not
> draw unless he intends to shoot, and that a direct note
> to Russia would violate that maxim.[30]

Roosevelt's position, as printed in the *American Hebrew*, was
that he was "confident that much good has already been done
by the manifestations throughout the country, without any
regard to creed whatever, of horror and sympathy over what
has occurred." He added:

I have been visited by the Russian Ambassador on his
own initiative, and in addition to what has been said
to Secretary Hay, the Russian Ambassador has notified
me personally, without any inquiry upon my part, that
the Governor of Kishineff has been removed; that between three and four hundred of the participants in the
outrages have been arrested, and he voluntarily stated
that those men would be punished to the utmost that
the law would permit. I will consider most carefully
the suggestions that you have submitted to me. . . .
Nothing that has occurred recently has had my more
constant thought, and nothing will have my more
constant thought, than this subject. In any proper way
by which beneficial action may be taken it will be
taken, to show the sincerity of the historic American
position of treating each man on his merits as a man,
without the least reference to his creed, his race, or
his birthplace.[31]

Thus did the president of the United States convey his views
on Kishinev to the Russian government via the American press,
at the urging of American Jewish leaders.

Scarcely had the B'nai B'rith leaders met with President
Roosevelt before Jacob Schiff suggested yet another possible
course of action toward the Russians. Writing directly to the
president on June 17, Schiff told him that he doubted "that
any diplomatic action can be devised, on the part of this or
any other Government, in the way of protest or representation
to the Russian Government, indignant though the people
through the country may feel, that such an outrage upon
humanity should be possible at the beginning of the twentieth
century." But if the Russian government could not be attacked
diplomatically over the Kishinev matter, in which American
interests admittedly were not involved, there was an area in
which the United States could go on the offensive. Schiff suggested that the United States government, to demonstrate its
own outrage over Kishinev, should now take up with the
Russians the question of the freedom of American Jews, bear-

ing U.S. passports, to travel as freely in Russia as other American citizens. "Indeed," Schiff wrote, "the time has come to insist that the American passport is good in the hands of any American citizen, and if this be not recognized, friendly intercourse with the offender must cease." He realized that this was an "extreme proposition," but he hoped that the President would agree "that nothing but extreme measures will bring Russia to the understanding that to be considered a civilized government, she must also act like a civilized government."[32] Thus, Schiff linked the Russian Jewish question with the passport issue as Secretary of State Blaine had done two decades earlier. But whereas Blaine had concluded that the passport question could only be resolved when Russia reformed its attitude toward its Jewish subjects, Schiff now proposed to reverse the process and force Russia to behave in a civilized manner by first insisting that the Russian government recognize the rights of American Jews to travel freely there.

While Schiff's approach would prevail before many years in response to further Russian atrocities, the American response to the Kishinev massacre developed along the lines first suggested by the B'nai B'rith leaders. Scarcely had the executive committee of that organization met with Roosevelt and Hay before other Jewish organizations requested similar meetings.[33] Pressed to formulate some response to the Jewish appeals, Roosevelt instructed Hay to write to Simon Wolf that the president had resolved to transmit the petition of American Jews to the Russian government, a draft of which had been presented to Roosevelt and Hay at the June 15 meeting with B'nai B'rith. As Hay wrote to Wolf on June 24:

> The matter which [the President] had to consider most seriously was whether or not such a proceeding would be to the advantage of your persecuted and outraged co-religionists in Russia. On this point he has decided to accept your opinion and that of the numerous and intelligent groups of American citizens of the Jewish faith whom you represent. He requests that you will send him the petition in due form at your earliest

convenience. Of course, you will understand that the
President cannot tell you what reception your petition
will meet with at the hands of the Russian Government.[34]

Later that same day Wolf met with the president. Roosevelt
told him that upon careful consideration he had concluded that
the United States government could comply with the request
of the executive committee of B'nai B'rith to forward their
petition to the czar, in order to appease the public sentiment
for some sort of action. He indicated to Wolf that he was also
giving consideration to the proposal of an international conference, as suggested by the B'nai B'rith leaders, and that the
State Department "would feel its way in Europe to see how
such a proposition would be received." The president was
"more than pleasant" and had words of praise for the committee. Wolf now suggested to Levi that he "have printed and circulated as quickly as possible the petition, principally in the
largest cities," and that not "every Tom, Dick and Harry" be
allowed to sign it, "but only people whose identity and position in the world cannot be disputed."[35]

Late in June Levi conferred with Oscar Straus. The latter
suggested to Wolf, through Levi, that Wolf meet again with the
president and secretary of state to solicit from them any suggestions that would be of benefit in obtaining the signatures. "In
fact," Levi wrote Wolf, "I should like to have any suggestions
that they or either of them has to make." He also asked Wolf
to tell the president and Hay that "the approval of their course
as expressed in the papers is faint compared to what the people
are saying on the street." Levi added:

> The Jews are especially jubilant. Mr. Schiff, three or
> four days ago, told me that he was not in accord with
> the policy adopted by the B'nai B'rith. He evidently
> thought that our mission to Washington would prove
> fruitless. I have seen him since, and while he did not
> disavow his former views, he evidenced such an interest
> in what the President has done, and admired it so
> strongly, that there can be no doubt about his present

state of mind. He is of the opinion that great good will
result from sending the petition forward no matter
whether it be received or rejected.[36]

This, however, was probably not a true reflection of Schiff's
views on the petition matter as will be seen. From the editor
of the *Jewish World*, however, came praise for Wolf's success
in his "efforts in behalf of our persecuted brethren in Russia."[37]

Enthusiasm was dampened late in June by press reports
"from authoritative sources" that the Russian government had
learned of the intention of the United States government to
forward the B'nai B'rith petition to St. Petersburg and would
not consent to receive it.[38] Roosevelt expressed himself to Hay
as "angered over what I regard as the impertinent action of the
Russians in this matter. They are endeavoring to appeal to the
people over our heads." He asked Hay to research the precedents for his action in forwarding the petition and concluded:
"Of course we must send the petition as we have decided to do
unless Russia officially notifies us in proper form that she will
not receive it."[39] Hay agreed that the Russians were seeking to
prevent the submission of the petition, "but we have given our
word [to the B'nai B'rith] and must send it if they wish it."
It was up to the Jewish leaders themselves to now decide
whether there would be any purpose served by submitting a
petition which would probably not be received, or whether
there would not be more advantage to be gained simply by
giving "the document the utmost publicity in this country and
in Europe as having been refused a hearing by the government
of the Tsar."[40] Meantime, the State Department issued a public
statement to make it clear that the delay in forwarding the
petition to St. Petersburg arose not as a result of the statements
from Russian sources but solely due to the fact that the B'nai
B'rith had not yet presented the document with all of its signatures to the State Department for transmission.[41]

Roosevelt suggested and Hay approved the course of instructing the American chargé in St. Petersburg to ask the Russian
government, in view of the expressions emanating from St.
Petersburg and the Russian embassy in Washington, whether

it would accept and submit to the czar "a petition couched in proper terms and signed by prominent citizens of the United States, if presented through the American Embassy." As Hay put it: "If they answer in the negative—which is virtually certain—we have complied with our engagement to the Jews of the country and the international incident is thereby closed, leaving you free to decide hereafter what notice you may think best to take of it. . . . I do not think the matter is as yet serious, and there is no reason why it should become so. They are acting the fool, but we should have no interest in precipitating a crisis at this time."[42]

Both Roosevelt and Hay obviously were anxious that the affair should be concluded as soon as possible, and when Levi informed the president that it was "utterly impossible" to have the petition ready for delivery as soon as Roosevelt desired, the President decided to meet with leading American Jews about the matter, this time including Oscar Straus in the consultation.[43] On July 11 Hay wrote to the president enclosing the draft of an instruction to Riddle, the chargé at St. Petersburg, to be used in the event Roosevelt decided to query the Russians by cable whether they would accept the petition. Hay added: "I rather hope you will conclude after seeing our friends, to make the inquiry by cable which will put a speedy end to the international incident. It is possible that Lamsdorff [the Russian foreign minister] may say, 'How can we tell, not having seen the document?' Of course they *have* seen it, but that cuts no ice. In that case, we shall have to send it over."[44] On the same day Hay wrote to Roosevelt that he had given to the press "a very gratifying despatch from the American consul at Odessa" which indicated that the Russians were acting with "apparent sincerity" and "most energetic severity" against those responsible for the Kishinev massacre. Hay concluded that "the protests from the United States, even if they never reached the tsar, have had a very great effect on the minds of the bureaucracy, just as we told our Jewish friends a month ago." Hay advised Roosevelt: "The less we do and say now and the sooner we get through with it, the better, in my opinion."[45]

At Roosevelt's request Straus, Levi, and Wolf traveled to

Oyster Bay to meet with him on July 14. Straus told the president that his reply to the committee at the meeting of June 15:

> so full of sympathy for the Jews of Russia and so complimentary to those in this country, had reached around the world, and that it was published in full in the leading European journals . . . and added that he had courageously taken a stand in humanitarian diplomacy which was as effective as it was new, and that I firmly believed that it had not only prevented further massacres in Russia, but that it would stay the hand of the oppressor in every country for many years to come, be the oppressed Jews or Christians, for the nations of the world had learned to know through him that the United States was not indifferent to human suffering brought on by persecution.

At the president's suggestion it was decided not to await the submission of the signed petition from the B'nai B'rith. The cable, which Hay had suggested be sent to St. Petersburg asking the Russian government if it would accept the petition, would include the text of the petition itself. By this ingenious device, the text of the petition would be placed in the hands of the Russian government even if it refused to accept the signed petition.[46]

On July 14 after the meeting with Straus, Levi, and Wolf, Roosevelt's secretary wired to Hay that Straus was carrying to him the text of the dispatch which the president wanted wired immediately to Riddle. The wire went on:

> The President entirely agrees with you that the despatch should be sent at once. Accordingly, he requests that the message of which the original and copy will be submitted to you, be cabled over tomorrow afternoon, if possible, and that Riddle at once present it, in accordance with your suggestion to the President, and then have the State Department announce that the action taken was on the suggestion of our friends. The

President says he thinks this meets exactly the point you raised in your letter to him, and yet the only point which made him hesitate about adopting your suggestion, and that was the desire to get the substance of the petition embodied in official form. The President feels that by the course adopted we, in the first place, show that we are meeting the wishes of the gentlemen who originated the petition; and are also getting the diplomatic incident closed as soon as possible.[47]

According to Straus, who carried the original and a copy of the dispatch from Oyster Bay to Washington, the secretary of state did not entirely approve of the president's course since he felt that "this is presenting the petition," and Hay "did not think the petition ought to be presented until we had asked."[48] On July 14, however, Hay wired Riddle in St. Petersburg:

You are instructed to ask an audience of the Minister of Foreign Affairs and to make to him the following communication:

"Excellency: The Secretary of State instructs me to inform you that the President has received from a large number of citizens of the United States of all religious affiliations and occupying the highest position in both public and private life, a respectful petition addressed to His Majesty, the Emperor, relating to the condition of the Jews in Russia, and running as follows:

"The cruel outrages perpetrated at Kischineff during Easter of 1903, have excited horror and reprobation throughout the World. Until your Majesty gave special and personal directions, the local authorities failed to maintain order or suppress the rioting.

"The victims were Jews and the assault was the result of race and religious prejudice.

"The rioters violated the laws of Russia.

"The local officers were derelict in the performance of their duty.

"The Jews were the victims of indefensible lawlessness.

"These facts are made plain by the official reports of, and by the official acts following the riot.

"Under ordinary conditions the awful calamity would be deplored without undue fear of a recurrence. But such is not the case in the present instance. Your petitioners are advised that millions of Jews—Russian subjects—dwelling in South-western Russia, are in constant dread of fresh outbreaks. They feel that ignorance, superstition and bigotry, as exemplified by the rioters, are ever ready to persecute them; that the local officials, unless thereunto specially admonished, cannot be relied on as strenuous protectors of their peace and security; that a public sentiment of hostility has been engendered against them and hangs over them as a continuing menace.

"Even if it be conceded that these fears are to some extent exaggerated, it is unquestionably true that they exist, that they are not groundless, and that they produce effects of great importance.

"The westward migration of Russian Jews, which has proceeded for over twenty years, is being stimulated by these fears, and already that movement has become so great as to overshadow in magnitude the expulsion of the Jews from Spain and to rank with the Exodus from Egypt.

"No estimate is possible of the misery suffered by the hapless Jews who feel driven to forsake their native land, to sever the most sacred ties, and to wander forth to strange countries. Neither is it possible to estimate the misery suffered by those who are unwilling or unable to leave the land of their birth; who must part from friends and relatives who emigrate, who remain in neverending terror.

"Religious persecution is more sinful and more fatuous even than war. War is sometimes necessary, honorable and just. Religious persecution is never defensible.

"The sinfulness and folly which give impulse to unnecessary war, received their greatest check when Your Majesty's initiative resulted in an International Court of Peace.

"With such an example before it the Civilized World cherishes the hope that upon the same initiative there shall be fixed in the early days of the Twentieth Century, the enduring principle of Religious Liberty; that by a gracious and convincing expression your Majesty will proclaim not only for the government of your own subjects, but also for the guidance of all civilized men, that none shall suffer in person, property, liberty, honor or law because of his religious belief; that the humblest subject or citizen may worship according to the dictates of his own conscience and that government, whatever its form or agencies, must safeguard those rights and immunities by the exercise of all its powers.

"Far removed from your Majesty's dominions, living under different conditions and owing allegiance to another government, your petitioners yet venture, in the name of civilization, to plead for religious liberty and tolerance; to plead that he who led his own people and all others to the shrine of peace will add new lustre to his reign and fame by leading a new movement that shall commit the whole world in opposition to religious persecutions."

At the end of the petition, Riddle was instructed to ask whether the petition would be received by the Russian government, in which case "the petition will be at once forwarded to St. Petersburg." Riddle was also instructed to "report at the earliest possible moment your execution of this instruction."[49]

Before Riddle could receive the instruction and act, however, this carefully contrived ploy to get the Jewish petition into the hands of those who were sure to reject it was finessed by the Russians. On July 15 the Russian minister for foreign affairs summoned Riddle. The American envoy recounted:

He had seen that a Jewish petition addressed to the Emperor of Russia was about to be forwarded to the Embassy under the auspices of the Government of the United States. As he wished to avoid all friction, and did not wish to be under the necessity of offering the least discourtesy to me personally, he thought it would be better to notify me informally that such a petition would not be received; if I delivered it to him in person he would at once hand it back without looking at it. If I sent it accompanied by an official note he would at once place it in an envelope and return it to me un-opened, unread; that the Emperor whose will is the sole law of this land had no need of information from out-side sources as to what is taking place within his domin-ions; and that even a respectful petition or prayer relating to internal matters could not be received from foreigners. The Emperor's kindly feeling toward America, and the Minister's own esteem for the Em-bassy, made them desirous of avoiding the smallest diplomatic incident.

This being the Russian attitude, Riddle felt on receiving the dispatch from Washington the next day that he had already re-ceived the answer of the Russian government to the question which he was now instructed to ask, and he wired the State Department that he would take no further steps unless ordered to by Washington.[50]

Hay and Roosevelt were willing to allow the issue to end on that note. On July 16 Hay told the president that Riddle's re-port had arrived. "You will see [the] Russian government refused to receive or even to read the petition before it arrived. I will announce to the press simply that the Russian govern-ment has refused to receive the petition and give no details—or I will give out anything you direct."[51] Hay regarded the Russians as "inept asses." The Russians, he told Roosevelt, "would have scored by receiving the petition and pigeonhol-ing it," but instead the president had scored by doing "the right thing in the right way, and Jewry seems really grateful."

Russia, Hay told the president, had more interest in good relations with the United States than this country had in such relations with the Russians, "and they will soon come around and lie to us as volubly as ever."[52] Roosevelt instructed Hay to release the entire cable sent to Riddle,

> and then add that at the very time this cable was received by our chargé in St. Petersburg, he was informed by the Russian Minister for Foreign Affairs that in view of what had happened in the newspapers, the Russian Government wished to notify him informally that the proposed petition . . . would not be received under any condition. . . . Also notify Messrs. Straus, Wolf and Levi of what has been done and say that they are now at liberty to say whatever they choose as regards the matter.[53]

Leo Levi's response, as reported in the *New York Times*, was that the action of the Russian government in refusing to accept the petition had come as no surprise. He added, however, that:

> The movement . . . has had all the good effects that were in contemplation, and even more. It has enabled the American people and the Government to make an enduring record of their views on the Kishineff horror. It has brought the emphatic expression of those views home, not only to the people of Russia, but to the Russian Emperor and his Ministers. They have become acquainted with the contents of the petition, not only by reading it in the press, but also, because its full text was communicated in the note which asked whether the original would be received.[54]

The latter, of course, was a misconception as the note had never been presented to the Russians. Simon Wolf agreed that the incident was "closed and exactly as we anticipated." He told the president that the Jews were "thoroughly content and in perfect accord with every step taken by you and Secretary Hay. Immediate great good has been accomplished, but more will result in the future."[55] Roosevelt was well satisfied with the way the affair had been handled. As he wrote Congressman Littauer: "I think we did that business pretty well. We certainly went to the limit in taking the lead on behalf of humanity."[56] The *American Hebrew* agreed that just the right thing had been done:

> Had the United States government been in a position to protest against the Kishineff outrage, it would have done so; from every statement issued from the White House, that fact is evident. Given the petition secured by the B'nai B'rith, it did the very best that could have been done under the circumstances, it tried every means at its command to present that petition, in order that the Russian government might see what is the opinion of the American people. It would have been the height of folly for us to insist on our government going any further. We cannot afford to involve our government in any controversy with Russia on a detail.[57]

The Kishinev petition was carried through largely by the B'nai B'rith, principally under the leadership of Leo N. Levi and Simon Wolf, although other individuals and organizations played important roles. Oscar Straus was not involved in the affair until called in late in the proceedings, but he expressed himself as "very much pleased with the entire management of this affair, also with its conclusion."[58] He wired Roosevelt his "heartiest congratulations" on the president's "most satisfactory disposition of the Kishineff petition," and added:

> Your action in this matter and in the recent Roumanian protest marks an era in the highest realm of diplomacy, the diplomacy of humanity which marshals the enlightened spirit of civilization against persecution and gives vitality and force to those beneficent principles in international relations which contribute to peace and happiness in every land.[59]

Jacob Schiff, however, did not agree, arguing that "both the Jews
in Russia as well as our people in the United States would be
better off if the dignified protests made by Christian America
at the Carnegie Hall meeting and other similar meetings throughout the country would have been permitted to remain the *final*
impression made in Russia and in the civilized world in
general."[60] Schiff made the same point to President Roosevelt:

> I and many with me have from the outset considered
> the recent action of Messrs. Levi, Straus and Wolf as a
> mistake. Mr. Leo Levi was so informed immediately
> after he first appeared before you with his committee,
> but my friends and I felt that, his action having re-
> ceived your high support, it was proper that we should
> give loyal support to what had been undertaken. Now,
> however, that all the excitement which was produced
> by the so-called Kishineff petition has passed, it is but
> right that you should become acquainted with other
> views than those which have been submitted to you.
> . . . *Petitions* to the Tsar's government profit no one,
> *protests* on the part of the civilized world, such as have
> so properly and dignifiedly been recently made at the
> Carnegie Hall meeting in New York and other cities,
> will not fail of their purpose. And what we particularly
> need are ambassadors at the court of St. Petersburg
> who shall not sacrifice to their social comfort the repre-
> sentation of the true spirit animating the American
> government and people. . . .[61]

Roosevelt did not agree with Schiff, answering that his own
view "was that the action of the government concerning the
petition was, in effect (only to an infinitely greater degree),
doing just what the Carnegie Hall meeting attempted to do.
It was a protest on the part of the civilized world with a
thousandfold the weight that the meeting in Carnegie Hall"
had.[62]

    Despite the apparently successful settlement of the Kishinev
affair during the summer, real and rumored pogroms continued

to appear in Jewish and diplomatic correspondence during the following winter. In September riots in Homel inflicted death and damage on Jews in that city, although not on the scale of Kishinev.[63] Late in December Straus wired the president that the afternoon newspapers contained reports from the *London Times* that outbreaks of violence against Jews in Kishinev had begun anew. Straus urged that the American ambassador in St. Petersburg, as well as the U.S. consul at Odessa, be queried to ascertain whether the reports were correct.[64] While Roosevelt was taking the matter up with the State Department, Simon Wolf and Adolphus Solomons were also pressing for action there.[65] On December 29 Straus learned from Roosevelt's secretary that the U.S. consul at Odessa had reported the rumors were groundless.[66] Straus responded that he was convinced that "the prompt inquiries the President caused to be made must have had a restraining influence on the authorities in Russia, and I assume awakened in them a sense of duty to check threatened outbreaks from the knowledge of the fact that this country was deeply concerned."[67]

From the perspective of the years following 1903, it seems reasonable to conclude that the efforts of American Jewish leaders like Schiff and others less well known had the greater long-term effect on relations between the United States and Russia by arousing American public opinion against Russia through such protests as that at Carnegie Hall. These efforts also marked a dramatic shift in the strategy of Schiff, at least. Until now the American Jewish leaders had agreed on the policy of arrogating to themselves the responsibility to intercede with the authorities in Washington as in the traditional *shtadlan* or "court Jew" approach.[68] In doing so they frequently sought the support of influential non-Jews as well. But in 1903 Schiff and other like-minded American Jewish leaders abandoned the *shtadlan* approach from their despair that the United States government could intervene effectively in the Kishinev matter. Instead they cooperated with Jews of east European origin and other American leaders in seeking to build a mass movement of Jews and non-Jews alike in a national protest. More effectively than ever before, the American Jewish community marshaled its forces for an exercise in pressure politics. Thus, the Kishinev protest marked a turning point both within the American Jewish community and in the marshaling of the larger non-Jewish population behind the cause of humanitarian treatment of east European Jews.[69] According to one source, seventy-seven protest meetings were held in fifty towns and cities in twenty-seven states.[70] Prominent Americans were visible as active participants in the protests, including former presidents, governors, mayors, senators, congressmen, and important figures in both the Catholic and Protestant churches.[71] The press also participated by carrying articles and news reports describing conditions in Russia in the most negative way. It was an impressive mobilization of concern and public opinion in response to an incident which, by comparison even with the pogroms in Russia 2-3 years later, was insignificant in terms of lives lost, and which would be dwarfed to microscopic size by the millions who died in the Nazi holocaust a few decades later. When war broke out between Russia and Japan early in 1904 this altered perception of Russia on the part of the American people would stand Japan in good stead. And the successful mobilization of American public opinion in 1903 would not be forgotten when American Jewish leaders sought to influence policy in later years.

NOTES

1. See, for example, stories in *American Hebrew*, May 1, 1903; and *New York Times*, April 24, 1903.

2. *New York Times*, April 26, 1903.

3. For one account of the Kishinev massacre see Dubnow, *History of the Jews in Russia and Poland*, 3 vols. (Philadelphia, 1918), vol. 3: *The Jews*, 69-75.

4. Schiff to Straus, May 5, 1903, Jacob H. Schiff Papers.

5. Hay to McCormick, April 29, 1903, *Diplomatic Instructions of the Department of State, 1801-1906, Russia*, National Archives Microfilm Publication M77, reel 140 (hereafter cited as DS M77/140).

6. Loomis to Wolf, May 5, 1903, Simon Wolf Papers.

7. Levi to Wolf, May 7, 1903, Wolf Papers.

8. *American Hebrew*, May 8, 1903.

9. Schiff to Low, May 8, 1903, Schiff Papers.

10. Schiff to Sabsovich, May 13, 1903, Schiff Papers.

11. *New York Times*, May 17, 1903.

12. McCormick to Hay, May 9, 1903, Department of State, *Despatches from United States Ministers to Russia, 1808-1906*, National Archives Microfilm Publication M35, reel 60 (hereafter cited as DS M35/60).

13. Schiff to Hay, May 19, 1903, Schiff Papers.

14. Hay to Schiff, May 20, 1903, John Hay Papers.

15. Schiff to Hay, May 21, 1903, Schiff Papers.

16. *New York Times*, May 20, 1903.

17. Straus to Hay, May 20, 1903, Oscar S. Straus Papers.

18. Straus to Wolf, May 20, 1903, Straus Papers.

19. Hay to Straus, May 22, 1903, Straus Papers.

20. *American Hebrew*, May 22, 1903.

21. Roosevelt to Hay, telegram, May 21, 1903, and Hay to Root, undated, Theodore Roosevelt Papers.

22. Roosevelt to Hay, May 25, 1903, Roosevelt Papers.

23. *New York Times*, May 28, 1903.

24. Straus to Hay, May 28, 1903, Straus Papers.

25. Hay to Straus, June 1, 1903, Straus Papers.

26. Schiff to Nathan, June 2, 1903, Schiff Papers.

27. Wolf to Levi, May 29, 1903, Wolf Papers.

28. Wolf to Hay, June 8, 1903, Wolf Papers.

29. Memorandum, "Touching the Kishineff Massacre in April, 1903, to be used by the Executive Committee of the Independent Order of B'nai B'rith in conference in Washington, D.C., with Secretary of State John Hay, by appointment, June 15, 1903," Wolf Papers.

30. *American Hebrew*, June 19, 1903.

31. Ibid.

32. Schiff to Roosevelt, June 17, 1903, Schiff Papers.

33. *New York Times*, June 16, 1903.

34. Hay to Wolf, June 24, 1903, Wolf Papers.

35. Wolf to Levi, June 24, 1903, Wolf Papers.

36. Levi to Wolf, June 29, 1903, Wolf Papers.

37. Editor of the *Jewish World* to Wolf, June 26, 1903, Wolf Papers.

38. *New York Times*, June 27, 1903.

39. Roosevelt to Hay, July 1, 1903, Roosevelt Papers.

40. Hay to Roosevelt, July 1, 1903, Hay Papers.

41. *New York Times*, July 2, 1903.

42. Hay to Roosevelt, July 3, 1903, Hay Papers.

43. Levi to Roosevelt, July 3, 1903, Roosevelt Papers.

44. Hay to Roosevelt, July 11, 1903, Hay Papers.

45. Hay to Roosevelt, July 11, 1903, Hay Papers.

46. Straus memorandum, "The President and the Kishineff Petition," in scrapbook, "Rumania and Russia, 1902-1903," Straus Papers.

47. Barnes to Hay, July 14, 1903, Roosevelt Papers.

48. Straus, "The President and the Kishineff Petition," Straus Papers.

49. Hay to Riddle, July 14, 1903, Hay Papers.

50. Riddle to Hay, July 16, 1903, DS M35/60.

51. Hay to Roosevelt, telegram, July 16, 1903, Hay Papers.

52. Hay to Roosevelt, July 16, 1903, Hay Papers.

53. Roosevelt to Hay, July 16, 1903, Roosevelt Papers.

54. *New York Times*, July 18, 1903.

55. Wolf to Roosevelt, July 18, 1903, Roosevelt Papers.

56. Roosevelt to Littauer, July 22, 1903, Roosevelt Papers.

57. *American Hebrew*, July 24, 1903.

58. Straus to Loomis, July 21, 1903, Straus Papers.

59. Straus to Roosevelt, telegram, July 18, 1903, Straus Papers.

60. Schiff to Adler, July 31, 1903, Schiff Papers.

61. Schiff to Roosevelt, August 6, 1903, Roosevelt Papers.

62. Roosevelt to Schiff, August 13, 1903, Roosevelt Papers.

63. Riddle to Hay, September 26, 1903, DS M35/60.

64. Straus to Roosevelt, telegram, December 28, 1903, Straus Papers.

65. Loeb to Straus, telegram, December 28, 1903, and Wolf and Solomons to Straus, telegram, December 29, 1903, both in Straus Papers.

66. Loeb to Straus, December 29, 1903, Straus Papers.

67. Straus to Loeb, December 30, 1903, Straus Papers.

68. For this tradition in Jewish history see Selma Stern, *The Court Jew* (Philadelphia, 1950).

69. See Zosa Szajkowski, "Jewish Diplomacy," *Jewish Social Studies* 22 (July 1960): 151.

70. Cyrus Adler, *The Voice of America on Kishineff* (Philadelphia, 1904), p. 123.

71. For accounts of the American response to the Kishinev massacre see ibid., as well as Isidore Singer, *Russia at the Bar of the American People* (New York and London, 1904); Taylor Stults, "Roosevelt, Russian Persecution of Jews, and American Public Opinion," *Jewish Social Studies* 30 (January 1971): 13-22; Philip Ernest Schoenberg, "The American Reaction to the Kishinev Pogrom of 1903," *American Jewish Historical Quarterly* 63 (March 1974): 262-83.

CHAPTER 4

The Russo-Japanese
War Years, 1904-1905

With the outbreak of war between Japan and Russia in February 1904, American Jewish sympathies quickly lined up in support of Japan. As the *American Hebrew* expressed the feeling of the Jewish community:

> It is but the veriest [sic] human nature that causes us to exult at the initial victory of Japan over Russia. Aside of the fact that Japan seems to have justice on her side in the conflict that she has precipitated, that Russia, who has defied all the decencies of civilization in her own land, should seek to assume to control territory in the Orient in the name of civilization leads us to hope that she will be brought abjectly to her knees in the present war. Meanwhile, the Jew may hope for some peace in Russia. The revolutionary and socialistic elements there will undoubtedly assert themselves and keep the local authorities busy so that the Jews will be left to breathe freely for the time being.[1]

So outspoken was the American Jewish press in championing Japan's cause against Russia that at least one American Jewish leader became concerned. As Cyrus Adler wrote to the editor

of the *American Hebrew*, soon after the above statement
appeared, the Jewish press ought to keep in mind that there
were five million Jews in Russia, and that the Russian embassy
in Washington monitored the American Jewish press. He suggested that American newspapers not go beyond the sentiment
being expressed in the general American press, namely that
Japan "may be doing the work of civilization in limiting the
spread of despotic Russia." The Kishinev incident, Adler
pointed out, had aroused American public opinion against
Russia and with that American Jews ought to be satisfied.[2]
The *American Hebrew* was not far in advance of general sentiment in the United States, however, which is clear from the
observation of one American periodical that it had "never
known a conflict in which the United States was not an active
participant where there was anything like the unanimity of
opinion or intensity of sympathy which is felt in the republic
for Japan."[3] As Adler observed, the Kishinev agitation was at
least in part responsible for the enthusiasm toward Japan's
cause against Russia.

The outbreak of the war in East Asia did not, however, quiet
American Jewish concern with future Kishinev-like outbreaks
in Russia. As spring of 1904 approached Schiff wired Straus
he had been told by Lord Rothschild in England of apprehension
that there would be a repeat of the Kishinev outrage in Odessa
during Easter. According to the report, pamphlets inciting such
outrages were being freely circulated there without interference
by the authorities. Rothschild was calling the matter to the
attention of the British government, and he requested the
American Jewish leaders also to ask the American government
to communicate with the Russians, through the U.S. ambassador at St. Petersburg, to express the hope that the impending
outrages should not take place.[4]

Straus immediately wired the substance of Schiff's message
to the president, adding that he trusted Roosevelt would "once
more invoke . . . humanitarian diplomacy."[5] The following day
Straus wired Schiff (who was then in Germany) that the "President made strongest possible representations through [Russian
ambassador] Cassini."[6] Straus then thanked Roosevelt's secre-

tary for the president's prompt and strong actions, adding:
"No President has made so large a contribution to the diplomacy
of humanity as President Roosevelt." He suggested making the
president's action public.[7] It was, after all, a presidential election year. To Straus's suggestion, Roosevelt's secretary replied
"the President would prefer to have it get out in some way
through you, without any appearance of its being an official
statement from Washington."[8] Straus's statement on the affair
cleverly took advantage of Russia's extremity in the war with
Japan when he indicated that:

> Apart from the humanitarian considerations that has
> [*sic*] actuated the President and Secretary Hay in call-
> ing Ambassador Cassini's attention to the alarm that is
> felt in this country, our Government in the interest of
> friendly relations desires to prevent any occasion for
> such manifestations of public opinion which would put
> a strain upon the strictly neutral attitude this country
> seeks to maintain in the present war between Russia
> and Japan.[9]

The appearance in the newspapers of the details of Straus's
successful intercession with the administration incensed Simon
Wolf, who had also interceded with the State Department over
the matter and was disturbed that Straus had obtained publicity for himself in a matter which Wolf had been careful to
keep confidential.[10]

Schiff reported to Lord Rothschild on the action taken in
the United States in response to his request, but told him he
felt it not to be good practice to make such representations to
the president each time there was a rumor of possible outbreak
of anti-Semitic violence in Russia, since Schiff feared that "we
might 'cry wolf' too often and thus weaken the weapon which
we should reserve in all its might and strength for the critical
time which is no doubt ahead of us." Schiff feared that difficult times were in store for the Jews of Russia and only hoped
for their sake, and for Russia itself, "that the conflict between
Russia and Japan will . . . lead to such an upheaval in the basic

conditions upon which Russia is now governed that the elements in Russia, which seek to bring their country under constitutional government, shall at last triumph." Schiff recited for the English financier his own successful efforts to bar Russian loans from the American securities market, refusing to cooperate with the Russians unless they first acted to improve conditions for their Jewish subjects. Further, he suggested that European Jewish bankers, too, ought not to be bought so easily with Russian promises, but ought to refuse to cooperate in floating Russian loans until there were real results demonstrated where the Jews of Russia were concerned.[11]

Anxious for an "upheaval" in Russia, Schiff was not one to let pass an opportunity to assist in creating such an upheaval. In addition to working to deny Russia the access to loans which were necessary for the prosecution of the war with Japan, Schiff actively assisted Japan in meeting her own wartime financial requirements. En route back to the United States from his visit to Germany, Schiff stopped in London. At a dinner he was seated next to Takahashi Korekiyo, the Japanese financial commissioner dispatched by his government to float a $50 million bond issue in Great Britain with which to finance the war with Russia. Takahashi had sounded out the prospects for American financial assistance while in New York en route to London, but had been disappointed by the response. In London, too, he was unable to interest British bankers in underwriting more than half of the amount sought by his government, a total of $25 million. After listening to Takahashi's description of Japan's requirements, Schiff notified him the next day that Kuhn, Loeb and Company would underwrite the other $25 million that Japan needed. Schiff made no secret of the fact that his primary motive in assisting Japan was his desire to undermine the Russian autocracy which was oppressing Russian Jewry.[12]

The Japanese war bonds offered for sale by Kuhn, Loeb and Company were immensely popular in the American investment market—reflecting the enthusiasm for Japan and the antipathy for Russia in the United States. It is interesting to note the successful sale despite the fact that the United States was still a net capital importer and had almost no experience in handling the bond issues of foreign governments, and despite the risky nature of an investment in the war bonds of a nation that was a decided underdog in the war. The first bond issue was oversubscribed by 500 percent within twenty-four hours, and the Japanese were encouraged to float a second bond issue of $60 million. Schiff again agreed to underwrite half of the bonds—a total of $30 million—in the United States, and this flotation also was successful, with subscriptions for the bonds coming from as far away as San Francisco.[13]

Japan's victory at Port Arthur in January 1905, and the favorable trend of the battle for Mukden in the following months, gave a decided lift to Japan's credit with foreign bond buyers. In February Takahashi stopped in New York to consult with Schiff concerning a third bond issue. The American Jewish banker told him that New York would be able again to furnish half of the new Japanese war loan, and he assured Takahashi that if the other half of the loan could not be floated in London Schiff would call on his contacts in Germany to help put the entire loan over. These advance assurances by Schiff so eased the London negotiations for Takahashi that the details of the new bond issue were settled in only five days. The new loan of $150 million was again split evenly between London and New York.[14] The third bond issue was an even greater success than those that had preceded it: about $500 million in subscriptions were received for the $75 million American share of the bond issue, and subscriptions were received from cities all across the United States.[15]

Takahashi told the Associated Press in late March that the third bond issue would be adequate to support the Japanese war effort for at least a year, and perhaps for a year and a half. But the victory of Admiral Togo at the naval battle of Tsushima seemed to his government to offer an excellent psychological opportunity, in May of 1905, for yet another bond issue to be floated. Takahashi objected, but with the approach of peace negotiations his government became more insistent, arguing that the money would be needed whether or not peace resulted from the negotiations. Takahashi did not expect that either New York or London financiers would be pleased with an attempt to bring out a new loan so close on the heels of the large bond issue in March. When Schiff questioned why such a loan was necessary so soon, however, Takahashi argued convincingly that with the approach of peace negotiations Japan must make it clear to the Russians that she could finance the war for as long as might be necessary. Schiff not only agreed to help underwrite the new loan, but, while Takahashi wired London to sound out prospects there, Schiff wired his contacts in Germany to see if they would be interested in underwriting one-third of the proposed $150 million bond issue. The reply to Takahashi's inquiry of London was not encouraging, but the answer to Schiff's wire promised support from the German bankers. In Takahashi's words: "Mr. Schiff advised me to go to London and talk to the bankers. He said that if the British bankers refused to raise the amount, he would see to it that [$150 million] would be raised in the United States and Germany." With this assurance, Takahashi sailed for England where London financiers were finally induced to match New York and Berlin, with each of the three cities underwriting $50 million of the new loan. The fourth Japanese war loan was only slightly less popular than the March issue in the United States, being oversubscribed by about 500 percent. The addition of the Germans to the issue undoubtedly gave it greater prestige, since Germany had previously served as a market for Russian bonds.[16]

There were thus a total of four bond issues by the Japanese government floated in the foreign market during the Russo-Japanese War in which Schiff and his syndicate participated. The four loans underwritten in the United States totaled $180 million in face value. Because of the discount at which the bonds were sold, the actual investment by those purchasing the bonds was closer to $160 million. In addition to the actual amount of such American support for Japan, however, the total of subscriptions offered in the United States for the Japanese war bonds should be noted. Total subscriptions in the United States for the four war loans probably amounted to nearly $850 million—an amount very nearly equal to the entire cost of Japan's war with Russia.

Finances were a critical factor of the war between Russia and Japan. It was the view of Count Witte of Russia as the war began that:

> if we should succeed, in the end, in defeating the
> Japanese, it would be by virtue of our superior finances.
> The Japanese cannot resist our finances. I have nothing
> to say of the two other factors—the army and the navy.
> Perhaps the Japanese can carry on the war one and a
> half, two, at the most two and a half years. Other factors
> being left out of account, the Japanese can therefore
> be brought to sue for peace by their financial ruin.[17]

Yet, as Witte recorded in his memoirs later, less than a year had passed after this optimistic statement before he was on his way to Portsmouth, New Hampshire, to represent his country at the peace conference, by which time his Russia "had exhausted all our means and had lost our credit abroad. There was not the slightest hope of floating either a domestic or a foreign loan. We could continue the war only by resorting to new issues of paper money, that is by preparing the way for a complete financial and consequently economic collapse."[18] Ambassador McCormick in St. Petersburg reported in March 1905 that the failure of Russia in its foreign financing and the strain on Russian finances had led the Russian minister of finance to counsel the Czar to enter into peace negotiations with Japan.[19]

By contrast with this deterioration of Russia's financial standing in foreign money markets, Japan's credit stood stronger in those markets at the end of the war than it had at the beginning. As an American journal pointed out shortly before the peace conference was convened in 1905: "The strange point . . . is the fact that a 10 per cent increase in the Russian debt has been followed by a slump in Russian credit; while an increase of more than 160 per cent in the Japanese debt has been followed by a wonderful advance in the credit of that country."[20] To a considerable extent, then, the outcome of the Russo-Japanese War may be attributed to Japan's success in international finance, in contrast with Russia's failure. Both the success and the failure were, in considerable part, attributable to the influence of the Jewish banking community in the United States and Europe. Schiff's role had certainly been decisive in Japan's financial success, since it is extremely doubtful that London alone could or would have absorbed all of the Japanese war bonds had it not been for the American participation in the flotations.

On the other side of the coin, Schiff had exerted all of his influence to block Russian access to loans. Since the turn of the century the Russians had sought to find a market in the United States for their government bonds. Those efforts had always been checked by the American Jewish banking community, which demanded of the Russians a quid pro quo in the form of greater rights for Russia's Jewish subjects in the form of actions and not promises. The enormous financial expenditures of the war with Japan caused Russia to seek loans again in the international market and to make a renewed effort to tap the American bond market which was showing itself so receptive to the bonds of Russia's enemy. It was almost certainly from such reasons that the Russian minister of the interior, von Plehve, expressed in June of 1904 a desire to meet with Schiff to discuss measures which might be taken in Russia to improve the condition of the Jews. That initiative, taken through Dr. N. Katzenelsohn, brought a reply from Schiff setting forth the conditions under which he would make such a visit to Russia. Schiff told Katzenelsohn, for the Russian minister of the interior, "The unwillingness of American money markets to take up Russian financing, and the antipathy which has recently been revealed by the American people toward Russia, are due purely to the disgust that is felt here against a system of government which permits such things as the recent Kishineff episodes and the legal discrimination which is the order of the day in Russia." Schiff explained he would not "enter a country which admits me only by special favor, and which is closed to all members of the Jewish faith except by such special favor." If he were to go to Russia, "the existing restrictions against the visé of passports for foreign Jews must first be abolished. Only when that is done can any foreign Jew enter Russia without loss of ordinary self-respect." Two weeks later Schiff wrote Katzenelsohn that he "must now wait to see to what extent the gentlemen in St. Petersburg are prepared to meet the conditions upon the fulfillment of which I have agreed to visit Russia."[21]

The assassination of von Plehve nipped this initiative in the bud, but it did not alter the basic tone of conciliation exhibited by the Ministry of the Interior. Von Plehve was succeeded by Prince P. D. Sviatopolk-Mirsky as minister of the interior in August 1904. Ambassador McCormick found the new minister conciliatory toward the Jews in his discussions with him. In an interview with the Associated Press, published in Russian newspapers and forwarded to the State Department by McCormick, Sviatopolk-Mirsky expressed his concern with the condition of the poorer class of Jews and an earnest desire "that they be given larger opportunities for their life work." McCormick noted this conciliatory attitude had been linked in some foreign newspapers with a desire "to pave the way for loans in the United States." The ambassador, whose sympathy for the Russian government he made no attempt to conceal, felt that: "The real friends of the Russian people, including those of the Hebrew persuasion, can render genuine service to their fellow-men of both races in this country by accepting this declaration at its face value and not attributing ulterior motives to the new Minister and indulging in carping criticism before he has had an opportunity to prove his words by his deeds."[22] A few days later there appeared to be even more tangible confirmation of the new direction that Russian policy was taking toward the Jews when McCormick was told by the Russian minister of foreign affairs that the Ministry of the Interior had appointed a special commission with the mandate to revise generally the passport regulations of Russia.[23] The tide of reaction, however, was already building in Russia. In January of 1905 McCormick found Sviatopolk-Mirsky "not the same Prince Mirsky with whom I had talked three months before almost to a day," with the liberal reforms "nipped in the bud."[24] It was the skepticism of the Jews and other opponents of the Czar's regime that had been validated and not McCormick's optimism.

When yet another overture from Russia to Schiff was forthcoming in March 1905, the American Jewish banker responded again that Russia's attempts to raise funds in the United States had always been unsuccessful,

> firstly, because of the want of sympathy on the part of the American people with Russian methods of administration, and secondly, because my own firm, which is more or less leading in finance in the United States, has deemed it its duty to discourage favorable reception to Russian financial overtures so long as Russia persisted in its harsh attitude towards its Jewish subjects and in its mortifying discriminations against foreign Jews.

With the reestablishment of peace between Japan and Russia, Schiff suggested, a market could be found in the United States for Russian bonds, "provided the special laws still existing and which debar the Russian Jewish population from civil rights are swept aside and the Jew is placed on a parity with all other subjects in the Tsar's domain." Unless this was done, "every effort to regain American sympathy for any purpose whatsoever must prove in vain." Schiff hoped that the restoration of peace would bring civil rights to Russian Jews and, if so, then he would "no longer withhold the cooperation . . . sought from me for making possible the entry of Russian finance into the markets of the United States."[25]

At first glance, however, it did not appear that European Jewish bankers exhibited the same concern displayed by Schiff in their own relations with the Russians. Americans—Jews and non-Jews alike—were discouraged by the seeming willingness of European banking houses bearing Jewish names to back the czar's government financially even while that government persecuted its Jewish subjects. The matter, however, proved not as simple as it appeared to Americans. Responding to Schiff's own criticism of European Jewish willingness to support Russia financially, Lord Rothschild reported that his own firm had refused to participate in any Russian loan since 1875. Bankers on the continent, however, were another

matter, he pointed out, because they were frequently subjected to pressures from their governments to lend money to
friendly or allied countries. Moreover, some of the continental
banking firms bearing Jewish names were, in fact, operated by
Christians.[26] When former ambassador Andrew D. White criticized the willingness of European Jewish banking houses to
support Russia, his criticism touched off a study of the question by American Jewish leaders which confirmed Rothschild's
observations.[27] The study found the major Jewish banking
houses of England and France had indeed refused to handle
Russian issues, and the only participating Jewish firms in
France or Germany either were operated by Jews who had
been baptized as Christians or those whose Judaism "hangs so
loosely upon them that they should not be charged to us."[28]
The French Rothschilds, it was found, had participated in a
Russian loan in 1901, partly under pressure from the French
government and partly due to certain promised concessions
by the Russian government in its treatment of Russian Jews,
but not since.[29] The Jewish financial boycott, then, was rea-
sonably effective during the war years and certainly contributed
to Russia's deteriorating financial position during the war.

Facing election to the presidency in his own right in 1904,
Theodore Roosevelt naturally was receptive to many of the
wishes of American Jewish leaders. He had acted quickly in
response to the rumors of anti-Jewish riots in Odessa in late
March 1904. Now American Jewish leaders began to press once
again an issue long dear to them—the elimination of Russian
restrictions on the free travel of Jews bearing American passports. Using the obvious favoritism being displayed toward
Japan and against Russia in the United States during the Russo-
Japanese War, Secretary of State Hay took up the matter with
Ambassador Cassini in April 1904. According to Hay's diary
for April 7, 1904: "I opened again the subject of the Jews
passports, which agitated him greatly. He said, as usual, the
time was most inopportune &c. I told him that this was one
of the elements of the feelings of distrust in this country
against Russia and removing it would do only good."[30]
Again on June 11 Cassini responded with the same alibi. Hay

called his attention to the fact that the United States government had been pressing for a solution to the problem for many years, only to be told on each occasion that it was "an inopportune time." The secretary of state told Cassini that the passport issue was a source of "great annoyance to us," and "that a great part of the ill-feeling in this country towards Russia came from the question of passports—and absolutely no advantage to Russia."[31] The Russians would not move.

In April the House of Representatives adopted a resolution requesting the government to enter into negotiations with "the governments of countries where discrimination is made between American citizens on the ground of religious faith or belief" to obtain recognition of American passports, no matter by whom they were held, "in order that all American citizens shall have equal freedom of travel and sojourn in those countries, without regard to race, creed, or religious faith." The resolution obviously was aimed at Russia, and on July 1 it was forwarded to Ambassador McCormick for presentation to the czar's government. The Russian position in St. Petersburg was, however, as intractable as that exhibited by Ambassador Cassini in Washington. The passport question was an internal Russian matter, McCormick was told, and "the Russian Government could not extend privileges to members of the race in question which were denied to those domiciled within the Empire."[32] The matter rested there until the somewhat encouraging news in October that the passport question was being taken up for study by a special Russian commission.

Meanwhile, on May 9 Simon Wolf wrote to Straus that Roosevelt had asked him for a draft of a plank to be included in the Republican national platform in regard to the passport question. Wolf asked Straus to prepare the draft.[33] Straus did so, but on May 18 he lunched with the president at the White House, at which time Roosevelt brought up Wolf's request for a statement in the Republican platform on the passport question. According to Straus' memorandum of the meeting: "The President said—You know, Mr. Straus, I am prepared to do anything that I can for all of our citizens—regardless of race or creed—but we can not go to war with Russia on this subject— besides to put such a question in the platform would look like

an effort to catch votes—as it could not be regarded for any
other purpose in that such statements in platforms are of no
avail." It was obvious that Wolf had misrepresented the matter
to Straus and others by claiming that the request for the platform statement had emanated from the president, when it was
in fact, in Straus's words, "a scheme concocted in his own brain
and no such request or suggestion had been made or even referred to by the President." When Roosevelt said that he could
no longer confer with Wolf "with any assurance of reliability,"
Straus sought to explain the source of the misunderstanding
to the president. "I replied that friend W[olf] may mean al-
right—but he suffered from megalomania, I feared. What I did
not say, we in New York, such as Schiff, Cyrus Adler & others
well know that—Wolf had constituted himself as the spokesman for the Jews at the capital for his own advantage and
glorification." Straus told Roosevelt on this occasion that he
had characterized the president's actions on behalf of east
European Jews as the "Diplomacy of Humanity" and Roosevelt
"liked the name and would use it, as it expressed the feelings
that activated him in these several instances."[34]

Despite Roosevelt's apparent reluctance and the misconception between Wolf and the president, the passport question was
addressed in the platforms of both the Republican and Democratic parties in 1904, with Jacob Schiff writing a draft plank
for the Democrats.[35] The *American Hebrew* featured the two
planks in a story, "Democracy and the Passport Question,"
and editorialized that the plank of the Democratic Party was
even stronger than that of the Republicans. "Now that both
political parties have placed themselves on record in the
matter," the *American Hebrew* said, "we hope that Russia will
be compelled soon to allow American Hebrews to travel in her
country without hindrance."[36]

At least substantially as a result of his apparent willingness
to act in diplomacy as requested by American Jewish leaders,
Roosevelt's bid for election to the presidency in his own right
in 1904 was strongly supported by the American Jewish community. When asked by one of the Roosevelt campaign committees to give expression to his own views concerning Roosevelt,
Schiff responded:

> I am personally a great admirer of the President, be-
> cause of the many sterling qualities he possesses and
> which he gives constantly evidence of. Contrary to
> what is stated by his adversaries, the President is a man
> of deep deliberation upon questions and matters which
> claim his attention, though when he has once reached
> a conclusion as to what is right and just and proper, no
> one and nothing can sway him from the path he has
> decided upon—consider, for instance, his course when
> some two years ago he so vigorously protested on be-
> half of the American people to Roumania because of
> the persecutions practiced upon her Jewish subjects.

Schiff recounted the events of the Rumanian protest of 1902,
and of the president's action in response to the Kishinev massacre, and added that he had every expectation that "the President will make every effort to hasten the time when the
Russians can no longer deny recognition to the American passport by whomsoever it may legitimately be presented, in order
to secure the right of unmolested travel in the Tsar's dominion."
Furthermore, "no narrow construction of the immigration laws
has been permitted under President Roosevelt's administration,"
nor need there be any fear that there would be any negative
modifications during his presidency because Roosevelt felt
that "the opportunities of this country should be open to all
who choose to come and who are physically and morally fitted
to profit by these opportunities." Schiff concluded that he
was convinced "that the Jewish citizen should and will consider the duty to his race, to cast his vote for the continuance
in office of President Roosevelt, and that he will be glad of
the opportunity to show his appreciation of the President's
intense patriotism, and of his fearless courage on behalf of the
oppressed and persecuted."[37]

Oscar Straus told Roosevelt that though he had always been
a liberal Democrat, or latterly a Cleveland Democrat, his ad-
miration for Roosevelt's "fearless devotion to right in its
highest sense, and my esteem for your wisdom and courageous
executive conservatism" had converted him into a campaign

worker for the president's election.[38] Both Straus and Schiff
were invited by Roosevelt to see him formally notified of the
Republican nomination.[39] The president also asked Straus
for his comments concerning the portion of his letter of acceptance which dealt with the passport question.[40] At Hay's suggestion, Roosevelt also approved the publication of the
diplomatic correspondence on the Jewish question with Russia,
but only after consulting with Jewish leaders like Straus and
Schiff since "they would all be greatly flattered."[41]

The *American Hebrew*, while not openly endorsing the election of Roosevelt, reprinted on its editorial page on October
14 a laudatory statement reprinted from the London *Jewish
Chronicle*, which hailed Roosevelt as "the nearest approach
to the political knight errant that exists in the latter day
world," and which concluded that the Jews of America
would not "withhold from him the gratitude due for his labors
in their behalf." The *American Hebrew* concluded: "This
testimony from the chief organ of English Jewry is eloquent
evidence of how our brethren abroad regard President
Roosevelt's endeavors to be of service to our people."[42] The
message was clear.

After Roosevelt's election Straus spent a night at the White
House in mid-November as a guest of the president. Roosevelt
asked him to comment on incomplete drafts of his forthcoming message to Congress. According to Straus's memorandum
of the evening:

> He first read us what he had to say on foreign relations;
> the action taken in regard to Russia and Roumania,
> in order to inform Congress what had been done. He
> placed his action upon the high humanitarian ground.
> Before reading this, he said: "Mr. Straus, I should like
> to have you pay special attention to this, as I have con-
> sulted you all along in regard to the action that I have
> taken." He then stated our action in regard to Russia
> and Roumania has been criticized as interfering with
> the internal affairs of other nations, and the statement
> has been repeatedly made, how would we like it if

other nations would criticize us for the negro lynchings in the South, and he said in the first place the
lynchings are comparatively few; those few were here
and there, one at a time, and though bad enough, were
nothing compared with the cold-blooded wholesale
murder under official recognition, if not at the instigation of the ruling powers, such as the Kishineff massacre. But he said, my answer to all of these criticisms
is this: only a short time ago I received a remonstrance
or petition from a society in Great Britain regarding the
lynchings in this country. I did not reject it. On the contrary, I answered it most politely, and expressed my
great regret for these unlawful and unjustifiable acts
with which neither I nor the government had any sympathy. On the contrary, the government does everything
in its power to prevent these outrageous and unlawful
acts. He concluded then by saying: "Mr. Straus, I author-
ize you to make use of this information whenever the
occasion arises."[43]

After the evening with the president, Straus recommended to
him the advisability of appointing a minister to Rumania rather
than to continue the practice of being represented to that
country through the U.S. minister to Greece. Roosevelt promised
to do his best to comply with Straus's suggestion.[44] The president also promised Straus that he would consult with him when
the question arose of the appointment of a new ambassador
to Russia.[45]

The Russo-Japanese War years saw the resurrection of the
American Society of Friends of Russian Freedom, moribund
since 1894. The English *Free Russia* announced in its issue of
April 1904 that the "revival of interest in Russia and Russian
affairs in the United States has called into active life the American Friends of Russian Freedom."[46] Actually, the resurrection
had begun in the summer of 1903 as a consequence of the
Kishinev incident. The extent of the involvement of Straus
and Schiff in the resuscitated movement is unclear, but one
activity undertaken under the auspices of the organization was

very clearly Schiff's. At the suggestion of George Kennan, Schiff furnished the funds to spread revolutionary propaganda among Russian prisoners of war in Japan. According to Kennan, Schiff financed the propaganda campaign among the Russian officers and enlisted men in the prisoner of war camps in 1906, "sowing the seeds of freedom in perhaps a hundred different regiments of the Russian Army," and also enabled Kennan and Dr. Nicholas Russel "to take care of all the Russian political convicts the Japanese released when they took possession of the island of Saghalin and whom they turned over to us."[47]

The principal work was done by Dr. Nicholas Russel, a Russian by birth and a naturalized American citizen, who had been president of the first territorial senate of Hawaii. According to the *New York Times* Russel:

> obtained adequate funds and a great mass of Socialistic literature from the "American Friends of Russia [*sic*]," of which Charles W. Folk and Julia Ward Howe are respectively President and Vice President; from the "Committee of the Revolutionist Socialist Party of New York," a branch of the famous Russian organization, and from other similar societies. After the fall of Port Arthur Dr. Russel was sent to Japan to spread among the Russian captives the ideas of his party. According to members of the local society he had succeeded beyond all expectation, as is shown by the fact that he has organized under the banner of Socialism nearly all of the Russian soldiers taken prisoners by the Japanese, who are now in detention camps in Japan awaiting transportation to their homes. . . . Wherever they go, it is to be expected that the men from Japan will act as a leaven and that, hard as the authorities may try, they will be unable to eradicate the effect of the awakening which the prisoners have undergone in the course of their long sojourn in their captors' country.[48]

Late in March of 1905 it became apparent that the war between Russia and Japan was approaching its end, and Schiff
expressed the hope that the Jews of Russia could now expect
better times. He felt surely the Russian government had learned
from its experience during the war that "international Jewry
is a power after all, and that if Russia wants to have the goodwill of the leading Jews in the world, she cannot continue to
withhold the barest human rights from her own Jewish subjects."[49] Whether or not the government of the czar had
learned this lesson, the Russian people appeared not to have;
in May 1905 the press carried new stories of Jewish massacres
in riots at Melitopol, in south Russia, and in Zhitomir, in
southwestern Russia.[50] There were also reports of outbreaks
in Russian Poland. In response to a cable from Paul Nathan
in Germany, Schiff quickly contacted President Roosevelt but
was forced to report to Nathan that the president was unable
to take any initiative at present. Roosevelt had, however, promised Schiff confidentially that upon the arrival of the new
Russian ambassador, Baron Rosen, he would "try to impress
upon him at the first opportunity that if Russia wants to gain
the goodwill of the United States, she will have to change com-
pletely her attitude toward her Jewish subjects." Since it
seemed obvious that Baron Rosen had been named to replace
Cassini from a desire on the part of the Russians to improve
relations with the United States, Schiff considered it to be
"of great moment if President Roosevelt explains to the new
Russian Ambassador from the very outset what has to be done
to establish better relations." As for the riots in Russia, Schiff
told Nathan that the impression in the United States, rightly
or wrongly, was that they had "been instigated against the
wishes of the St. Petersburg government."[51] Simon Wolf, too,
had communicated with the State Department to ascertain
whether the reports of anti-Jewish riots were true.[52] The State
Department did query the embassy in St. Petersburg concerning the reports but took no further action.[53]

The anti-Jewish actions in Russia in mid-1905 led Adolf
Kraus, the new president of B'nai B'rith, to seek an interview
with Count Witte when the latter was in the United States
representing Russia at the Portsmouth Peace Conference. Kraus

invited Schiff, Isaac N. Seligman, Adolph Lewisohn, and Straus to join him in the conference with Witte.[54] Schiff was not sanguine about any results that might be obtained from such a talk and was concerned lest it be said that he had discussed financial matters with Witte. There was, he felt, "only one thing we can do, to give as hard knocks to Russia as we can whenever opportunity offers, to accept no promises in return for our aid as bankers when this is asked for, and to do nothing for Russia until she has *actually* given civil rights to her Jewish subjects."[55] But Schiff did participate in the meeting, which was held on August 14 in Portsmouth. Simon Wolf, although not invited to participate, expressed his own sentiments in a letter to Witte, writing:

> Russia at this juncture needs two important elements to inspire its future prosperity and happiness: money and friends. The Jews of the world, as citizens of their respective countries, control much of the first and would make a magnificent army of the latter. There is no use disguising the fact that in the United States especially the Jews form an important factor in the formation of public opinion and in the control of the finances. . . . By virtue of their mercantile and financial standing in this country they are exercising an all potent and powerful influence. . . . Understand me distinctly that this power is not used to subvert or destroy but to resent aggression on the one hand and defend right on the other, and thus, owing to the lamentable and deplorable conditions of the Jews in Russia, your Government suffers a loss not only of prestige but of influence and friendship.[56]

At the meeting the Russian side was represented by Count Witte, Baron Rosen, and Gregory Wilenkin, an official interpreter who was a Russian Jew. According to Kraus's account of the conference, which lasted for three hours, Schiff pointed to Wilenkin and asked Witte: "Will you please tell me why you, as a Russian, have full rights in your country, while he, also a Russian, has none?" Witte replied that he agreed the restric-

tions against the Jews in Russia were unjust, but to do more
than repeal them gradually might create a revolution in that
country. One objection to repealing the laws was that young
Jews were leaders among the revolutionists in Russia, Witte
argued, but Schiff responded that the Jews had good reason
for becoming revolutionists since they were denied justice
under the czar. Witte argued that the revolutionists could not
succeed, and that the Romanov dynasty would "rule Russia
for at least another hundred years."[57] According to Schiff's
account of the meeting, sent to Philip Cowen by telegram:

> We honestly sought to impress [Witte] with [the] neces-
> sity [of the] prompt granting [of] full civil rights and
> stated without reserve that unless this [was] granted
> the steadily growing Jewish influence in America would
> be thrown against Russia, nor could [the] good will of
> American people be regained until Russia has given equal
> rights to Jewish subjects. We feel we have made an im-
> pression on Witte personally. Whether this will have
> any effect on Russian government [the] future must
> show. Witte avers that Jews do have rights to vote
> for members [of the] national assembly and can be
> elected as members of the assembly. He says latter when
> constituted will decide [the] entire Jewish question
> and is hopeful of [its] outcome. . . . Russian loan rumors
> are nonsense.[58]

After the interview Schiff, Straus, and the others addressed
a lengthy letter to Witte, dated September 5, in which they
reiterated their concern with the status of Russian Jewry and
the other points which they had made at the meeting with him.
In one paragraph they again made the point:

> The people of the United States, as must be known to
> you, are close observers of all that is taking place in
> Russia during this momentous period of her existence.
> Their sympathies are, for the time being, alienated from
> Russia because, liberty- and justice-loving, they have

recoiled from the horrors of Kishineff and from the terrible conditions which, though long existing, have only now been fully disclosed. Jewish influence in the United States, especially political, already carries great weight, and is steadily increasing, being constantly recruited from the large immigration of Russian Jews. Can it be expected that the influence of the American Jew upon public opinion will be exerted to the advantage of the country which systematically degrades his brethren-in-race, making their fate almost unendurable?[59]

For his part, Schiff continued to agitate against any issuance of Russian bonds in the United States. In late August of 1905, when it was reported that National City Bank was considering participation in a Russian bond issue, Schiff wrote James Stillman of that bank: "while I wish in no way to interfere with what may be considered the interests of your stockholders, it is but right that I should say to you if the report is correct, self-respect will necessitate my withdrawal from the board."[60] Late in 1905 the Russian government invited George W. Perkins and J. P. Morgan to St. Petersburg to discuss American participation in a Russian international loan. That initiative, however, was aborted by the wave of anarchy which swept Russia during the winter of 1905 to 1906.[61] In November of 1905 the outrages against Russian Jews began which dwarfed the Kishinev incident and stunned Jews and non-Jews alike throughout the civilized world.

NOTES

1. *American Hebrew*, February 12, 1904.
2. Adler to Cowen, February 16, 1904, Philip H. Cowen Papers.
3. *The Arena*, May 1904, p. 519.
4. Schiff to Straus, March 31, 1904, Oscar S. Straus Papers.
5. Straus to Roosevelt, March 31, 1904, Straus Papers.
6. Straus to Schiff, April 1, 1904, Straus Papers.

7. Straus to Loeb, April 4, 1904, Straus Papers.

8. Loeb to Straus, April 5, 1904, Straus Papers.

9. *American Hebrew*, April 15, 1904.

10. Wolf to Cowen, April 9, 1904, Cowen Papers.

11. Schiff to Rothschild, April 5, 1904, copy in Cowen Papers.

12. Gary Dean Best, "Financing a Foreign War: Jacob H. Schiff and Japan, 1904-05," *American Jewish Historical Quarterly* 61 (June 1972): 314-15.

13. Ibid., pp. 315-16.

14. Ibid., pp. 316-17.

15. Ibid., pp. 317-18.

16. Ibid., pp. 318-20.

17. Quoted in *Forum*, April 1905, p. 527.

18. *The Memoirs of Count Witte* (Garden City, N.Y., 1921), p. 135.

19. McCormick to Hay, March 24, 1905, Department of State *Despatches from United States Ministers to Russia, 1808-1906*, National Archives Microfilm Publication M35, reel 62 (hereafter cited as DS M35/62).

20. "The Financial Facts About Russia and Japan," *The World's Work*, July 1905, p. 6347.

21. Schiff to Katzenelsohn, July 21, 1904, Jacob H. Schiff Papers.

22. McCormick to Hay, October 1, 1904, with attachment, DS M35/62.

23. McCormick to Hay, October 7, 1904, DS M35/62.

24. McCormick to Hay, January 18, 1905, DS M35/62.

25. Schiff to Wilenkin, March 27, 1905, Schiff Papers.

26. Rothschild to Schiff, April 7, 1904, Schiff Papers.

27. White to Wolf, May 12, 1905, copy in Cowen Papers.

28. Cowen to Wolf, May 17, 1905, Cowen Papers.

29. Seligman to Cowen, July 3, 1905, Cowen Papers.

30. Hay Diary, April 7, 1904, John Hay Papers.

31. Hay Diary, June 11, 1904, Hay Papers.

32. McCormick to Hay, August 14, 1904, DS M35/61.

33. Wolf to Straus, May 5, 1904 and "Suggestions for a Plank in the Republican Platform," Straus Papers.

34. Memorandum, "At Luncheon with President Roosevelt at the White House, May 18, 1904," Straus Papers.

35. Schiff to Wiley, June 27, 1904, Schiff Papers.

36. *American Hebrew*, July 15, 1904.

37. Schiff to Lipsky, October 5, 1904, copy in Cowen Papers.

38. Straus to Roosevelt, July 18, 1904, Straus Papers.

39. Roosevelt to Straus, July 19, 1904, Straus Papers.

40. Roosevelt to Straus, August 5, 1904, Straus Papers.

41. Roosevelt to Hay, September 10, 1904, Theodore Roosevelt Papers.

42. *American Hebrew*, October 14, 1904.

43. "Memorandum of a Night at the White House as a Guest of the President, November 16, 1904," Straus Papers.

44. Straus to Roosevelt, November 18, 1904, and Loeb to Straus, November 19, 1904, Straus Papers.

45. Roosevelt to Straus, December 16, 1904, Straus Papers.

46. *Free Russia*, April 1904.

47. Kennan to Schiff, April 11, 1917, George Kennan Papers, Library of Congress.

48. *New York Times*, November 12, 1905.

49. Schiff to Nathan, March 29, 1905, Schiff Papers.

50. *New York Times*, May 10 and 11, 1905.

51. Schiff to Nathan, May 19, 1905, Schiff Papers.

52. *American Hebrew*, May 26, 1905.

53. Loomis to Meyer, May 19, 1905, and June 14, 1905, *Diplomatic Instructions of the Department of State, 1801-1906, Russia*, National Archives Microfilm Publication M77, reel 140 (hereafter cited as DS M77/140).

54. Edward R. Grusd, *B'nai B'rith: The Story of a Covenant* (New York, 1966), p. 134.

55. Schiff to Cowen, August 7, 1905, Schiff Papers.

56. Quoted in *American Hebrew*, August 18, 1905.

57. Adolf Kraus, *Reminiscences and Comments* (Chicago, 1925), pp. 156-57.

58. Schiff to Cowen, telegram, August 16, 1905, Cowen Papers.

59. Schiff, Seligman, Straus, Lewisohn, and Kraus to Witte, September 5, 1905, in Cyrus M. Adler, *Jacob H. Schiff: His Life and Letters*, 2 vols. (Garden City, N.Y., 1928), 2: 129-32.

60. Schiff to Stillman, August 29, 1905, Schiff Papers.

61. Meyer to Root, November 6, 1905, DS M35/64.

CHAPTER 5

Russia, 1905-1906

Witte had barely concluded his talks with the American Jewish leaders before fresh reports of atrocities against Jews in Russia appeared in American newspapers.[1] The reports increased, and in November black headlines told of massacres of Jews in Odessa and elsewhere in Russia. The *New York Times* reported that men, women, and children had been slain in Odessa, that 5,657 were in hospitals, and that the number of dead "may never be known—mutilated bodies are still lying in the streets."[2]

A first response by American and European Jewish leaders was monetary relief for the suffering in Russia and an "open door" for up to 500 Russian Jewish orphans.[3] On November 7 a meeting was held at Temple Emanu-El in New York City to launch the relief effort. It was, reported the *American Hebrew*, "one of the most remarkable meetings ever held in this country by Jews," in that all elements of the Jewish community were represented, including not only the uptown Jewish element, but also the East Side, Socialists, Zionists, "almost the entire local rabbinate," the heads of Jewish institutions, "the supporters of our institutions, men who had for years given of their time and money to relieve the distress of our brethren." On the results of the meeting, the *American Hebrew* reported:

The following officers of the meeting were elected:
Oscar S. Straus, chairman; Cyrus L. Sulzberger, secretary; Jacob H. Schiff, treasurer. Mr. Straus took the
chair and gave the floor to Mr. Schiff, who gave a con-
cise, a vivid account of what had been done to co-operate with European committees and to enlist the active
sympathy of President Roosevelt. He said it was necessary to act, not to talk. . . . It seemed that the Russian
central government had lost control and that intervention would be of no avail for there seemed to be
no government able to do anything. Mr. Schiff had
telegraphed to Washington knowing that the President
could do nothing. He had then called the meeting in
conjunction with Straus.

Not only Schiff, but Straus and Simon Wolf as well, had contacted the administration in Washington regarding possible diplomatic intercession by the United States, and all had been
disappointed. Schiff had wired Roosevelt that the reports of
the massacres in Russia were "so revolting that reluctantly as
I do so I feel to be justified in asking whether . . . any expression on the part of this government might be of any avail in
inducing vigorous measures on the part of the Russian authorities to stop these terrible atrocities." He was, he told the president, perfectly aware of the difficulties of the situation, "but
when humanity stand[s] aghast, conventionalities must stand
aside."[4] Schiff had even cabled Count Witte, now premier of
Russia, that: "The American people stand aghast at atrocities
in Odessa and elsewhere. No government should expect the
moral support of other nations which under any condition
permits such a situation to continue." Witte, however, replied
that the Russian government was itself "horrified at these outrages," and told Schiff he should know "that I less than anyone
can sympathize with such savage outbreaks." He was, he told
Schiff, doing everything that could be done, "but as long as the
country is in such excited states, the local authorities are often
powerless."[5] Clearly diplomatic intervention of any kind

would be useless since the Russian government was obviously
helpless in its attempts to bring about order in that country.
Straus, however, had traveled to Washington to confer with the
president "to learn his views." Roosevelt was "full of
sympathy," but concluded from Witte's cable to Schiff, a copy
of which Straus showed him, that nothing could be done by
the United States government under the circumstances which
could be of any benefit to the Jews of Russia.[6]

Simon Wolf had explored the possibility of an American
diplomatic initiative with the State Department, but was told
by Secretary of State Elihu Root that "at this juncture any
action by this Government looking to the relief of your coreligionists in Russia would be inopportune and unavailing."
Root told Wolf he hoped, however, that the establishment of
a more liberal form of government in Russia and the reestablishment of control over the country would lead to "a
practical response" to America's "repeated solicitations of
freer treatment of American Hebrews," and that the United
States might then "be in a position to exert efficient good
influence toward the more liberal treatment of all Jews in
Russia and their better protection from the consequences of
deep lying racial antagonism." The problem was one, he
assured Wolf, "which strongly attracts the sympathetic attention of this Government."[7] Of interest is the fact that Root
apparently gave priority to the passport question, and only
after the resolution of this issue was the United States government to seek to improve the condition of the Jews in Russia.

Reporting his efforts to Schiff, Wolf wrote that "unfortunately our government is not in a position to affirmatively do
anything, although I feel confident the President is at work
trying to do something."[8] At a meeting which he called in
Washington in behalf of the fund raising effort, Wolf told his
audience that, while he realized President Roosevelt could not
interfere in the domestic affairs of Russia, Roosevelt had an
enormously influential personal side such as he had revealed
in orchestrating the Portsmouth Peace Conference. It was that
side which Wolf hoped could now be mobilized in behalf of
Russian Jewry, "that he may be able through the force of his

own striking personality, genius, talents, and power to bring
about some concert of action on the part of men as great as
himself to put an end to the massacre of the Jews in Russia."[9]
The image of knight errant, once attributed to the president,
was difficult to shake.

Largely in response, apparently, to Wolf's inquiry, the State
Department was in fact monitoring the situation in Russia. On
November 22, Root wired the embassy in St. Petersburg: "Many
influential Hebrews in this country are greatly distressed over
reports of Jewish loss of life and suffering in recent outbreaks
and are endeavoring to raise relief funds." Root asked the embassy for reports on the outrages, including the numbers killed,
sick, wounded, and destitute and the losses sustained.[10] Spencer
Eddy, the chargé, responded with reports gleaned from consular
sources of Jewish casualties in Warsaw, Riga, Rostoff, and other
cities—with the greatest damage in Odessa where he reported
560 Jews killed, 2,000 in hospitals, and the suffering and destitution great.[11] Handwritten at the bottom of the telegrams were
instructions that they should be shown to Simon Wolf. A few
weeks later Ambassador George von Lengerke Meyer reported
to the State Department: "Russian nation appears to have gone
temporarily insane; government practically helpless to restore
law and order throughout the country."[12] If the Russian government could not impose its will on the nation then diplomatic
pressure upon that government clearly would be pointless.

American Jewish leaders concentrated their efforts on relief
and, in the aforementioned relief meeting at Temple Emanu-El,
received over $50,000 in pledges, with Schiff guaranteeing this
sum out of his own pocket to the London relief committee in
advance of the actual payment of the subscriptions.[13] The resultant organization, known as the National Committee for the
Relief of Sufferers by Russian Massacres, quickly sought to enlist the cooperation of the entire Jewish population in its effort
to raise funds for the relief of Russian Jews.[14] Under the leadership of Straus, Sulzberger, and Schiff, local committees were
established in numerous towns and cities to generate contributions for the National Committee.[15] The goal was set at one
million dollars.[16] At the same time, responsible Jewish organs

like the *American Hebrew* called for the formation of a permanent organization "to represent the American Jewish people in all matters that affect their interests and brethren in distress in foreign countries." It sought an organization that would contain delegates from all the Jewish organizations in the United States.[17] In this way the pogroms of 1905 set in motion the forces that would lead to the creation of the American Jewish Committee.

During November contributions poured in to the National Committee. By the twentieth the fund had already passed the half million dollar mark. Straus reported that the committee had sent telegrams to 454 communities, and in all of them "the work of collecting funds began within a few hours after our communication was received." He was now confident that the fund would easily reach the goal that had been targeted.[18] By early the following month the committee had received one million dollars with nearly half the amount collected from within New York City itself. The balance included contributions of $80,000 from Chicago; $60,000 from Philadelphia; $22,000 from Baltimore; $27,000 from St. Louis; $20,000 from both San Francisco and Boston; $17,000 from Cincinnati; $14,000 from Kansas City; $15,000 from Cleveland; and $10,000 each from New Orleans and Pittsburgh. In fact, the committee confessed to the *New York Times* that it had not really expected to collect more than one-fourth of the one million dollar goal. As the *New York Times* reported the campaign:

> Mr. Schiff sent telegrams to more than 400 cities for immediate help, and advices showed that not a moment was lost after the appeal was received. A black-bordered appeal was sent to thousands of individuals, to synagogues, lodges, clubs, and various Jewish organizations throughout the United States. Lodges and synagogues pledged large sums, and then called on their members to make good the pledges. . . . From the first Mr. Schiff kept the remittances ahead of the actual cash on hand. He announced from the start of the fund that he would

do this on account of the urgency of the situation, and
the act was warranted by the pledges made on all sides.[19]

Strong support also was furnished by the American Jewish
press, which not only carried the appeals of the National Committee for funds, but also exhorted its readers through editorials
to send subscriptions to the committee.[20]

Schiff, however, was not content with furnishing relief.
Simple diplomatic protest appeared impracticable so the highly
agitated Schiff sought a precedent in American intervention in
Cuba seven years earlier for something more extreme than a
simple unilateral diplomatic protest.[21] Thus, given the state of
anarchy evident in Russia, Schiff wrote to Roosevelt that he
doubted "even if our and other Governments would unite in a
note of remonstrance to Russia, that any actual result would
follow such action." Still, Schiff believed it was becoming daily
more apparent that something must be done and soon. He concluded that if American action had been justified in Cuba in
1898, as it doubtless was, then surely it was now "the duty of
the civilized world to intervene so that the slaughter" in Russia
might be brought to an end. Schiff believed, he told the president, that if Roosevelt would simply ask authority from Congress "to take such measures as may become advisable, in cooperation with other Governments, to prevent the continuation
and further spread of the conditions now prevalent in Russia,"
then the action would be "heartily endorsed by the American
people." In addition, it "would have the immediate effect of
establishing a different order of things in Russia than now
exists; that it would rally national self-respect in Russia, would
help to make possible the constitution of a proper party of law
and order, so that actual measures on the part of our own
Government and other Powers would probably not be necessary."[22] In the extremity of his concern with the fate of Jews
in Russia, Schiff clearly was making an outrageous request in
calling for what was at the least an audacious bluff which, if
it failed, might well have led to a forceful remonstrance by the
United States—preferably in league with other powers—and
perhaps if all else failed, to even unilateral or joint military
intervention in Russia.

Roosevelt naturally was appalled by Schiff's suggestion and responded that such an action "would make the United States Government ridiculous, and so far from helping the condition of the Jews, would have hurt them in Russia *and would have tended to hurt them here.*" Given the state that Russia was in, the president pointed out, it was impossible that anything he might do would accomplish anything constructive. He added:

> When the governmental authorities in Russia are wholly unable to protect themselves—when there is revolt in every quarter of the empire, among every class of the people and bonds of social order everywhere are relaxed—it is idle to suppose that anything could be done by diplomatic representation. The idea of a European coalition in which we should join is, of course, wholly chimerical. What would such a coalition do? Enforce liberty or order—restore the autocracy, or install a republic? There, it is evident, we could do nothing, and where we could do nothing, I have a horror of saying anything. We never have taken—and while I am President, we never will take—any action which we cannot make good.

Roosevelt told Schiff he would "take no action until I know that any action I take will do good instead of harm, and I shall announce no position which I may have to abandon at the cost of putting the United States Government in a humiliating and ridiculous attitude." He believed, the president said, in the old plains adage: "Never to draw unless you mean to shoot." In a postscript he added: "I sympathize thoroughly with your feelings, wrought up as they are and ought to be at the dreadful outrages committed on the Jews of Russia; anything I can do I will do, but I will not threaten aimlessly and thereby do harm."[23]

To a cooler-headed Oscar Straus, Roosevelt wrote that "our good friend Jacob H. Schiff became hysterical over what I could do about the dreadful atrocities perpetrated upon the Jews in Russia." He enclosed a copy of the reply he had sent to

Schiff and told Straus: "Thank Heaven, you kept your head,
as you always do, my dear fellow!"[24] Straus responded that he
had "endeavored to act to the best of my efforts as a buffer
for you in the matter of the Russian massacres, but the fact is
that it is difficult to persuade many that you, who have done
so much, cannot accomplish any and everything that humanity
might dictate; in other words, they crown you with a halo of
international omnipotence." Straus had, he told the president,
made exactly the same points that the latter had made in his
letter to Schiff, that "in the present revolutionary condition
of affairs, interference from without could do no good, but it
might do harm, it might irritate rather than allay conditions."
Certainly the United States could not intervene in Russia,
either alone or in league with other nations, "for many obvious
and conclusive reasons."[25]

Despite Schiff's plea for the administration to undertake
with European powers some concerted protest or action against
Russia, it was clear that the latter, at least, was out of the question—the United States would not and could not abandon its
traditional independence in foreign policy in this instance,
and to agitate openly for such a course of action would only
redound, as Roosevelt had hinted, to the detriment of American
Jews. Perhaps from a belated appreciation of this, in late December 1905 Schiff opposed proposals emanating from European
Jewish organizations for an international Jewish congress which
was to be held in Brussels to take up the Jewish problem in
Russia. As he wrote to one of the organizers, the National Committee for the Relief of Sufferers by Russian Massacres had decided to turn down the invitation to attend the conference
because the executive committee had decided "that we in this
country ought to do nothing which would give the American
people the impression that it is the intention of international
Jewry to create an organization which—in order to render
assistance in the difficult situation in which our Russian coreligionists unfortunately find themselves—will adopt measures
for relief which might ignore or injure the justified, or even
unjustified, interests and desires of this country." Schiff warned
that "the whole state of affairs must be handled with great dis-

cretion if we are not to jeopardize the important work which can and must still be done in the United States for the alleviation of the lot of our oppressed Russian coreligionists—especially in the matter of receiving great numbers of them here."[26] To another European Jew Schiff wrote that he believed the United States could still absorb "a large portion of Russian immigration," and this was crucial since he viewed the dreams of some Jewish leaders of establishing a Jewish state in East Africa as "pure madness." If millions of Russian immigrants were to be absorbed as a result of conditions in that country, they would have to be accommodated in a location "where conditions are already settled, as in the United States, in Canada, or in Argentina." It was to avoid jeopardizing such immigration, Schiff reported, that the American committee had declined the invitation to the Brussels conference.[27]

There was good reason to be concerned about possible restrictions being imposed on immigration. An awakening of nativist sentiment in the South and the Far West, together with restrictionist sentiment on the part of the American Federation of Labor, had led to a resurgence in 1905 of the movement to limit immigration. American Jewish leaders were stimulated by the situation in Russia to take "unprecedented action on behalf of a liberal immigration policy."[28] They were also alert to provide no fuel for the restrictionist fire. Schiff's concern about the possible backlash against immigration as a result of excessive agitation on the part of American Jews in favor of American intercession in the Russian situation did not, however, extend to such agitation from other quarters. He did not object when Congressman William Sulzer wrote him in mid-January 1906 that he had organized "a committee of distinguished citizens in Washington" to put together "a monster demonstration to protest against Jewish outrages in Russia and to urge the administration to use all in its power to put a stop to these atrocities." The meeting was to be addressed by a number of U.S. Senators and Congressmen, and Sulzer was confident that the meeting would "go far to bring about the consummation we all have so much at heart."[29] The meeting was held on January 21 with Senators Patterson (Colorado), Overman (North Carolina), and Clark (Arkansas), as well as Congress-

men Sulzer and Bennet (New York), Rainey (Illinois), Hinshaw
(Nebraska), Taylor (Alabama), Moon (Pennsylvania), and
Trimble (Kentucky), occupying seats on the platform.[30]
   Meanwhile, Roosevelt had resolved to appoint Oscar Straus
to his cabinet. What is interesting about the appointment is
the president's attempt to link it to the current tragedy of
Russian Jews. As Straus recalled his conversation with Roosevelt,
the president told him:

> Straus, you know I like you very much. I suppose you
> know I am going to make you a member of my cabinet
> and the reason is, first, because I have a very high esti-
> mate of your character, your judgment and your ability,
> and I want you for personal reasons. There is also a
> second reason—I want to show Russia and such countries
> what we think of a Jew in this country. . . . I could not
> see my way clear of doing any good, and perhaps it
> would be doing harm, to make any public display or
> utterances regarding the dreadful massacres in Russia
> under the present disorganized condition of affairs there.
> I could not see any good coming out of it, and I did not
> want to do anything which might sound well here and
> have just an opposite effect there. I think it is a much
> more effective evidence of my interest to place a man
> like you into my cabinet, which will doubtless have
> an influence more than words would have in all coun-
> tries where there is an unreasonable prejudice.[31]

Thus President Roosevelt professed to view his appointment of
Straus to the cabinet as a form of indirect attack on the prejudice that was at the root of the Jewish problem in Russia.
   In addition to its activities in mobilizing relief for the suffering Jews in Russia, the National Committee also was monitoring
the migration of Jews from that country to the United States.
The committee was concerned that nothing should be done
which might lead to exclusion of Jewish immigrants or to pressures for restrictive immigration legislation, and so it advised
immigrants to the United States to be "properly equipped" for
entrance into this country.[32] However, the National Committee

scrupulously refused to allow the allocation of any of its relief funds for the payment of transportation for immigrants to the United States, since to do so would be to violate the provision of American immigration law prohibiting "assisted immigration." If even a few cases were assisted and discovered, the committee feared that "the entire movement of Jews to this country would be thrown under suspicion of being assisted," and were this to happen, "a serious check might be given to the free admission of unassisted immigration, which for many years past has aggregated from six to one hundred thousand Jews annually."[33]

Early in 1906 reaction was clearly gaining the upper hand in Russia, the authority of the government gradually was reasserted, and excesses against the Jews diminished, but in March of that year serious concern began to be expressed by Russian Jews about the possibility of renewed pogroms to coincide with Easter. The Russo-Jewish Committee in London once again solicited the assistance of the National Committee in bringing diplomatic pressure to bear upon the Russian government to prevent renewed outbreaks of violence. Since the situation was different now, with the authority of the Russian government reestablished, the London committee had been successful in moving the British government to consult with the Russian ambassador about the problem. London expressed hope that the National Committee would be able to achieve a similar success with the United States government. As the president of the Russo-Jewish Committee expressed to Straus:

> I am aware that our good friend Mr. Jacob H. Schiff has already in vain invited the assistance of your President, but having regard to the fact that contrary to all previous precedents, our Government has actually solicited the Russian minister to afford protection to the Jews, and has, contrary to all expectations, received a satisfactory assurance from him, I am of the opinion that a like assurance should be solicited, and, if possible, obtained, by your Government through your ambassador in St. Petersburg.[34]

When no response was forthcoming, the London committee wired Straus again a week later that pogroms were expected everywhere in Russia at Easter and asked him to encourage the U.S. secretary of state to instruct the American ambassador in St. Petersburg to intercede with the Russian government, following the British precedent, "so as to prevent a recurrence of pogroms."[35] In response to the second plea from London Straus arranged an appointment with President Roosevelt for April 7, 1906, after which he wired the London committee that the president had directed the American ambassador to Russia to cooperate with the British ambassador there, and that he had also promised to take the matter up with the Russian ambassador in Washington. Straus wrote to the London committee:

> The President has several times taken action at my instance in these Russian and Roumanian matters and he, with his humanitarian sense, immediately instructed the Secretary of State to communicate with our ambassador at St. Petersburg to confer with Spring-Rice [the British ambassador] and take immediate action. I also prevailed upon the President to have an unofficial conference with Baron Rosen here and to impress upon the latter the President's deep concern that every step shall be taken by his government to prevent a repetition of the massacres; that if such should occur, it would have a most unfortunate effect as far as Russia is concerned in this country.[36]

On April 7, 1906, the State Department cabled the embassy in St. Petersburg: "Grave apprehensions felt by numerous relatives in this Country that mob disturbances and unlawful attacks upon Jews are planned for Easter. What information have you as to what precautions have been taken to avert renewal of the distressing events of former years?" The wire also informed the embassy that the State Department understood that Great Britain was making similar inquiries, and it asked the embassy to confer with British ambassador Spring-

Rice.[37] Ambassador Meyer responded that Premier Witte appeared "to be very sanguine that there will be no Jewish troubles," and that the minister of the interior had sent a circular to "all the Governors instructing them to prevent Jewish disturbances and to hold the police responsible."[38] A copy of Meyer's wire was forwarded to Straus by William Loeb, Jr., Roosevelt's secretary, with instructions to make no "public use" of the cable, but to "show it privately to anyone to whom you think it wise to show it."[39] Meanwhile, under further prodding from Straus, Roosevelt reported that he had seen the Russian ambassador, Baron Rosen, and had received from him "the positive statement that Russia was fully alive to the situation and was taking every step to prevent any trouble to the Jews." Rosen had spoken "warmly" of Straus's "courtesy and consideration," but had told the president that "another prominent Jewish gentleman in New York City had prejudiced Witte against the cause of which he was pleading by his attitude." The "prominent Jewish gentleman" was clearly Jacob Schiff, as Straus indicated in an initialed marginalia.[40]

Straus was congratulated by the Russo-Jewish Committee in London for his success in initiating action from the president, as the committee felt "that the humanitarian attitude adopted by yourself and your President will go far to prevent the recurrence of the lamentable events which plunge all Jews in common into such deep grief."[41] When Easter passed uneventfully in Russia, the Russo-Jewish Committee wrote Cyrus Sulzberger that it had "not the slightest doubt that the action [taken by the Russian Government] was due to the lively interest evidenced by your President at the instance of our friend, the honorable Oscar Straus, and the President's representation made to the Russian government through its ambassador at Washington." It was, the chairman of the Russo-Jewish Committee pointed out, the first Easter in almost twenty years when Russian Jews "were not, in some place or other, victims of outrage of more or less importance."[42] Clearly the Russian government had exerted its influence to prevent any incidents, and the obvious concern exhibited by the United States government may have influenced the Russians to that end.

Yet the Russo-Jewish Committee recognized that Roosevelt's action, at Straus's initiative, had not been the only factor in the peaceful Easter in Russia. The Russian government in 1906 once again was seeking a loan in the international money market.[43] American and European Jewish bankers bent their efforts in 1906 to block as far as possible the Russian attempts to obtain funds. Straus, too, lobbied against the Russian effort, lunching with a partner of J. P. Morgan and Company and obtaining his "solemn word that his firm would not take part in the Russian loan, certainly not until authority for such loan shall have been given by the Duma," the new Russian parliament.[44] A few days later Straus positively confirmed that Morgan would not participate in the Russian loan, and he asked the Russo-Jewish Committee to encourage Lord Rothschild to throw his influence against the loan in Europe.[45] Despite the fact that the Rothschilds refused to participate, as well as the German banks and Morgan in the United States, the Russian loan was negotiated successfully through French financial institutions and Baring Brothers in London.[46] The "treachery of Germany and of the American syndicate of bankers headed by Morgan," as Witte later put it, reduced the amount of the Russian loan, however, from 2.750 billion francs to 2.250 billion francs, a reduction of nearly one-fifth. Still, the "loan that saved Russia," as Witte referred to it, was the largest foreign loan ever floated to that time in history.[47] The Russian bonds were not popular with investors, however, and according to one account Baring Brothers was left with about $50 million of the bonds on their hands, being unable to find buyers for them. Ernest Cassel, a close Jewish friend of Jacob Schiff's, saved Baring Brothers from bankruptcy by taking the bonds off their hands. Cassel invited Schiff to participate in the business, arguing that to do so would doubtless prove beneficial to Russian Jews. Cassel brushed aside Schiff's attempts to dissuade him from aiding the Russians, since he was sure that after he saved Russia's credit he could obtain an interview with the czar and could then obtain concessions for Russia's Jews. In that expectation, however, Cassel was proved wrong by later events.[48] Thus, while the efforts of Jews to block the Russian loan of 1906 may have contributed to the

loss of some funds for the Russians, they were unable to prevent the Russian government from obtaining the money it
needed.

Jewish fears that a renewal of atrocities against Jews in
Russia would not long be held in check once the Russian government was again financially secure soon had confirmation. New
atrocities at Bialystok led Schiff to appeal once again to President Roosevelt for assistance. On June 18 he wired Roosevelt
that he had received "the most heart-rending cablegrams from
Russia and elsewhere," copies of which he was sending to the
president, which described "a most horrid state and a renewal
of their atrocities in their worst form." English Jews were seeking the intervention of their government and hoped for similar
action from the United States. While recognizing, he said, "the
hopelessness of the situation," Schiff prayed that Roosevelt
would "not hesitate to act if it is at all practicable on the part
of our government to do anything in the way of intervention."
But in his letter of the same date, forwarding to Roosevelt the
cables which he had received regarding the situation, Schiff
added that he knew "in advance that, unfortunately, nothing
can be done by our Government." Still, he wanted to bring the
situation to the president's attention "in the faint hope that
possibly you and also Secretary Root might be able to see
some way in which pressure can be brought upon the Russian
Government." Schiff felt, he said, "mortified that I have again
to address you on this depressing subject, but the unfortunate
situation as it exists must be my excuse."[49]

Roosevelt, whose irritation had already been revealed at
Schiff's repeated appeals for action in prior situations when
the government had been powerless to bring about any improvement, now responded that he would take the matter up
with Root. The president expressed to Schiff his own shock
and horror at what was happening in Russia, but added: "you
know . . . how well nigh impossible it is to accomplish but
harm by interference."[50] Simon Wolf received substantially
the same response when he, too, took up the Bialystok affair
with the president.[51] Jews in Britain failed in their attempts
to get action from the British government, and Schiff was

seized once again by a feeling of powerlessness about the events in Russia. The situation there, he told one correspondent, "occupies my mind day and night, but I am utterly unable to point out the way in which we could do anything in this country at this time of effective value to prevent these horrible occurrences." All of the influence of American Jewish leaders with the Roosevelt administration was for naught if the United States government, itself, was powerless to alter the situation.[52]

Nevertheless while even Schiff was convinced that Roosevelt could "do absolutely nothing at this juncture to intervene in the horrible state of affairs in Russia," and that it was a mistake continually to ask the president for assistance, he resolved to make yet another effort.[53] In response to Schiff's latest entreaty, Roosevelt wrote on June 26 intimating that he had indeed been seeking to bring pressure to bear on the Russians.[54] Roosevelt had, in fact, instructed Secretary of State Root to cable the embassy in St. Petersburg that: "The President wishes you to take the earliest occasion to ascertain informally whether the reports of acquiescence of local authorities" in the Jewish massacres at Bialystok were true and, if so, to learn "whether steps are not being taken by the Russian Government to show its condemnation of such action in a way to do away with the present unfortunate effect upon American public opinion." The American people, Root reported, had been showing an increasingly sympathetic attitude toward Russia and her attempts to establish "peace and order on a sound constitutional basis, and we much regret any check to that feeling." The United States government, the wire continued, was sure the Russian government was making every effort to prevent such outrages, but "it is impossible that this should be the general view unless the true attitude of the Russian Government is exhibited by so dealing with the inculpated local officials as to make misunderstanding impossible."[55] The United States, then, only would be satisfied that the Russian government did not countenance such attacks as at Bialystok if it acted to deal with the officials responsible.

In seeking to carry out the instructions from the State Department, Ambassador Meyer found that the Russians were already familiar with the contents of the cable, having apparently broken the code, and that they were unwilling to discuss the matter with him. Instead, Meyer was referred to an official communication issued by the minister of the interior to the prefectural governors and published on June 23, which read:

> To avoid excesses, in reference to the occurrences in Byalostock, warn all your subordinates, high and low, that I expect absolute fulfillment of their duty from them. Disorders of any kind, whether agrarian or anti-Jewish must be prevented, and in the case of their occurrence must be suppressed in the most decisive manner. Nipping such movements in the bud means lessening the number of victims. All who are inefficient or inactive will be held strictly accountable.

The British ambassador experienced a similar response when he called on the Russian foreign minister concerning the same matter.[56] Secretary of State Root concluded: "Russia appears to have treated our message about Byalostok very much as we would have treated a proposition from Russia to discuss lynching."[57] Several months later Schiff confided that Roosevelt had told him, "in confidence—and I repeat, in confidence— that after Bialystok, our ambassador in St. Petersburg tried to make representations which the minister to whom he was speaking interrupted replying that Russia was unwilling to permit foreign powers to interfere in such matters." From this Roosevelt had concluded "it was entirely impossible after such a rebuff to make further such representations."[58]

In July 1906, however, renewed atrocities in Russia brought yet another request from the Russo-Jewish Committee in London asking Schiff if it were not possible for the United States government to deliver a diplomatic protest. Of the request, which came from Lord Rothschild, Schiff wrote Cyrus Adler that, while he knew that the president could do nothing, he had nevertheless immediately sent him the original of Rothschild's cablegram. Upon receipt of the cablegram, Roosevelt sent for Schiff's son, Mortimer, who lived near his

Oyster Bay home, and met with him for nearly an hour. Roosevelt told him that the Russian attitude of snubbing American attempts to intercede and refusing to receive any representations from the United States government made it pointless to attempt any further initiatives. Schiff concluded that he could "see that further appeals to the President will not do any good, if they may not possibly do harm, and I freely confess that I am at my wits end."[59] Schiff thanked the president for meeting with his son and asked him to forgive his continued importunations which were caused, he told Roosevelt, by "the unfortunate situation in which we find ourselves, but you will at least have the confidence of knowing that my confidence that you would assist us if you could is of the utmost."[60] Schiff understood it was Roosevelt's position that, in Schiff's words, "so long as the United States and other Powers are not prepared to back up their intervention with ships and troops, it can serve no purpose and can only do harm to make further representations to the Russian Government."[61] If the Russian government was determined to snub American attempts at remonstrance and to maintain its indifference to diplomatic initiatives, further such initiatives were clearly pointless. The alternatives were then to do nothing, or to press remonstrances backed by force. Even the most agitated American Jewish leaders recognized the latter was impossible.

From their feelings of powerlessness, American Jewish leaders poured their energies into other channels. In January 1906, at the instigation of a group of prominent New York Jews including Cyrus Adler, Cyrus Sulzberger, and Louis Marshall, a call was issued for a meeting of leading Jews from all over the United States to meet the following month in New York City to take up the question of forming a national organization representative of American Jewry. The general consensus was that some form of national organization was needed, although Adolf Kraus at least was unwilling to see the B'nai B'rith swallowed up by such a national body and Simon Wolf would only agree not to oppose its formation. A larger problem, however, was disagreement over how the new body was to be constituted. The conflict centered around two proposals.

Louis Marshall sought a genuinely democratic body and favored a national convention representative of Jewish congregations across the country which would then choose an executive committee. Oscar Straus countered by arguing, in Naomi Cohen's words, "for ability rather than democracy" and favored the appointment of an executive committee of fifteen members which would be empowered to increase its numbers. Jacob Schiff sided with Louis Marshall in seeking to broaden the base of Jewish leadership and make it more democratic. The conference voted for the Straus plan, but by the close vote of 16 to 13, which indicated in the interest of unity a compromise was desirable between the two plans. On May 19 a smaller conference was held in New York which adopted a compromise proposal offered by Dr. Cyrus Adler. Adler proposed the appointment of an executive committee of fifteen with the power to increase its number to fifty and which would co-operate with the existing national Jewish organizations. Chairman Mayer Sulzberger and five others were authorized to appoint the committee of fifteen. These fifteen then chose thirty-five additional members, and on November 11, 1906, the American Jewish Committee was launched at its first meeting.[62]

As Naomi Cohen has pointed out, however, the formation of the American Jewish Committee did not immediately alter the existing approach to Jewish problems significantly, nor did it immediately bring about any significant changes in the dramatis personae of Jewish leadership. Judge Mayer Sulzberger served as president of the American Jewish Committee, with valuable assistance from Cyrus Adler, but Jacob Schiff and Oscar Straus remained powerful figures because of their personal prestige, their extensive contacts, and their wealth of experience in dealing with the successive administrations in Washington. Adolf Kraus and Simon Wolf likewise continued to be influential voices for the American Jewish community even after they resigned from the American Jewish Committee in 1907 over the failure of attempts to delineate the "spheres of activity" of the American Jewish Committee, B'nai B'rith, and the Union of American Hebrew Congregations.[63] As long as powerful figures like Schiff, Straus, Kraus, and Wolf remained active, their personal prestige would be more influential in agitating with the administrations in Washington than would the organization of a committee.

During the unprecedented anti-Semitic violence of 1905-1906 in Russia, the activities of American Jewish leaders had produced little result. Some scholars have suggested that the failure of the Roosevelt administration to act more energetically in these years in response to the pogroms in Russia was due to the presence of Secretary of State Elihu Root, who, it is argued, was less inclined to make political use of the State Department than had been John Hay, and perhaps because of the fact that Roosevelt had no further political aspirations.[64] Such a judgment rests upon a comparison between the relative inactivity under Root in 1905-1906 with the presumably greater activity displayed in 1902 and 1903 under Hay. Such judgments are unfair, however, in that they credit Hay with greater activity than is warranted by the record, and ignore the very different situation that prevailed in Russia in 1905-1906 by comparison with the situation in Rumania in 1902 and that in Russia in 1903.

It is clear from the record that informal representations by President Roosevelt to the Russian ambassador in Washington and through the embassy at St. Petersburg were not noticeably less frequent under Root than under Hay. Secretary of State Hay's reputation for activity rests primarily with the Rumanian notes of 1902 and the transmission of the Kishinev petition of 1903. He is deservedly credited with seeking to bring Rumania's actions into accord with its obligations under the Berlin Treaty. In the case of the Kishinev pogrom of 1903, however, his activity was limited to his unsuccessful attempt to transmit to the Russian government a petition conceived and executed not by the State Department but by American Jews. The forwarding of a petition scarcely qualifies as a diplomatic initiative by the State Department. Thus it is hard to fault Secretary of State Root for being less responsive to the Jewish problem in Russia than Hay. In Root's behalf it must also be added that the situation in Russia was profoundly different in 1905-1906

from what it had been previously, and it was, moreover, markedly different from that in Rumania in 1902. Rumania in 1902
and Russia in 1903 possessed governments which ruled. In the
Rumanian case, the issue was governmental policy; in the
Russian case it was the connivance of local authorities in a
massacre. The first of these was a matter that could be dealt
with through diplomatic remonstrance, the second did not lend
itself well to such a protest. The situation in Russia through
the worst of the pogroms in the winter of 1905-1906 found
the country in a state of anarchy in which the government was
powerless, and protests by other governments could be but
unavailing.

American Jewish leaders were fully as aware as Roosevelt
and Root that Russia was in the midst of a revolution and
utterly incapable of imposing its will in the countryside for
any purposes, least of all in behalf of despised minorities. As
Cyrus Adler somewhat cold-bloodedly, but realistically, observed to Straus, there should be no surprise that Jews and
others were suffering under the revolutionary conditions then
prevailing in Russia. Adler pointed out:

> For a long time all Jews everywhere had been hoping
> for some sort of a revolution in Russia. The Jews in
> Russia had distinctly worked for it. I know of my own
> knowledge a considerable number who have been direct-
> ly and openly, and I may say properly, associated with
> all the revolutionary movements. In the public opinion
> which has been formed throughout the world against
> Russia for her treatment of the Jews, the Jews of the
> world have openly and properly played a leading part,
> and do you now really think that a revolution of the
> magnitude which is going on in Russia at the present
> day among 140 millions of people has one chance in a
> thousand to get through without bloodshed? The
> changes that have taken place and that are going to take
> place there are greater changes than were wrought by
> the French revolutions; not only because they are
> among a greater number of people, but also because of

the diversity of races and the long standing animosities in this ill-assorted empire. I have been told by people in absolute touch with the situation, that there have been as many Armenians killed in the Caucasus as Jews in Bessarabia.[65]

Straus and Schiff were not quite as willing to accept the brutal fact of the Jewish sacrifice in the cause of revolution and continued to go through the motions of pressing Washington in the hope that something might be done. They, too, however, recognized the impossible situation for diplomatic solutions that was created by the turmoil in Russia. As Schiff wrote Lord Rothschild in November 1905:

When a week ago the horror of the situation in Russia began to dawn upon us here, we hoped at first that it would be possible by some diplomatic action of our government to induce the Russian Government to use its authority in Russia to stop the ruthless proceedings of the populace in Odessa and other Russian towns. It became, however, very promptly evident that the central government in Russia had lost its control over the local authorities, who, no doubt seeing power slipping away from them and perceiving the end of the old regime, stirred up the lowest passions of the populace against the Jews in revenge for the latters' aid to the liberal movement. The aid of the American government having thus become impracticable, nothing remained but to take immediate steps for the organization of efficient material relief to those who in Russia had become overwhelmed by these terrible atrocities.[66]

Thus, it was not a change in the stewardship of the State Department, or an absence now of political ambition on the part of the president, that prevented an effective protest by the United States. Instead it was the changed circumstances in Russia itself, and American Jewish leaders were fully cognizant of the problem posed by those changed circumstances.

In November of 1905, at the apparent height of the revolution
in Russia, Schiff expressed optimism in the czar's "imminent
fall" and the belief that further large scale emigration from
Russia by Jews would no longer be necessary. The revolution,
toward which Schiff had bent his efforts during the Russo-
Japanese War, seemingly would solve the Jewish problem in
Russia.[67] The gradual recovery by the Russian government during 1906, however, ended Schiff's optimism. Renewed pogroms
in October 1906 led Schiff to address new entreaties to the
Roosevelt administration for diplomatic action. On October
22 he forwarded to the president a letter he had received from
Dr. N. Katzenelsohn, a leading Russian Jew, in which
Katzenelsohn told Schiff:

> Surely something *must* be done, to save the Jews in
> Russia, and the only place from which we may expect
> anything is—there can be no doubt about that—America.
> As Mr. Straus informs me, important diplomatic steps
> have actually originated from Washington, which, how-
> ever, have evidently had no results or even negative re-
> sults. Like all weaklings, the Russian Government clings
> particularly to its "rights" and its "independence," and
> is especially jealous where it is a question of "interfering
> with its internal affairs." What, then, can be done? I
> argued with Mr. Straus whether the attempt could not
> be made, that President Roosevelt send a private letter
> to the Tsar, in which he would point out to the latter,
> as amicably as energetically, the awful policy of Russia
> toward the Jews. Such a letter has many advantages
> over diplomatic negotiations. In the first place, the
> Czar *must* know of it; secondly, it would be no "inter-
> ference," but an act of friendship, and, thirdly,—we
> must try everything—alas, we have nothing to lose.

Straus, who was now part of Roosevelt's cabinet, had been impressed by the idea, and had suggested that Katzenelsohn submit it to Schiff for possible transmission to the president.[68]
 Schiff forwarded the letter to Roosevelt, noting there was

nothing he could add to what Katzenelsohn had said, and leaving it to the president's "own judgment and decision whether the suggestion that you address a private letter to the Czar is feasible."[69] The president forwarded the correspondence to Secretary of State Root who responded with a copy of a dispatch from the embassy in St. Petersburg reporting on an interview with the Russian premier Stolypin. The premier had "expressed the hope that the Siedlec riots would constitute the very last ordeal for the Jews," and had stated "he would shortly introduce a bill extending Jewish rights and leaving it to the Duma to bestow absolute equality."[70] There seemed, then, little necessity for the action by Roosevelt which Katzenelsohn had suggested. Schiff, however, noted that the proposed legislation, as published in the press, continued in existence the Jewish Pale of Settlement, which meant that Russian Jews must still find it impossible "to sustain themselves properly so long as they remain crowded into a narrow pale."[71] Having heard similar concessions publicized by the Russians in the past, Schiff linked them once again to Russia's desire to float a foreign loan.[72] Henceforth, Schiff would concentrate his efforts on seeking to solve the Russian Jewish problem in America—through immigration and through the campaign to obtain for American Jews the right to travel in Russia on a basis of equality with other American citizens.

NOTES

1. See, for example, *New York Times*, August 27, 1905.

2. Ibid., November 2, 3, and 5, 1905.

3. Schiff to Sir Samuel Montagu, cable, November 8 and 27, 1905, National Committee for the Relief of Sufferers by Russian Massacres Papers (hereafter cited as NCRSRM) American Jewish Historical Society Library.

4. *American Hebrew*, November 10, 1905.

5. Quoted in Adolf Kraus, *Reminiscences and Comments* (Chicago, 1925), p. 162.

6. *New York Times*, November 8, 1905.

7. Ibid., November 9, 1905.

8. Wolf to Schiff, November 11, 1905, NCRSRM.

9. *New York Times*, November 11, 1905.

10. Root to American Embassy, St. Petersburg, November 22, 1905, *Diplomatic Instructions of the Department of State, 1801-1906, Russia*, National Archives Microfilm Publication M77, reel 140 (hereafter cited as DS M77/140).

11. Eddy to Root, November 25 and 26, 1905, Department of State *Despatches from United States Ministers to Russia, 1808-1906*, National Archives Microfilm Publication M35, reel 64 (hereafter cited as DS M35/64).

12. Meyer to Root, December 13, 1905, DS M35/65.

13. Schiff to Montagu, November 8, 1905, NCRSRM.

14. Lasker to Schiff, November 20, 1905, NCRSRM.

15. See, for example, Schiff to Staab, November 22, 1905, NCRSRM.

16. *New York Times*, November 10, 1905.

17. *American Hebrew*, November 10, 1905.

18. *New York Times*, November 20 and 21, 1905.

19. Ibid., December 3, 1905.

20. *American Hebrew*, November 17, 1905.

21. This course was suggested in an article by Judge Samuel Greenbaum of the New York State Supreme Court in *American Hebrew*, December 1, 1905.

22. Schiff to Roosevelt, December 8, 1905, in Cyrus M. Adler, *Jacob H. Schiff: His Life and Letters*, 2 vols. (Garden City, N.Y.: publ., 1928), 2: 136-38.

23. Roosevelt to Schiff, December 14, 1902, Jacob H. Schiff Papers.

24. Roosevelt to Straus, December 14, 1905, Oscar S. Straus Papers.

25. Straus to Roosevelt, December 15, 1905, Straus Papers.

26. Schiff to Wolsohn, December 28, 1905, Schiff Papers.

27. Schiff to Nathan, December 29, 1905, Schiff Papers.

28. Sheldon M. Neuringer, "American Jewry and the United States Immigration Policy, 1881-1953" (Ph.D. diss., University of Wisconsin, 1969), pp. 82-85.

29. Sulzer to Schiff, January 16, 1906, NCRSRM.

30. *New York Times*, January 22, 1906.

31. "Memorandum of a Luncheon with the President at the White House on January 6, 1906," Straus Papers.

32. Spero to Sulzberger, January 23, 1906, NCRSRM.

33. Sulzberger to Tenenholz, January 24, 1906, NCRSRM.

34. Montagu to Straus, March 30, 1906, Straus Papers.

35. Montagu to Straus, April 6, 1906, Straus Papers.

36. Straus to Montagu, April 9, 1906, Straus Papers.
37. Bacon to American Embassy, St. Petersburg, April 7, 1906, DS M77/140.
38. Meyer to Root, April 9, 1906, DS M35/66.
39. Loeb to Straus, April 9, 1906, Straus Papers.
40. Roosevelt to Straus, April 10, 1906, Straus Papers.
41. Spero to Straus, April 9, 1906, Straus Papers.
42. Joseph to Sulzberger, April 25, 1906, Straus Papers.
43. Ibid.
44. Straus to Montagu, April 9, 1906, Straus Papers.
45. Straus to Montagu, April 11, 1906, Straus Papers.
46. Montagu to Straus, April 12, 1906, Straus Papers.
47. *The Memoirs of Count Witte* (Garden City, N.Y., 1921), pp. 294-95, 297.
48. Wolf to Adler, July 27, 1926, copy in Schiff Papers.
49. Schiff to Roosevelt, telegram and letter, June 18, 1906, Schiff Papers.
50. Quoted in *American Hebrew*, June 22, 1906.
51. *New York Times*, June 21, 1906.
52. Schiff to Hallgarten, June 21, 1906, and Schiff to Jaros, June 20, 1906, Schiff Papers.
53. Montagu to Schiff, June 22, 1906, NCRSRM; Schiff to Jaros, June 25, 1906, Schiff Papers.
54. Schiff to Roosevelt, June 27, 1906, Schiff Papers.
55. Root to American Embassy, St. Petersburg, June 23, 1906, DS M77/140.
56. Meyer to Root, June 27, 1906, DS M35/66.
57. Quoted in Aryeh Yodfat, "The Jewish Question in American-Russian Relations, 1875-1917 (Ph.D. diss., American University, 1963)," p. 100.
58. Schiff to Nathan, December 21, 1906, Schiff Papers.
59. Schiff to Adler, July 25, 1906, Schiff Papers.
60. Schiff to Roosevelt, July 26, 1906, Schiff Papers.
61. Schiff to Nathan, July 26, 1906, Schiff Papers.
62. Naomi W. Cohen, *Not Free to Desist* (Philadelphia, 1972), pp. 1-16.
63. Ibid., pp. 25-27.
64. See, for example, Philip G. Jessup, *Elihu Root* (New York, 1938), 2: 65.
65. Adler to Straus, November 13, 1905, Straus Papers.
66. Schiff to Rothschild, November 10, 1905, Schiff Papers.

67. Schiff to Zangwill, November 21, 1905, Schiff Papers.

68. Katzenelsohn to Schiff, October 1, 1906, in *Numerical and Minor Files of the Department of State, 1906-1910*, National Archives Microfilm Publication M862, reel 115 (hereafter cited as DS M862/115).

69. Schiff to Roosevelt, October 22, 1906, Schiff Papers.

70. Loeb to Root, October 29, 1906, and Root to Schiff, October 30, 1906, DS M862/115.

71. Schiff to Root, November 1, 1906, Schiff Papers.

72. Schiff to Nathan, November 22 and December 20, 1906, Schiff Papers.

CHAPTER 6

Seeking a Solution Through Immigration, 1907-1914

The inadequacy of diplomatic remonstrance as a device for aiding the Jews of Russia had been amply demonstrated by the events of 1905-1906, and the triumph of the reaction there offered a dismal future for Russian Jews. The American Jewish leadership did not fail to continue to appeal to the administration in Washington for assistance when it seemed called for, but Schiff in particular began to search for other ways in which the plight of Russian Jews might be solved. If the situation of the Jews in Russia could not be improved in that country, then the only apparent solution was to remove them from that country.[1] Beginning in 1906 Schiff began to bend his efforts and a part of his wealth toward finding new ways for the United States to absorb the millions of Russian Jewish immigrants who he felt must escape to the United States. Despairing that the conditions of Russian Jewry could ever be improved in their homeland, Schiff wrote Israel Zangwill of the Jewish Territorial Organization (ITO) in late 1905 that, if reaction set in against the Jew in Russia, "then the time *will* have arrived for him to leave Russia as our forefathers have left Egypt and Spain and then, too, the fate of Russia will become sealed as has been the case with every country that has driven out the Jews."[2] Should emigration become necessary, the United States with its liberal immigration laws offered the only prospect for the quick absorption of large numbers of Russian Jews, but not if those immigrants continued to pile up, as in the past, largely in New York City.

The problem resulting from the tendency of Jewish immigrants to congregate in New York City had already resulted in the early 1890s in efforts by New York Jews to "remove" some immigrants from the unhealthy and crowded conditions of the ghettos to the interior of the country. The efforts were carried out through a variety of programs. Agricultural colonization was attempted in a number of states from New Jersey to Oregon. The creation of the Baron de Hirsch Fund in 1889 brought funds from Europe to aid in the solution of the problem. This fund of $2.4 million was contributed by the Baron Maurice de Hirsch, a wealthy German Jew, and according to its historian the trustees of that fund "tried out almost every possible solution—agricultural colonization, suburbanization (on a small scale), the removal of industries to outlying districts, the transportation of families to . . . smaller towns and industrial centers, and so on." But all such efforts continued to be dwarfed by the size of the immigration of the 1890s, and the resettlement of a few hundred immigrants per year scarcely made an imprint on the crowded and unhealthy conditions in New York City and the other large northeastern port cities. In a further attempt to cope with the problem, the Industrial Removal Office (IRO) was organized in New York City by the de Hirsch Fund. The IRO sent agents to various sections of the country to find employment for New York Jews willing to migrate to the interior. With such "requisitions" in hand from inland communities, the IRO sought out likely candidates in the ghettos to fill the jobs and then aided in their relocation. Close cooperation was fostered between the IRO in New York and the local Jewish communities throughout the United States. In the first years of its operation the IRO was able to remove nearly 2,000 persons to 250 communities throughout the United States.[3]

At this time there were primarily three different approaches by those who viewed emigration as the solution to the problems of Russian Jewry. The Zionists advocated the reestablishment of a Jewish nation in Palestine. The Jewish Territorial Organization, which had split off from the Zionists, was led by Jewish writer Israel Zangwill and sought to create autonomous Jewish territories wherever practicable. The Jewish Colonization Society (ICA), financed by the Baron de Hirsch, assisted east European Jews in emigrating to new lands—primarily to Argentina. Jacob Schiff regarded both the Zionists and Territorialists as impractical and utopian, particularly in their inability to respond quickly and on the scale necessary to meet the problem which was emerging in Russia in 1906. But more than this, Schiff disagreed with the basic philosophy of both the Zionists and Territorialists. Schiff argued that "the Jew must maintain his own identity—not *apart* in any autonomous body, but *among* the nations, where alone he can fulfill the mission which is assigned him to promote the unity of God and the brotherhood of man among the people of the earth." Jews should not seek to live apart in ghettos, even if they were self-governing states, but should instead integrate themselves into the life of the nation in which they found themselves.[4]

As reaction against Jews began to gain the upper hand in Russia in 1906, Schiff sought to divert Zangwill's ITO from what he regarded as philosophically incorrect and impractical objects into more correct and immediately useful channels. It was no longer enough, he decided, to remove Jews from the eastern port cities as they accumulated there. If the United States was to absorb the two million Jewish immigrants who might have to be accommodated in this country, those immigrants should be "removed" directly into the interior of the United States by diverting them through ports other than those on the east coast. This was necessary, Schiff believed, because the eastern port cities offered such attractions to the Jewish immigrants that they rarely bestirred themselves to move elsewhere. The large Jewish population of New York City, which made it by the early twentieth century the largest Jewish city in the world, meant the existence of a full religious, cultural, and social life for the Jewish arrival, no matter what his language. This contrasted markedly for him with the alien environ-

ment of the rest of the country.[5] There had been, as yet, little
negative reaction to the growing Jewish population in the eastern
cities, but Schiff and others feared that further immigration,
on the scale necessary to relieve conditions in Russia, must
inevitably lead to demands for restrictions on immigration if
Jewish migrants continued to crowd into the unhealthy and
highly visible ghettos in the large eastern cities.

Thus, to preserve the United States as a destination for
Jewish immigrants fleeing oppression in eastern Europe, the
rest of the United States had to be opened up more fully to
them. But that would require a mechanism in Russia and Europe to propagandize destinations alternative to New York City
and to make the necessary arrangements for transporting
immigrants to those locations. The ideal mechanism, as
Schiff saw it, was the Jewish Territorial Organization. Schiff
promised Zangwill if the ITO would take up the Russian part
of the operation he would contribute as much as $500,000 to
the American end of the operation. He believed if the operation
were properly handled up to four million Russian Jews could
be moved into the interior of the United States and into
Canada within five or ten years, with two million of those
accommodated in the United States. Movement on such a scale
would largely solve the Jewish problem in Russia, Schiff felt,
while simultaneously relieving further congestion in the eastern
cities. Moreover, Schiff was sure that the United States government would give such an effort "full moral support."[6]

According to Schiff's understanding, more than 60 percent
of the 1.5 million Jews in the United States were living in New
York City and other eastern port cities, while "not ten per cent
are located West of a North to South line, drawn through a
point fifty miles west of Chicago."[7] However, it bears repeating
that Schiff was not concerned only with deflecting immigration
from the east to the interior of the country. As Zosa Szajkowski
has pointed out, Schiff was primarily concerned with making
possible a larger Jewish immigration into the United States.[8]
As he wrote to Judge Mayer Sulzberger, Schiff was concerned
with the question: "What can we do . . . not only to divert the
stream of Russo-Jewish immigration into the American 'Hinter-

land,' but even to promote a considerably larger immigration than we now receive, into this territory?'' Schiff had good reason to believe that cooperation, or at least an understanding attitude, would be forthcoming from Washington. Oscar Straus was serving the Roosevelt administration as secretary of commerce and labor, under which department operated the Bureau of Immigration and Naturalization. The commissioner general of immigration, Franklin P. Sargent, had suggested just such a diversion of immigrants, preferably through the port of New Orleans, when Schiff talked with him early in 1906.[9]

While Schiff hoped initially for the European end of the effort to be handled jointly by the ICA, ITO, and the German Hilfsverein der Deutschen Juden, he soon discovered that Zangwill was unwilling to cooperate with non-territorialists like the ICA. In the end the European aspect of the movement was handled by the ITO, which propagandized Schiff's choice of Galveston, Texas, as an entry point for Russian Jews seeking to immigrate to the United States. The ITO then handled their transportation as far as Bremen, Germany, where they were temporarily cared for by the Hilfsverein until they could be placed on steamships destined for Galveston. In the United States the placement of the immigrants across the country was entrusted to the Industrial Removal Office working in much the same way as it handled the transferring of Jews from New York City. Incoming Jews would be met at Galveston, matched with "requisitions" from the inland communities arranged by the IRO, and then sent on their way to their new homes. Immigrants would be sent into the interior almost immediately after they arrived at Galveston, making their journey a continuous one. Since the agency at Galveston would have a manifest containing all the relevant information concerning the immigrants at least a couple of weeks before their arrival, sufficient time was available for arranging for their distribution into the interior. The "continuous journey" would not only spare Schiff's group the expense of boarding the immigrants in Galveston but would also prevent their developing any attachment for that city.[10]

In a trip to Washington late in January 1907, Schiff found

Secretary Straus strongly supportive of the Galveston plan.
More encouraging was the support of President Roosevelt. As
Schiff wrote to Paul Nathan of the Hilfsverein: "President
Roosevelt was particularly happy that we are making this
effort to open this new door to immigration to the United
States instead of concentrating it in the north Atlantic ports
as has been the case hitherto."[11] This evidence of support
from the federal government was important for the prospects
of success of the operation. There existed a great variety of
laws governing immigration and the officials were permitted
considerable latitude in the interpretation and application of
those laws. A friendly attitude on the part of the authorities
thus could help to ensure the success of the Galveston operation, while a hostile authority could doom it. From the
beginning, therefore, Schiff insisted that the immigration laws
must be scrupulously honored since, he explained, "everything
must be avoided which can possibly induce our officials to
place obstacles in the way of the proposed immigration." Thus,
Schiff reprimanded Nathan for assuring some immigrants that
part of their traveling expenses would be paid if necessary. He
was willing only to assure them that, if the situation required
it, the American end of the movement would contribute to the
expense of their transportation from Galveston to their ultimate destination.[12]

The first shipment of immigrants arrived, belatedly, on July
1, 1907, when fifty-four ITO-sponsored Russian Jews debarked
at Galveston. The movement had scarcely been launched, however, before a severe financial recession developed in the United
States, making it impossible for the American end of the movement to place anything but a handful of immigrants. Disappointed, Schiff wrote Cyrus Sulzberger in December that it was
a shame, "just as we could see the assured success of the movement in sight, this setback should have come."[13] To Zangwill
he explained that he had "never seen such a sudden change
from prosperity to general depression and discouragement."[14]
Only because Schiff felt that a handful of immigrants, at least,
should continue to be sent through to keep the machinery in
operation, were any immigrants sent at all.[15] Not until the end

of 1908 did Schiff begin to regain hope that conditions would
improve sufficiently by March or April of 1909 to restore
operations to the maximum level.[16]

Then, just as economic conditions appeared to be improving
in the United States, making it possible for the American end
of the operation to resume accepting as many immigrants as
the ITO could send, the European end of the operation faltered
when the ITO ran afoul of the Russian authorities and was
branded illegal. Schiff wrote Zangwill that he expected that
Galveston would be able to absorb larger numbers of immigrants by the summer of 1909, and that he hoped, therefore,
"when the moment comes that the ITO will have become
legalized in Russia, or failing that, which I would deeply regret,
that arrangements can be made to place the Galveston work
where it can most efficiently be looked after."[17] The latter,
of course, would have meant a transfer of the Russian end of
the operation to the ICA and would have been a confession of
failure by the ITO. In the summer of 1909 the ITO was able
to reestablish its legality, but despite Galveston's requests for
additional immigrants there was no response from the ITO,
bringing from Schiff a gentle reminder to Zangwill of an earlier
promise by the latter that if ever the ITO was unable to handle
the task adequately it would call upon the ICA for assistance.[18]

The summer of 1909 also brought an organizational change
at the American end. Schiff had come to the conclusion that
some more efficient means must be found to coordinate the
arrangements at Galveston, and so he formed a permanent
Galveston committee. The membership was to consist of
Schiff, Cyrus Sulzberger, Professor Morris Loeb, David Bressler,
and Morris Waldman and the committee was to "give regular
attention to all questions which may present themselves in
connection with the Galveston plan." Schiff reiterated that he
was "anxious to place myself and my means into accomplish-
ing all that can be done to open the wide territory beyond the
Mississippi to a large Jewish immigration."[19] A few weeks later
he announced to Zangwill the formation of the committee
which included, in addition to the above named, Reuben
Arkush, president of the Industrial Removal Office, and the

Rabbi Henry Cohen of Galveston.[20] In another letter to
Zangwill, Schiff established the terms under which he would
regard the Galveston movement as a success. Unless the movement reached the point where it was placing an average of 200
immigrants a month or 2,500 per year—meaning an inflow of
approximately 25,000 in a decade—he could not, he told
Zangwill, regard the movement a success.[21] These figures were,
of course, considerably in excess of the numbers of immigrants being furnished by the ITO. While the American end of
the operation increased its ability to handle immigrants and
called for more of them, the ITO failed to provide immigrants
sufficient to meet the requisitions being received by the
Industrial Removal Office from inland communities.[22]

By mid-1910, however, under the new Taft administration
the United States government had become a prime deterrent
to the success of the Galveston movement. The arrival of
Alfred Hampton, a new inspector-in-charge, in Galveston early
in 1910 quickly brought an end to the friendly relations which
had heretofore existed between Schiff's Jewish Immigrant's
Information Bureau and the immigration authorities in that
city. On May 6, 1910, Hampton wrote to the commissioner
general of immigration concerning the Galveston movement,
"the alleged purpose of which is to divert Jewish immigrants
from the Northern ports," and told him:

> Upon assuming charge of this district recently I was
> surprised to learn that it had been the custom each
> month to admit at this port many destitute Jewish
> aliens, that is, Jewish aliens without money, and with-
> out friends or relatives in this country, upon assurances
> being given by the representatives of the aforesaid
> Jewish Immigrants' Information Bureau that said aliens
> would be cared for during their temporary detention
> in this city, and provided with the necessary transpor-
> tation, provisions, and funds to reach certain designated
> southwestern points, where upon arrival they would be
> given work.

Hampton furnished his superior with such information as he had been able to gather concerning the European end of the operation and concluded that an investigation was called for "in order to ascertain whether the Jewish Society is acting as agency of the steamship company in soliciting immigration and whether the steamship company is secretly reducing rates, or whether the Jewish Society is . . . soliciting immigration and supplying a portion of the passage money as a charity." Hampton expressed concern that the immigrants arriving under ITO sponsorship might "come under the class of assisted aliens, or paupers, or contract laborers, as the case may be." He asked for guidance from his superiors on the extent the government wished him to "recognize the Jewish Immigrants' Information Bureau in its capacity of self-appointed guardian of Jewish alien arrivals in this country, without funds or money."[23] In response to Hampton's inquiry and suspicions about the Galveston movement, the federal bureau ordered an investigation to determine whether the promises of jobs made by the JIIB to the arriving immigrants were actually being fulfilled while the secretary of commerce and labor requested an investigation by the Justice Department.[24]

Meanwhile, in contrast to the policy of the authorities at Galveston during the first three years of the movement, Hampton began to exclude aliens who arrived at the port without "adequate" funds, despite the guarantees furnished by the JIIB, which triggered appeals and protests from Schiff and the other members of his committee. Schiff sought the assistance of Congressman William S. Bennett of New York in intervening with Secretary of Commerce and Labor Charles Nagel, explaining to Bennett:

> We are . . . now facing governmental methods at Galveston . . . which, if persisted in, are certain to break up the movement through Galveston, and will result in throwing back upon New York and other northern ports the entire stream of immigration which we have been taking such pains to deflect and which the large

American hinterland can digest to such better advantage than the East.[25]

The immediate issue was the exclusion of some thirty immigrants who had arrived on the SS *Hanover* on June 23. Acting Secretary of Commerce and Labor Benjamin S. Cable defended the department's position to Congressman Bennett, writing:

> These aliens were excluded by the board mainly on the ground that they were likely to become public charges. This appears to be a proper ground in some of the cases, but there is another good reason for exclusion, namely, that all of them "have been induced or solicited to migrate to this country by offers or promise of employment." . . . The records show, and it seems to be an established fact, that the Jewish Immigrants' Information Bureau [does] advertise and distribute literature in Russia, and by this means and through their agents or correspondents there, advise Russian Hebrews to go to Galveston rather than New York, that they do not have to show any money at Galveston; that many Jews have gone to Galveston and that the Jewish Society would take care of them and provide them with work in Galveston or elsewhere. . . . Our investigation shows that while work has been secured for the aliens admitted to the Jewish Bureau in the past, it is of a temporary nature and they are frequently changing, also that they are sometimes out of work.

Cable indicated that he did not believe the practice should suddenly be instituted of excluding such immigrants, in view of the fact that such cases had been admitted for several years before this, "but there is no reason why the law should not, within a short time, be administered at Galveston as at other ports."[26] From Galveston, Inspector Hampton similarly argued that the impression must be corrected that Galveston was more lax in its enforcement of immigration laws than the other ports of entry.[27] Clearly the sympathetic attitude on the part of the authorities, which Schiff had all along understood to be important to the success of the Galveston experiment, was no longer to be forthcoming if the views of Cable and Hampton were to prevail.

Through the summer and into the fall of 1910, the Galveston committee attacked the Cable-Hampton position on the legality of the actions of the JIIB. The movement, through its representatives and immigration lawyers, was compelled once again to argue that the immigration from Russia was not solicited or stimulated, but rather came as a result of the "intolerable conditions" existing in Russia. To the extent that the immigrants were "solicited" or "induced," they pointed out, it was for the purpose of deflecting them to Galveston in preference to the crowded eastern ports. Immigration was not being increased, they asserted, but rather deflected; the immigration to Galveston had not increased the total immigration to the United States "by one person," since the arrivals at Galveston otherwise would have gone to the eastern ports. Finding jobs for the immigrants was not a violation of the law, they pointed out, and moreover the practice had been "recognized and tacitly approved" by the government at the time the Galveston movement had been inaugurated. Nor was there any violation of the law involved in assisting the immigrants through private charity once they arrived, as long as they did not become *public* charges.[28] Simon Wolf, immigration lawyer Max J. Kohler, and New York Supreme Court Justice Nathan Bijur provided additional arguments on behalf of the Galveston movement.[29]

Obtaining little satisfaction in altering the Cable-Hampton position through the force of their arguments, the Galveston committee began in August to move in the direction of political pressure. On August 22, 1910, Jacob Schiff dispatched a long letter to Cable in which he traced the motivation and history of the Galveston movement, including its initial inspiration from the Bureau of Immigration itself. He defended the movement against all the charges made against it within the Department of Commerce and Labor. In such an undertaking, he argued, the movement "had every right to expect the good will of the authorities, and until recently this appears not to have been withheld." But recently, "and for no satisfactory reason," the Department of Commerce and Labor had begun

to throw "needless difficulties in the way of the admission of
those who arrive at Galveston," and if that policy was maintained the movement would break down. If such a breakdown
did occur, Schiff warned Cable, the Taft administration would
be "held responsible by a considerable section of the American
people, and because of this I am sending a copy of this communication to the President for such consideration, if any, as
he may himself desire to give to this not unimportant subject."
He also asked that his letter be placed before Cable's superior,
Secretary of Commerce and Labor Charles Nagel, when he returned from his vacation.[30] The fact that this letter was intended
primarily for the president's eyes rather than for Cable is clear
from Schiff's account of the episode to Zangwill, in which he
wrote: "I have just addressed the President—for the letter I
have written to Assistant Secretary Cable . . . is meant to a
greater degree for the President than for the Department of
Commerce and Labor."[31]

Cable's reply to Schiff's letter gave the Galveston committee
no satisfaction, since the assistant secretary simply pointed out
that if his position was incorrect "the courts would probably
set me right upon proper application," thus encouraging Schiff
and the Galveston committee to take the matter to the courts.
Schiff's position, however, was that litigation would be fatal
to the movement, since the spectacle of drawn-out judicial
proceedings would destroy the confidence of the emigrants
from Russia. The success of the movement had just come into
sight, Schiff told Charles D. Norton, secretary to President
William Howard Taft, when Cable had stepped in and "wanton-
ly" crushed it. The only means by which confidence could be
restored in the Galveston movement, he told Norton, was
through the "retirement" of Cable from his office. Linking the
problem with the difficulties which the Jewish community was
also experiencing with the president over his unkept promise
during the 1908 campaign to secure the right of American Jews
to travel to Russia on American passports like other American
citizens, Schiff wrote Norton:

> We have in other respects experienced keen disappoint-
> ment because of the nonfulfillment thus far of platform

pledges and personal promises made during the last
Presidential campaign, and if I now write so unreserved-
ly, it is partly because I do not wish to see the President, whose loyal supporter I have been ever since he
was nominated, placed into a false position or lose the
goodwill of the important section of the American
people for whom I venture to speak in this.[32]

"If the Galveston Movement is broken down," Schiff wrote to
Simon Wolf, "someone is going to be punished for it—not the
man lower down, but the man higher up."[33] To another correspondent he argued: "We may have to employ earnest measures
in order to make our friends in the administration understand
that we are not to be trifled with and that platform pledges
and campaign promises must stand for something more than
for campaign consumption only, and must be made good."[34]
     The pressure on the top level of the Taft administration was
soon having obvious effect. From the president's secretary
came word that he had "gone over Mr. Schiff's letters with the
President, who is in full sympathy with what Mr. Schiff is trying to do," and as a result the administration was arranging
for a conference between representatives of the Galveston committee and the secretary of commerce and labor.[35] Meanwhile,
President Taft visited the immigration station at Ellis Island,
New York City, on October 18 and made remarks which were
taken as a hopeful sign by Schiff. In his talk there, Taft expressed support for the deflection of immigration away from
the eastern port cities and into the interior, leading Schiff to
feel encouraged in the belief that the president had the Galveston movement in mind as he spoke.[36] Perhaps Secretary of
Commerce and Labor Nagel interpreted the president's remarks
in the same way, for his correspondence with Taft's secretary
grew conciliatory in the latter part of the month. Nagel confessed he could see no provision of the immigration laws that
was being violated "strictly speaking" by the Galveston movement, even though he still had the impression that "as a whole
it does result in the kind of immigration which it is for the
Bureau to scrutinize closely and perhaps to discourage."[37]
     In December the oft-postponed meeting finally was held

when Schiff, Kohler, Bressler, and Elkus sat down with Nagel, Cable, and Attorney General George Wickersham for a meeting which lasted for two hours. As Schiff described the meeting to Zangwill a month later:

> Mr. Kohler made the very able opening argument while I did the summing up. I gave them the full history of the development of the Galveston movement and I ended by saying that we had endeavored in every way to keep within the law and believed that we had done so; that we had expected encouragement on the part of the government in the undertaking, which was at once humane and patriotic; that we had the assurance of the President that he was in sympathy with our work, and that it would have his support in every way in which it could lawfully be done; that we felt not we but the Department of Commerce and the immigration authorities were on the defense, and finally that if present methods were to be continued, of which we ought in justice to be frankly advised, we would close up our Bureau at Galveston and leave the responsibility for this to the present federal administration, which I thought in the face of the statement of the President in his message to Congress, that everything should be done to better distribute immigration, was a pretty heavy responsibility to take. When I had finished, Secretary Nagel made at first a show of being very much offended because of the aggressive manner in which I had spoken. The Attorney General took me aside and said to me, "Mr. Schiff, try not to make them antagonistic here; I will help you if I can." And finally Mr. Nagel calmed down and gave us the assurance that it was his desire to do what could be done under the law to help our work.[38]

According to Max Kohler's recollection years later of the meeting:

> Annoyed at the technicalities which were being gone into before the two Cabinet Officers, [Schiff] suddenly

jumped up and said, shaking his finger at Secretary
Nagel, "You act as if my organization and I were on
trial! You, Mr. Secretary, and your department are on
trial, and the country will rue it if this undertaking—so
conducive to promoting the best interests of our country, as well as humanity—is throttled by your Department's unreasonable obstacles!"[39]

Almost coincidental with the meeting, Washington's policy
was put to the test when in mid-December Galveston authorities excluded Jewish immigrants on grounds of "inability
to speak English, insufficient funds for transportation to
points where they might work, no friends or relatives to assist."
The JIIB at Galveston reported the organization had been
"utterly disregarded" by the authorities there in making their
decision.[40] The question now was whether the authorities in
Washington would sustain these exclusions or show evidence
of a new cooperative attitude toward the Galveston movement
as a result of the political pressure which had been brought to
bear upon the Taft administration. The latter was the case. On
December 23 Secretary Nagel wrote to the president's secretary that the meeting with Schiff and his counsel had been
held in obedience to the president's instructions and that it
had been decided to give "just as much consideration as can be
given to Mr. Schiff's enterprise." Nagel enclosed a memorandum
giving his general views on the Galveston movement, which
was to guide immigration policy during the balance of the Taft
administration. Nagel's memorandum stated:

> The inquiries which have been made both at the hear-
> ing [held] on the 14th day of December and in other
> ways do not bear out the conclusion that this immigra-
> tion is assisted, or induced, or solicited in the proper
> sense of the law. We have the unqualified assurance that
> these immigrants are not encouraged to come to this
> country, but that they are merely advised to go to
> Galveston instead of New York after their decision to
> come to this country is formed. Such activity is in keep-
> ing with the policy of the Department, and so long as

the agency that has interested itself in this immigration restricts its efforts to the purpose just indicated there appears to be no objection. . . . My conclusion is that these aliens should be admitted, and that so long as the system is followed substantially as has been represented and conditions otherwise remain the same future cases may be passed in accordance with this rule. . . . The conclusion is arrived at after conference with the Assistant Secretary who has given careful thought to the matter and who is in accord with the decision.

As for the excluded immigrants of mid-December, Nagel admitted thirteen of them at once and the remainder were admitted later.[41]

After four years characterized by limited success and considerable frustration, the leaders of the Galveston movement were encouraged in the beginning of 1911 that the Secretary of Commerce and Labor was endeavoring to be fair and reasonable, and that his apparent support for their activities would "give notice to the immigration authorities in Galveston not to be too hasty in excluding immigrants." Schiff now felt for the first time that "we have turned the corner and that henceforth immigrants will not be turned back except for physical illness or other incapacity to become wage earners." No longer would the amount of money brought with them by the immigrants be a factor in determining whether or not they should be admitted. Schiff now exhorted Zangwill to "accelerate the movement" of Jewish immigrants into Galveston since the "small parcels" which had been coming were hardly sufficient to maintain the machinery of the operation there.[42]

The movement encountered little further difficulty with the authorities over these issues through the remainder of the Taft administration, but the great frustration was once again the inability of the ITO to furnish immigrants in sufficient numbers and of adequate quality to satisfy the requisitions which were being obtained from inland communities. Late in 1911 Schiff again raised with Zangwill the possibility of ITO cooperation with the ICA, or of replacing the ITO entirely with the ICA.[43] While agreement was reached to continue the affiliation with the ITO alone at least through 1912, the poor health of the immigrants being sent, of which Schiff had for some time been complaining, began gradually to result in increased deportations. While his correspondence makes it clear that he had for some time been concerned about the quality of the people the ITO had been sending, Schiff now began to lash out at the authorities again, this time over the high number of deportations that were taking place from Galveston in early 1912 for health reasons.[44]

Complaints were also reaching the JIIB concerning the quality of the steerage accommodations on the North German Lloyd steamers which brought the immigrants from Bremen and the callous treatment to which the immigrants were subjected while on board. These were conditions which, if allowed to persist, were certain to discourage immigrants from entering the United States through Galveston.[45] Schiff wrote Zangwill of the complaints and asked that pressure be brought in Bremen to improve the situation, but his effort was without effect. The numbers continued to be unsatisfactory, and for Jacob Schiff, whose financial contribution was being drained away by salaries, rents, and other expenses, the meager number of immigrants flowing through the mechanism from Russia was a constant frustration.[46] In mid-1912 he wrote Zangwill: "We must have more immigrants of a proper sort if the movement is to be kept alive instead of gradually fizzling out." The ITO was averaging only about ninety persons per month, he pointed out, and they should be sending twice that number.[47] Late in the year Dr. David Jochelmann, director of the ITO emigration work in Russia, visited the United States to observe the Galveston operation. Afterwards Jochelmann reported to the Galveston committee that a new problem had arisen to plague the Russian end of the operation—a lack of money. With sufficient funds, he told the committee, an adequate number of immigrants could be sent, but the fund upon which the emigration work had been drawing was nearly exhausted.[48]

The Galveston committee was much encouraged by the report of David M. Bressler, who had accompanied Jochelmann on his inspection tour of the settled immigrants. According to Bressler's brief account of the trip, they had interviewed at least 600 of the immigrants in midwestern and southwestern cities and found "with the exception of not more than ten," that all of them were gainfully employed and earning respectable wages, while quite a number were engaged in small businesses and were earning even more. Quite a number of the immigrants were found to own their own homes, and some even owned other real estate as well, while practically all of them had bank accounts. They found numerous complaints among the immigrants—with the facilities at Bremen, with their treatment aboard the North German Lloyd steamers, with the long trip between Bremen and Galveston, and with the quality of the assistance provided them in some cities by the Jewish communities there. As a result of these complaints it was found most of the immigrants who had sent for their families had brought them in through the eastern ports rather than through Galveston. Still, Bressler felt that despite these complaints there was universal approval among the immigrants of the concept of the Galveston movement and a belief that its purpose could be realized more readily if the hardships of the journey between Bremen and Galveston could be reduced. Bressler concluded that the work of the Galveston movement had been "highly successful" and he found no evidence that any considerable number of the immigrants brought via Galveston had subsequently moved east to the Atlantic port cities.[49] Thus encouraged, Schiff wrote Zangwill that $350,000 still remained of the original $500,000 dollars he had pledged to the Galveston movement and that the JIIB was now prepared to settle a minimum of 250 immigrants monthly.[50]

The ITO, however, consistently failed to furnish immigrants in either the quantity or quality sought by the Galveston movement. Attempts to transfer the operation to the ICA failed, and Schiff began to despair that the movement would ever achieve the success he had contemplated originally. Schiff began to look ahead to the 10,000 figure as a possible terminal point in the Galveston operation, a figure which he estimated, in October, 1913, could be reached within a year.[51]

Meanwhile a new problem had reared its head at Galveston. Deportations for physical and health reasons were on the increase, especially for hernia. Schiff wrote Zangwill that he could not see why, "with the insistence of our immigration authorities to exclude those afflicted with hernia, those still continue to be sent on in such large numbers." The ITO had been warned repeatedly not to send such immigrants, but Schiff charged that the warnings were not being heeded.[52] While the hernia problem was almost certainly a legitimate objection on the part of the authorities at Galveston, as evidenced by Schiff's own complaints to Zangwill, the scrupulousness with which the physical examinations were carried out and interpreted by the authorities there was influenced almost certainly by the reassertion of Inspector Hampton's misgivings concerning the legality of the Galveston operation now that the Taft administration had been replaced by that of Woodrow Wilson. A letter from Hampton, reciting for his new superiors his long-time concerns about the operation, set off a flurry of renewed interest within the Bureau of Immigration in determining the legality of the Galveston operation.[53] Interestingly when Assistant Commissioner General F. H. Larned, a holdover from the Taft years, was asked by the new commissioner general for an opinion on the Galveston movement he did not cite the Nagel memorandum which had been the basis of the Bureau's policy toward the movement in 1911 and 1912. Instead, Larned cited the opinion of the former assistant secretary, Benjamin Cable, in opposition to the operation. Cable's position, reported Larned, was "that the immigration of Jews through Galveston under the auspices of the Jewish Society there was a violation of the immigration laws," and he added: "I believe the officials of the Bureau have always concurred in Mr. Cable's views with respect to this matter."[54] At Hampton's suggestion a detailed report was requested from the medical examiner at Galveston and an investigation was ordered of the activities of the ITO in Russia.[55]

In confronting the new problems for the Galveston movement, Schiff recognized that the situation was less promising for effectual protest than in 1910. President Wilson had signed into law an act creating separate departments of Commerce and Labor. The Bureau of Immigration had been placed under the Department of Labor, headed by Secretary of Labor William B. Wilson who was a former labor official and a restrictionist where immigration was concerned. Thus, the situation at Galveston was only an example of what was happening in lesser degrees at the other ports of entry.[56] The situation at Galveston, however, continued to worsen and, while the leaders of the movement did not question the fact that the doctor in that city was "a thoroughly conscientious official," they also had no doubt that he was "unduly severe in his examinations." In addition, they felt that he magnified "minor ailments to the point of unfairness," with the result that the "percentage of exclusions at Galveston" had become "the highest from any port in the U.S.," and it was easy to understand why the Galveston route was losing its popularity among immigrants from Russia.[57]

The combative attitude of 1910 no longer was present in the Galveston committee when it faced this new governmental challenge in 1914. The chronic problems of the movement, especially at the ITO end, had already led Schiff the previous year to tentatively project the end of the movement with the arrival of the ten-thousandth immigrant, expected to reach Galveston late in 1914. Now, at a meeting of the Galveston committee in January of 1914, Schiff suggested that the time perhaps had come to discontinue the work.[58] At that meeting the other members of the committee convinced Schiff it would be a mistake to do so, but three months later at yet another meeting of the committee Schiff made a convincing argument for ending the movement. After seven years of existence, he pointed out, "five of which might be called the active years," the Galveston movement had expended $235,000 in distributing almost 9,000 immigrants through that city. During this period of time, however, the volume of immigration through Galveston had not increased appreciably, and at no time "had the yearly numbers coming to Galveston exceeded 3% of the total Jewish immigration for one year." The committee concluded that two factors principally were responsible for the limited success of the movement: 1) the inadequate steamship facilities between Europe and Galveston, and 2) the unduly severe enforcement of the immigration laws and regulations at Galveston. Despite attempts to correct the former problem, there had been no improvement in the steamship service between Bremen and Galveston. As to the latter, it had been demonstrated convincingly that not only were exclusions and deportations at Galveston significantly higher than at the northern ports, but enforcement was becoming progressively more severe and more rigorous as time went by. Schiff's view was that these two factors "constituted an insurmountable handicap to the realization of the purpose for which the movement was started," and he argued again that the time had come to discontinue the operation. The committee decided to end the movement after September 30, 1914, except that assistance would continue to be extended to the wives and children of the JIIB immigrants, in meritorious cases, until the end of the year.[59]

In reporting the results of the April 9 meeting to Zangwill, Schiff blamed the medical examinations at Galveston, but also pointed out that the ITO representatives in Russia and in Bremen appeared to be "unable to prevent a considerable number of immigrants who do not come up to the standards set by our immigration laws and government regulations to embark for Galveston." Nor had the Galveston movement been successful in improving conditions on the North German Lloyd steamships. Thus, Schiff privately expressed three reasons for the failure of the movement—the inability of the ITO to perform its function properly being the third reason, and the one not publicly expressed because of Zangwill's sensitivity.[60]

Various schemes were advanced during the summer of 1914 for continuing the deflection of immigration away from the eastern ports without the JIIB, but all such discussions were rendered academic by the outbreak of war in Europe late that summer.[61] On November 2, 1914, Schiff addressed identical letters to his colleagues on the Galveston committee, in which he wrote:

> Now that the Galveston Committee has closed its work, I want to express to the members of the committee my deep appreciation of the cooperation and valuable

advice I have received from you as . . . my colleagues
on the committee in the effort on our part to solve an
important problem of great and lasting value both to
the immigrant, as well as to our own country. In this I
believe we have a right to feel that we have, in a measure,
succeeded, for aside from the fact that we have settled
almost 10,000 immigrants in the vast hinterland of the
United States, every one of whom is likely to form
more or less a center of attraction for others to follow,
we have acquired experience which is certain to be
most useful in further efforts which must come to deflect immigration into and through the overcrowded
cities of the north Atlantic coast to ports where it can
be more practically distributed over the sections of the
United States, where the immigrant is actually needed
and where his well-being can be better assured than in
the large centers of the eastern part of the United
States.[62]

From this it seems clear that Schiff contemplated further
efforts to deflect immigration after the war ended. His death
in 1920, however, and the restrictive immigration legislation
of the 1920s, put an end to the deflection movement.

From despair that the problem of Russian Jews could be
solved in their homeland, Schiff had turned to immigration to
the United States as the solution. In an effort to increase the
immigration to this country, he sought to deflect that immigration into the heartland of America by routing it through the
city of Galveston. Despite the difficulties posed for the success
of the movement by the U.S. government and by the inadequacy
of steamship facilities between Europe and Galveston, it is
apparent from Schiff's correspondence that his greatest frustration was with the unwillingness or inability of the Jewish
societies in Europe to close ranks and work with him without
regard to the "isms" and jealousies which divided them. To this
must be added his frustration at the unwillingness of European
financial sources, like the Rothschilds, to support the European
end of the operation to the extent that it could be properly

handled. While the Galveston movement did not live up to Schiff's expectations in 1906 and 1907, though, it did attain modest success. At an expenditure of approximately $250,000 the 10,000 Jewish immigrants settled through Galveston did become the "nuclei" Schiff had sought for larger Jewish communities later. This was less than half the 25,000 Schiff had planned on (but at an expenditure of half what he had contemplated), and it did not spark the great movement of Russian Jews to the inland United States for which he had hoped.[63] Nor was the movement successful in defusing agitation for restrictive immigration laws as he had hoped. Still, for the 10,000 concerned and for their families, friends, and other Jews drawn by their presence, their deflection into the interior rather than into the eastern port cities was highly significant.

NOTES

1. Zosa Szajowski, "Paul Nathan, Lucien Wolf, Jacob H. Schiff and the Jewish Revolutionary Movements in Eastern Europe, 1903-1917," 2 pts., *Jewish Social Studies* 29 (January 1967), 2: 4-10, describes the impact of the events of 1903-1906 on the thinking of Jewish leaders.

2. Schiff to Zangwill, November 21, 1905, Jacob H. Schiff Papers; see also Szajkowski, "Nathan, Wolf, Schiff," pp. 22-23.

3. Samuel Joseph, *History of the Baron De Hirsch Fund* (n.p., 1935), pp. 184-87.

4. Schiff to Zangwill, November 21, 1905, Schiff Papers; see also Naomi Cohen, "The Reaction of Reform Judaism to Political Zionism (1897-1922)," *American Jewish Historical Quarterly* 60 (1950): 361-94.

5. For a description of Jewish conditions in New York City, see Moses Rischin, *The Promised City: New York's Jews, 1870-1914* (Cambridge, Mass., 1962).

6. Schiff to Zangwill, August 24, 1906, Schiff to Nathan, August 27, 1906, Schiff to Sulzberger, September 27, 1906, Schiff Papers.

7. Schiff to Sulzberger, September 27, 1906, Schiff Papers.

8. Szajkowski, "Nathan, Wolf, Schiff," pp. 21-26; see also Zosa Szajkowski, "The Yahudi and the Immigrant: A Reappraisal," *American Jewish Historical Quarterly* 63 (September, 1973): 13-14.

9. Schiff to Sulzberger, September 27, 1906, Schiff Papers.

10. Gary Dean Best, "Jacob H. Schiff's Galveston Movement: An Experiment in Immigrant Deflection, 1907-1914," *American Jewish Archives* 30 (April 1978): 48-50.

11. Schiff to Nathan, February 25, 1907, Schiff Papers.

12. Schiff to Nathan, January 23, 1907, Schiff Papers.

13. Schiff to Sulzberger, December 2, 1907, Schiff Papers.

14. Schiff to Zangwill, December 4, 1907, Schiff Papers.

15. Schiff to Bressler, June 15, 1908, Schiff Papers.

16. Schiff to Zangwill, December 30, 1908, Schiff Papers.

17. Schiff to Zangwill, March 11, 1909, Schiff Papers.

18. Schiff to Bressler, July 6, 1909, and Schiff to Zangwill, July 7, 1909, Schiff Papers.

19. Schiff to Sulzberger, July 12, 1909, Schiff Papers.

20. Schiff to Zangwill, August 9, 1909, Schiff Papers.

21. Schiff to Zangwill, August 30, 1909, Schiff Papers.

22. "Minutes of Meeting of October 29, 1909," in Galveston Immigration Plan Papers (hereafter cited as GIPP), American Jewish Historical Society Library; Schiff to Zangwill, November 11, 1909, Schiff to Zangwill, December 2, 1909, Bressler to Schiff, December 13, 1909, Schiff Papers.

23. Hampton to the commissioner general, May 6, 1910, Record Group 85, File 52779/29, National Archives (hereafter cited as RG 85-52779/29 NA).

24. Keefe to Hampton, June 13, 1910, and Secretary of Commerce to Attorney General, June 16, 1910, RG 85-52779/29 NA.

25. Schiff to Warburg, June 28, 1910, Felix Warburg Papers, American Jewish Archives.

26. Cable to Bennett, July 14, 1910, RG 85-52779/29 NA.

27. Hampton to Commissioner General, July 16, 1910, RG 85-52779/29 NA.

28. "Statement of Facts Submitted by David M. Bressler, Esq., Honorary Secretary, 'Jewish Immigrants' Information Bureau,' July 21st, 1910, on Rehearing of Galveston Appeals," RG 85-52779/29 NA.

29. Simon Wolf to Bressler, August 3, 1910, GIPP; Schiff to Kohler, August 15, 1910, Max J. Kohler Papers.

30. Schiff to Cable, August 22, 1910, Schiff Papers.

31. Schiff to Zangwill, August 23, 1910, Schiff Papers.

32. Schiff to Norton, August 29, 1910, Schiff Papers.

33. Schiff to Wolf, August 30, 1910, copy in GIPP.

34. Schiff to Kraus, September 1, 1910, Schiff Papers.

35. Norton to Kohler, September 9, 1910, Kohler Papers.

36. Schiff to Kohler, October 19, 1910, Schiff Papers.

37. Nagel to Norton, October 27, 1910, RG 85-52779/29 NA.

38. Schiff to Zangwill, January 11, 1911, Schiff Papers.

39. Kohler to Mortimer Schiff, October 14, 1924, Schiff Papers.

40. JIIB to Schiff, December 15, 1910, Schiff Papers.

41. Nagel to President Taft, December 23, 1910, with enclosures, RG 85-52779/29 NA.

42. Schiff to Zangwill, January 11, 1911, Schiff Papers.

43. Schiff to Bressler, September 27, 1911, Schiff Papers.

44. Schiff to Zangwill, January 2, 1912, Schiff Papers; Schiff to Cohen, January 22, 1912, Rabbi Henry Cohen Papers, American Jewish Archives.

45. Schiff to Cohen, August 30, 1912, Cohen Papers.

46. Schiff to Zangwill, February 2, 1912, Schiff Papers.

47. Schiff to Zangwill, May 7, 1912, Schiff Papers.

48. "Minutes of the Meeting of November 30, 1912," GIPP.

49. Bressler, "Brief statement with regard to trip," GIPP.

50. Schiff to Zangwill, December 3, 1912, Schiff Papers.

51. Best, "Schiff's Galveston Movement," pp. 70-73.

52. Schiff to Zangwill, October 27, 1913, Schiff Papers.

53. Hampton to Commissioner General, August 21, 1913, RG 85-52779/29 NA.

54. Larned to Commissioner General, September 8, 1913, RG 85-52779/29 NA.

55. Commissioner General to Hampton, September 12, 1913, RG 85-52779/29 NA.

56. Schiff to Zangwill, November 24, 1913, Schiff Papers.

57. Bressler to Schiff, March 31, 1914, GIPP.

58. "Minutes of the Meeting of January 12, 1914," GIPP.

59. "Minutes of the Meeting of April 9, 1914," GIPP.

60. Schiff to Zangwill, April 14, 1914, Schiff Papers.

61. See, for example, Bressler to Schiff, July 29, 1914, and Schiff to Bressler, August 4, 1914, GIPP.

62. Schiff to Sulzberger, November 2, 1914, Schiff Papers.

63. The breakdown of the expenses of the Galveston movement can be found in "Financial Statement of receipts and disbursements on account of the Galveston Committee, New York City, January of 1907 to October 14, 1914," Schiff Papers.

CHAPTER 7

The Treaty Fight, 1907-1912

While Schiff was seeking to divert Russian Jewish immigration to the interior of the United States in order to make possible the absorption of a larger number of such immigrants into this country, he and other American Jewish leaders were active also on other fronts. Renewed turmoil afflicted Rumania in the winter of 1906-1907, but the failure of their entreaties in the face of pogroms in Russia in 1905 and 1906 caused American Jewish leaders to be chary about demanding action of the government toward Rumania. Jacob Schiff held that it was "not well at present to urge too much on our government in connection with Rumanian or Russian affairs, and that whatever be done in this respect had better be handled with great deliberation." His impression was that, while it was the Jews who were suffering the most in Rumania, "the whole agitation is more agrarian in general than purely anti-Semitic," and he suggested that the American Jewish community might best concentrate its efforts on material relief for those Jews affected.[1]

Nevertheless, the American Jewish Committee requested of the State Department that it inquire into the Rumanian situation and use its good offices, if possible, to prevent any pogroms there.[2] According to the *American Hebrew*, however:

The attitude of the administration, it is said, is that the
United States cannot afford to play the role of school-
master, and be continually proferring advice to foreign
countries as to how they can best deal with local disturbances, and as to what they should do for the protection of their own subjects. All the advices which
come to the State Department indicate that the
Roumanian Government is putting forth its best efforts
to end the troubles and to maintain its supremacy, and
it is held that any suggestions from this government
might be resented and perhaps properly so. Accordingly,
no action will be taken at this time concerning the
appeals.[3]

Clearly the American Jewish leadership must hereafter be more
selective in its appeals for action by the government. By the end
of April 1907 reports indicated that the situation in Rumania
had quieted down without any remonstrances from the United
States.[4]

One activity in which American Jewish leaders were involved
was the dissemination of propaganda materials in Russia. Schiff
was involved in helping to finance such work at least as early
as 1906.[5] One such effort was the attempt to influence public
opinion in Russia in favor of Russian Jews. This was done
through a Russian newspaper, *Rjetsch*, which was subsidized
until 1908 by the Baron Edmund de Rothschild and the Jewish
Colonization Association. As Samuel Montagu of the Russo-
Jewish Committee in London explained to Cyrus Sulzberger
of the National Committee for the Relief of Sufferers by Russian Massacres, the great advantage of the newspaper was that
it had a daily circulation of 50,000 copies in Russia. Since each
copy was purchased it was bound to be read by more people
and to exert a greater influence than pamphlets which were
"more often than not thrown away without even being looked
at."[6] Montagu asked for the support of the American National
Committee in granting a subsidy of 2,000 pounds sterling
(about $10,000) from the Central Fund for the newspaper.

The National Committee agreed to the expenditure of the funds, which was kept secret and was not included in the balance sheet of the Russo-Jewish Committee.[7]

In mid-1907 the American Jewish Committee concluded that the state of affairs in Russia made it an inopportune time to press the administration over the passport question which had been an issue among American Jews for decades.[8] American Jews, however, were outraged when they became aware of a circular issued by the Department of State on May 28, 1907, which included the statement:

> Jews, whether they were formerly Russian subjects or not, are not admitted to Russia unless they obtain special permission in advance from the Russian Government, and this Department will not issue passports to former Russian subjects or to Jews who intend going to Russian territory, unless it has the assurance that the Russian Government will consent to their admission.[9]

This incredible statement not only established clearly the acquiescence of the United States government in Russia's policy of discriminating against Jews bearing American passports, but made it appear that the State Department would hereafter assist the Russian government in enforcing that policy. When asked his opinion of this circular, Secretary of Commerce and Labor Oscar Straus responded that he entirely disapproved of it, that it was "contrary to the spirit and traditional policy of our government," and was, moreover, "in opposition to express law." He had, he said, placed the matter before the president and he believed that Roosevelt shared his views.[10] Only a few days later Straus was able to report: "I am informed this morning by a letter received from Dr. Cyrus Adler that the President has ordered the cancellation of the circular issued by the Department of State in May last, containing a notice to American citizens of Jewish faith who contemplate visiting Russia."[11]

Professor Naomi Cohen, in her definitive study of the abrogation of the 1832 treaty between the United States and Russia, has described the State Department circular of 1907 as "the catalyst in crystallizing the change in demand from diplomatic protest to outright abrogation" of the treaties with Russia as a means of defending the rights of American Jews to travel to Russia on a plane of equality with other American citizens.[12] But even now, as when Schiff had brought the subject up with President Roosevelt at the time of the Kishinev massacre, the passport question was not viewed in isolation. While American Jews justifiably were irate over Russia's discrimination against them, they viewed the passport question also as a means by which the condition of Russia's Jews might also be improved. As Schiff wrote Rabbi Stephen Wise in 1910, "If Russia be compelled to live up to its treaties and to recognize the foreign passports without discrimination, it will before long have to do away with the so-called "pale of settlement," for it is not to be assumed that foreign Jews will be permitted to freely enter and travel in Russia without the Russian Jew himself obtaining the same right from his government."[13] The assault on Russian restrictions upon American Jews, then, was basically also an assault on the disabilities under which Russian Jews were forced to live.

On May 18, 1908, Mayer Sulzberger, president of the American Jewish Committee, addressed a long letter to the president setting forth the arguments of American Jews for abrogation of the 1832 treaty between the United States and Russia:

> The commercial disadvantage to us of the expiry of the treaty of 1832 is not appalling. International trade like all other trade, is not in its bulk based on favoritism, but on mutual interest. We cannot sell what Russia does not want, nor do we buy what we do not expect to use advantageously for ourselves. The laws of commerce will in the end prevail over mere fancies or momentary estrangements. But the promotion of commerce, though a high function of statesmanship, is not its exclusive duty. A point in international relations may be reached when a first class power can better afford to lose a substantial advantage than tamely submit to the domination of a foreign power formidable for population

and resources. Russia is such a first-class power. . . . But
we also owe something to the dignity of our own country. Our Government, we fondly believe, is the greatest
on earth with respect to freedom, equity and justice.
Other nations have their ideals, which we must view
with respect, and, if possible, with sympathy. No nation can or ought to ask us to adopt its antithetical
views and yield our own. And if a request so unreasonable be made, either in words or by a course of conduct,
it is our duty energetically to refuse and repel it. Our
prayer therefore is that due notice be given to Russia
of the intended termination of the two treaties afore-
said, and that no new treaty be made unless all the
provisions covering both subjects and such others as
may be agreed on, are contained in one instrument
which shall likewise contain practical provisions to
secure its enforcement by denying its further benefits
to the party disregarding its obligation thereunder, or
any of them.[14]

The State Department, which had been pressing the Russians
for years to end their discriminatory practices toward American
Jews seeking to travel to that country, had been attempting for
a year to negotiate a new naturalization treaty with Russia
which, presumably, would solve the problem. However, only
weeks before Sulzberger's letter, the State Department had
been informed by the American embassy in St. Petersburg that
the Russians considered it impossible to negotiate the treaty
at that time and that matters must await the formulation of a
new law of naturalization which was then under consideration
by the Ministry of the Interior.[15] Secretary of State Root could
only respond to Sulzberger's letter that his communication
would "receive attentive consideration."[16] Sulzberger waited
nearly two weeks before writing the secretary again, conclud-
ing his letter with the observation that what he had suggested
on May 18 was "a lawful, peaceful, regular, practical and
practicable way by which Russia may be persuaded of the
impolity of continuing its unfriendly conduct." The government should embark on that course "promptly and without

allowing itself to be diverted from the consideration of a great
and fundamental question to the discussion of side issues.''[17]

When William Howard Taft, Roosevelt's hand-picked successor, won the Republican nomination in 1908, Jacob Schiff
addressed him a long letter on the passport question in which
he suggested that Taft take up the passport issue in his forthcoming letter accepting the Republican nomination. Schiff
wrote:

> This is an open sore with my co-religionists, who, from
> administration to administration, have urged and waited
> that proper protection be secured them in their rights
> as American citizens. Even to those to whom, like my-
> self, this is of no practical import—for I have no need
> to go to Russia and I stay away from where I am not
> welcome—the acquiescence of the American Govern-
> ment in this insult offered to its citizens of the Jewish
> faith has become almost unbearable. . . . This is a sub-
> ject which will not down, and its treatment through
> platitudes and platforms and otherwise will not suffice
> much longer. I need not assure you, Mr. Secretary, how
> deeply desirous I am for the success of your campaign,
> and of my unfailing belief that your election will assure
> an excellence of administration of the country's affairs.
> It is because of this that I do not contemplate without
> anxiety the possibility that Mr. Bryan [the Democratic
> candidate], with the tendency so peculiar in him, might
> feel induced to intimate that if elected his administration
> would insist that Russia recognize the American pass-
> port—when properly issued—in the hands of any Ameri-
> can citizen, and if the refusal be persisted in this would
> be considered good ground for suspending relations.
> Should Mr. Bryan make such a declaration, it would
> throw to him the large majority of the 200,000 votes
> of Jewish origin in this state and thus decide the New
> York electoral vote in his favor. I do not know and do
> not hope that such a situation will be created, but I
> cannot shut my eyes to a danger which is not beyond

possibility of arising, and to which I thought I should
call your attention.[18]

Taft did touch briefly on the passport question in his acceptance
of the nomination and wrote Schiff to call his attention to it.
Schiff responded that he realized Taft's reference to the passport question was "probably all you could, with proper dignity,
have made on the subject for the time being," but he called to
Taft's attention the fact that American Jews had been listening
to such assurances as he had made in the platform of the Republican Party for years without any result. He expressed the
hope, therefore, that "something more tangible will be accomplished in this respect by the State Department upon your
initiative when you are in the Presidential chair."[19]

Some Jewish leaders like Simon Wolf were convinced that
President Roosevelt, being a "born politician" and aware that
"a certain contingent of votes in New York City can swing the
state, and the state may possibly be the pendulum in the coming election," would take some action himself before the election in order to ensure Taft's victory.[20] A brief flurry of diplomatic activity was, in fact, initiated by Secretary of State Root,
with ample publicity, apparently designed to woo Jewish voters.
The State Department indicated to the Russians a desire for
a complete revision and amendment of the treaty of 1832, and
so informed Schiff in a letter of September 15, 1908. Schiff
responded that he earnestly hoped that the action would result
in something concrete since "the existing condition is a standing insult both to our government and to every citizen, be he
of the Jewish faith or otherwise." Schiff told the secretary of
state: "As a warm supporter and well-wisher of the administration, I have deemed it well to make publication of your letter
so as to allay to some extent, at least, the irritation which
exists."[21] Thus, the administration's weak initiative had served
its apparent purpose and Root had shown that he was as adept
as anyone at making political use of the State Department. It is
possible that the Roosevelt administration might have been
driven to more determined action—or the candidate, William
Howard Taft, to more specific pledges—had the Democratic

candidate taken a strong position on the issue. However, William Jennings Bryan failed to come out forthrightly for treaty abrogation, echoing only the Democratic platform in arguing that no exceptions should be made for American Jews where freedom of travel to Russia under an American passport was concerned but offering no remedies to the problem.[22]

As the election grew nearer, however, Secretary of State Root made yet another effort to quiet American Jewish disaffection with the Republicans and to bind them to Taft on election day. In a letter to Schiff, Root wrote of the question of obtaining for American Jews equality of treatment where Russia was concerned:

> Our government has never varied in its insistence upon such treatment, and this administration has repeatedly brought the matter to the attention of the Russian Government and urged the making of a new treaty for the purpose of regulating the subject. We have but very recently received an unfavorable reply to this proposal, and we have now communicated to Russia an expression of the desire of this government for a complete revision and amendment of the treaty of 1832, which provides for reciprocal rights of residence and travel on the part of the citizens of the two countries. We have expressed our views that such a course would be preferable to the complete termination of the treaty, subjecting both countries to the possibility of being left without any reciprocal rights whatever owing to the delay in the making of a new treaty. The course which the administration is following in this respect is the one which appears to us to be best calculated to attain the end desired, an end which I beg to assure you the administration is in full and sympathetic agreement with you.[23]

Evidence of the political motivation behind Root's letter lay in the fact that Schiff "received an intimation from Washington . . . that the administration would be pleased if I made publication" of the letter, and he did release it to the press.[24] The *American Hebrew*, which printed the letter in its entirety, found it "most gratifying reading." The journal elaborated:

> The policy adopted by the administration on the pass-port question is along the lines suggested to the Presi-dent by the American Jewish Committee and is as vigorous as it should be. The expression on the part of our government that a complete revision and amend-ment of the treaty of 1832 "would be preferable to the complete termination of the treaty, subjecting both countries to the possibility of being left without any reciprocal rights whatever" is suggestive of much for the Russian government to ponder upon. Even that country will probably be alert to the disadvantage of terminating the treaty from which it has gained much and we little.[25]

If the Roosevelt administration had not come out, as the Jews had hoped, forthrightly for abrogation of the 1832 treaty, it had at least subtly threatened abrogation if the Russians did not cooperate in revising and amending the treaty in such a way as to put an end to the abuses of which American Jews were protesting. In behalf of the American Jewish Committee, Judge Mayer Sulzberger described Root's letter to Schiff as "the most important advance that has been made by our govern-ment to protect the rights of Jewish citizens of this country in Russia." He added:

> At last Secretary Root has boldly taken the position that Russia must observe the treaty of 1832, or other-wise this government will terminate it and the treaty of 1887, and thus leave Russia and ourselves without any treaty. The letter of Mr. Root to Mr. Schiff shows all this. Though veiled in the polite phraseology of diplomatic intercourse, it is perfectly plain to the Russian government. I think that this is the beginning

of the end of the passport question, which is big with
possibilities for the benefit not only of American Jews,
but also of Jews in Russia. The country owes a debt
of gratitude to President Roosevelt, to Secretary Root,
and to the whole administration for their manly insistence on the rights of American Jews.[26]

The reference to "the whole administration" was doubtless
intended to encompass William Howard Taft, the Secretary of
War and now the party's candidate for the presidency. Certainly
American Jews seemed to have good reason to vote for the
Republican Party in the election and to have high expectations
that a Taft administration would follow through with the policy
outlined in Root's letter to Schiff. Schiff believed that American
Jews had "Taft's firm assurance that he is going to proceed
energetically with the policy which has been adopted." Taft's
election, he observed, was "satisfactory to everyone and public
opinion has since become very confident."[27] Immediately
following the election, the American Jewish Committee geared
up for the effort to get the treaties abrogated.[28]

Taft's inaugural address continued to suggest that he would
move on the passport question. In that speech he declared:
"We should make every effort to prevent humiliating and de-
grading prohibition against any of our citizens wishing temporarily to sojourn in foreign nations because of race or religion."
The *American Hebrew* concluded: "Since the President usually
includes in his inaugural only those subjects which he considers
of chief importance it is gratifying to find this included in that
category."[29] Early in the month that Taft took office, Congress passed a resolution calling upon the administration to use
its best efforts to reach agreement with the Russians recognizing the validity of an American passport in the hands of an
American Jew. This, too, the *American Hebrew* hailed as "an
important step in advance." It observed:

> It is true that similar resolutions have been passed be-
> fore without immediate result but the hands of the
> Secretary of State cannot fail to be strengthened in his

negotiations with Russia when he has behind him this
unanimous expression of opinion by the representative
voice of the nation. Russia cannot much longer refuse
to listen to the American people when they make such
a demand, so obviously based upon all the principles
of international right and comity.

The resolution of Congress, combined with Taft's reference to
the matter in his inaugural speech, was regarded as the beginning
of the end of American acquiescence in this "insult to its dignity."[30]

A year of apparent inaction on the part of the Taft administration followed, however, which led American Jews to become
restive. A letter to Taft from the publishers of a Jewish newspaper expressed well the growing disillusionment and sense of
betrayal some American Jews were beginning to feel toward
the Taft administration:

> Your Excellency will perhaps recall that during the cam-
> paign for your election you pledged yourself to secure
> the recognition by the Russian Government, of the
> American passport in the hands of Jewish citizens.
> Your Excellency may also be aware that the main argu-
> ments which we made to our readers in behalf of your
> candidacy was this pledge. Your promise was accepted
> at face value, and with much gratitude and hope by the
> Jewish citizens, and we have reason to know that it was
> one of the chief causes for their almost unanimous sup-
> port of your candidacy. The present administration is
> now almost a year old, and so far as we have been able
> to ascertain, very little has been done with regard to
> this question, and the same invidious distinction which
> Russia has made in the past between Jewish and other
> citizens of the United States is still being made, with-
> out any protest on the part of the American State
> Department.

The publishers told Taft that they assumed that his administration was doing something in the matter, despite the apparent

inaction, and asked for a report of progress which they might publish in order to reassure the Jewish community that action was being taken in conformity with his pledges.[31]

The American Jewish Committee was similarly concerned. After Judge Sulzberger and Dr. Cyrus Adler had held a fruitless meeting with the president, Secretary of State Knox, and Ambassador-designate to Russia William W. Rockhill, the American Jewish Committee decided in February of 1910 to press for yet another meeting with Taft.[32] The renewed Jewish pressure caused a new flurry of activity within the State Department. Secretary of State Knox wrote to the president that the gradual transformation of the Russian government to a constitutional basis was leading to measures that would undoubtedly bring about "material amelioration of the restrictions to which Jews have long been subjected in Russia" and told him of the appointment in Russia of a new Imperial Commission to revise passport regulations. Nothing had yet been accomplished, he admitted, but the American embassy had been urged to make all possible use of any opportunity to "press with renewed earnestness for such treatment of American passports as will respond to the dictates of modern sentiment and international law."[33]

Knox cabled Ambassador Rockhill a week later that he was awaiting the ambassador's report "on status of negotiations for the recognition by Russian Government of American passports for Jewish citizens." Rockhill was instructed to take all possible advantage of the appointment of the Imperial Commission to revise the passport regulations, but his reply to Knox undercut all of the optimism of the State Department.[34] Rockhill found no evidence that any such commission as Knox had mentioned was "even contemplated."[35] Moreover, the "democratization" of Russia which Knox expected to bring improvement for Jews in that country seemed likely, Rockhill reported, to have exactly the opposite effect. The deep-seated anti-Semitic prejudices of the Russian people, he told Knox, meant that any representative body such as the Duma was likely to be even more reactionary and repressive in its policies toward the Jews than the old government had been. Indeed, the ambassador found evidence "that the Duma is not sympathetic with even such measures of tolerance as the Government is disposed to show towards the Jews."[36] Knox's information to the president had been woefully inaccurate.

Perhaps from discomfiture at the confusion within his State Department, Taft apparently had not responded to the request of the American Jewish Committee for a further meeting with him, leading Judge Mayer Sulzberger to suggest now that individual members of the executive committee should seek to call on the president to voice their individual views. Schiff, however, was opposed to such a course "which might embarrass us at some future time and in different instances."[37] He therefore decided against meeting with the president individually to discuss the passport question. This attitude apparently aborted a meeting which President Taft had finally scheduled with Judge Sulzberger and Schiff for April 7, 1910, since there is no indication that such a meeting was held.[38]

In the meantime, Rockhill had compiled a lengthy survey for the administration of the Jewish situation in Russia and the passport question. The memorandum reviewed the history of these questions beginning with the year 1904, which marked "the beginning of the present phase of our negotiations with Russia for the removal of existing discriminations against American citizens of Jewish race wishing to visit Russia." As in his previous message, however, Rockhill concluded that public opinion in Russia was distinctly not disposed to grant Russian Jews civil equality, in large part because Jews were identified with the revolutionary movement and the feeling that the revolution had been greatly assisted by Jewish money from overseas. Echoing the official line of the Russian government, Rockhill reported:

> The Imperial Government, through the present Minister of the Interior, has on several occasions in the last two or three years given it as their opinion that, should equal civil rights be now conferred on the Jews of Russia, it would result in a general massacre and pillage of the Jews throughout the Empire.

Rockhill's general conclusion was that there was little prospect at the present time of "either the abrogation of existing special laws against the Jews in Russia, or the adoption of any law facilitating the ingress or sojourn of foreign Jews in the empire or the consideration of any measure which might result in bringing up a discussion of the Jewish question." Rockhill did not believe it possible for the Russian Foreign Ministry to take up negotiations for a naturalization treaty with the United States, or to make a new commercial treaty which would grant better terms for American citizens visiting Russia than were contained in the treaty of 1832. Rather, he felt it was possible that the Russian government might be able to interpret and amend the laws in a more favorable light without consulting the Duma or Council of Empire. He had, therefore, submitted suggestions for such modifications to the minister of the interior, and "it was believed that modifications might be possible."[39]

When Ambassador Rockhill returned to the United States for a visit, he, President Taft, and Secretary of State Knox met with Sulzberger, Schiff, and Adler on May 25. The administration drew upon a memorandum prepared by the State Department and based upon Rockhill's dispatch as the basis for their defense of the administration's apparent inaction in pressing the passport issue vigorously. The American Jewish Committee representatives attacked the Rockhill report as inaccurate and presented their own plan of action. The committee wanted the negotiations for revision of the treaty of 1832 transferred to Washington. In addition, they felt the United States government should also reiterate Root's threat that if no progress were achieved the result would be the abrogation of the treaty, and if that had no effect in furthering the negotiations the treaty should, in fact, be terminated.[40]

Again months passed, however, with no apparent movement on the part of the Taft administration. State Department officials were pessimistic that any progress could be made in negotiations with the Russians. As Assistant Secretary of State Adee described the situation to the head of the Division of Near Eastern Affairs:

The case seems well nigh hopeless. The Czar's govt. can do nothing effective in the way of more liberal treatment without the sanction of the Duma, and it can apparently do nothing with the Duma. . . . We can do nothing except press for such liberal modifications of the existing foreign passport regulations as may be made without the necessity of submitting them to the Duma for its sanction. Such submission would not only result in a flat refusal of the Duma to give its sanction, but would be very likely to call forth peremptory enactments by the Duma enjoining even greater restrictions upon the entry of alien Jews.[41]

On October 18 President Taft wrote to Schiff once again outlining the administration's perception of the difficulties and suggesting that American Jews mount a petition drive such as they had undertaken in response to Kishinev in 1903. Schiff, who had opposed the petition in 1903, was equally skeptical of its efficacy in 1910, responded to Taft's suggestion:

Experience has shown that petitions to the Tsar or the Russian government such as you propose to circulate in this country and present to the Tsar in Russia, are absolutely useless and without effect upon the barbaric government of the Tsar. There is only one way in which the people of the United States can ever expect to make an impression upon the Russian Government: in obtaining, in the first instance, recognition of the American passport by whomsoever held, and as a consequence of this, justice to Russia's suppressed and persecuted subjects. This can only be assured by the renouncing on the part of our government of the treaties with Russia which the latter is constantly abusing. Petitions or friendly remonstrance will prove of no avail.[42]

The following month Schiff wrote Rabbi Stephen S. Wise:

What we expect at this time from our own government, and in which we are sure we shall have the support of

the American people in general, is that the pledges
which were made by *every* party in their respective
platforms during the last Presidential campaign, but
more particularly the Republican party and President
Taft personally in his speeches and in private letters,
that every endeavor should be made to compel Russia
to recognize the American passport irrespective of the
religious faith of its holder shall be carried out.

The American Jewish Committee, he told Wise, had given the
president and the secretary of state its suggestions as to how
this could be carried out and the committee was hopeful that
the government would follow them up. Schiff concluded:
"I believe if we can get the powerful influence of the Outlook
[magazine] and the press in general in insisting that the platform to which I have referred must be carried out, much will
be gained."[43]

Schiff revealed his sense of urgency over the condition of
Jews in Russia and the link to the passport question when he
wrote late in December:

We know quite well that the present policy of the
Russian government, namely a slow and deliberate repression of the Jews, is much worse and more destruc-
tive even than the policy of horrors of the last months
of the year 1905, which immediately evoked the attention of the whole civilized world and thereby made it
impossible to continue such a policy, whereas the
present quiet, but all the more inhuman policy of the
Russian government, will hardly be noticed by the rest
of the world and the tyrannical government of Russia
will therefore have a freer hand undisturbed by others.
We are aware of this situation and are making every
effort to prevail upon our government to do something
definite to compel Russia to settle the passport question.
Once it can be established that Russia is to be open to
Jews from foreign countries without restriction, she
will not long be able to deny such freedom to her own
Jewish residents.[44]

In October Schiff had prevailed upon the Reverend David H. Greer, Episcopal bishop of New York, to obtain from the general convention of the Protestant Episcopal Church the adoption of a resolution of protest against "the cruel and inhuman treatment of the Jewish subjects" of Russia.[45] That effort had been successful and was proof, Schiff wrote a correspondent, that the Jews of America were trying to do "everything which we think may in the end bring relief to our brethren in faith who live in Russia."[46]

Despite the pressures from the American Jewish Committee and others, however, the Taft administration moved slowly on the passport question, and when it formulated its position on the matter late in 1910, that position favored the negotiation of a new treaty with Russia which would contain the provisions desired by American Jewish leaders, but not the abrogation of the existing treaty which they had sought.[47] This was a curious approach to the problem in view of Rockhill's skepticism that a new treaty could be negotiated. Meanwhile, in January the opportunity was presented for the opening gun to be fired in the American Jewish Committee's final assault on the issue—to bring the issue to the public and, by the force of public opinion, to cause the desired action to be carried out by the Taft administration. Encouraged by private advice from Charles D. Norton, Taft's secretary, that such a public airing of the issue might be useful in influencing the president, and buoyed by the encouragement of American Jewish leaders, Louis Marshall accepted an invitation to address the convention of the Union of American Hebrew Congregations.[48]

Marshall's speech, says Naomi Cohen, "set the pattern both in content and tone for the entire campaign" for abrogation of the 1832 treaty with Russia.[49] In his speech Marshall reviewed the history of the passport question and the position taken, without effect, by the United States government since the administration of President Grover Cleveland and concluded: "Apparently we are today as far from a solution of this problem which goes home to every American citizen as we were thirty years ago." Diplomacy had failed, he told his listeners, and the United States stood "at the door of Russia, hat in

hand, pleading with it that it shall recognize and perform its
contract" under the treaty of 1832. Marshall emphasized that
it was not just the Jews of America who were insulted but all
Americans, and remedying the situation was not a Jewish question "but an American question." The Russians were legally
in the wrong, and the United States should press for the rights
of its citizens, putting ideals above commercial and financial
interests. Marshall argued: "It is within the power of a country
situated as ours is to isolate Russia and to terminate all treaty
relations with a government which fails to recognize the
solemnity and sanctity of its treaty obligations, and that is
exactly what should be done without further delay."[50] After
Marshall's speech the convention passed a resolution he had
drafted:

> ... it is the sense of this Council, speaking not as a repre-
> sentative of Jews, but as a body of citizens having at
> heart the preservation of the honor of the Nation ...
> that the President of the United States, the Depart-
> ment of State and Congress be respectfully and earnest-
> ly urged to take immediate measures, in conformity
> with the express terms of the treaties now existing
> between the United States and Russia, and in accord-
> ance with the law of nations, to terminate such treaties;
> to the end that if treaty relations are to exist between
> the two nations, it shall be upon such conditions and
> guaranties only, as shall be consonant with the dignity
> of the American people.[51]

The resolution of the convention of the Union of American
Hebrew Congregations was soon followed by one from the
Cooper Union audience of the Peoples' Institute in New York
City, which petitioned the secretary of state "to use all proper
and lawful means in his power to persuade the Russian govern-
ment to cease from commission of further crimes against the
Jews within the borders of the Russian Empire," and to de-
mand that they cease their discrimination against American
Jews. Though the advisory council of the People's Institute

included such prominent American Jews as Jacob Schiff, Edwin and Isaac Seligman, Lillian Wald, and Paul Warburg, the great majority of the council consisted of non-Jews.[52]

Schiff, meanwhile, could report progress on another front. At a meeting with some of the leading members of the American Society of Friends of Russian Freedom, Schiff managed to mobilize that group behind the treaty abrogation fight. At a meeting which included Dr. Lyman Abbott (of *Outlook* magazine), Lillian Wald, and George Kennan it was decided that the society would "take up propaganda for the termination of the extradition treaty between Russia and the United States," and a committee was formed "to arrange, if practicable, for the establishment of an information or news bureau to furnish the American press in general regularly with news as to the political happenings in Russia." George Kennan was to head the press bureau. The society chose to agitate against the extradition treaty between the United States and Russia which it had opposed in the 1890s, rather than the treaty of 1832 since it was considered "that making propaganda for the termination of the extradition treaty would be more effective than if the passport question was taken up by the society, since the two treaties more or less must stand and fall together." The real reason, Schiff perceived, was that the society wished to help all it could but did not wish to encourage the belief that it was dominated by Jewish influences. The recruitment of the American Society of Friends of Russian Freedom brought articulate and influential allies to the side of the fight for abrogation.[53]

With the pressures increasing for abrogation, President Taft sought a way to build bridges to the American Jewish leaders. According to Simon Wolf's memoirs, it was he who suggested to the president a further meeting with American Jewish leaders to discuss the passport issue, and after Wolf had recommended the names of those who should be invited the president "then and there instructed his secretary to telegraph to each one, apprising them of the luncheon and conference."[54] Invited to the meeting on February 15, 1911, were Jacob Schiff, Congressman Henry M. Goldfogle, Louis Marshall, Adolf Kraus,

Philip Stein, Jacob Furth, J. Walter Freiberg, Bernhard
Bettman, and Simon Wolf. Marshall expressed concern that
some of the Jewish leaders would be so flattered by the president's invitation that they would "readily concede that everything has been done that can be done" and would stop short
of calling for abrogation of the 1832 treaty. He expressed
particular contempt for "Mr. Wolf's ordinary policy, to say
'Amen' to anything that the government authorities may
suggest," and told Schiff there was only one position the Jews
could take "with any degree of self-respect," which was to
press for fulfillment by the government of the resolution
adopted by the convention of the Union of American Hebrew
Congregations calling for the termination of the treaties between the United States and Russia.[55]

After a pleasant luncheon with the president the group met
in the library of the White House. To the "astonishment and
keen disappointment" of the Jewish leaders, the president did
not wait for them to make their points but rather read to them
his conclusions in the form of a written statement. Taft's position was that his administration had pledged only to "use
every proper effort" to make the American passport "a certifi-
cate of good treatment the world round, with an equality of
opportunity and a recognition of equality without reference
to creed or race anywhere." This, of course, was a far cry
from the advanced position taken by Root during the 1908
campaign, and which American Jews had been led to believe
would be followed by the Taft administration. The question
of Russian treatment of passports in the hands of American
Jews, Taft told his listeners, had been "under consideration"
ever since he began his administration. But, he argued, "We
have no international right to object to any nation's excluding any of our people, assuming that there is nothing of a
treaty obligation between us." Some U.S. secretaries of
state, notably Blaine and Everett, had consistently taken the
position that the treaty of 1832 did not permit Russia to treat
one category of American citizens differently from another
simply because they were Jews, but Taft maintained that
other secretaries of state had been somewhat doubtful on the

question. Russia, Taft noted, had consistently taken the position that it could discriminate, and had done so not only under the treaty with the United States but also under identically worded treaties with other nations. Other nations had acquiesced in Russia's interpretation of the treaties, he pointed out, and there the matter had stood, in the American instance, since 1832.

But now American Jews were asking Russia to abide by *their* interpretation of the treaty or else face the possibility of a renouncement of the treaty by the United States. The relationship between the United States and Russia, the president argued, was one of long standing, and one under which "property rights have been acquired, investments have been made, and a status established in respect to a great many things which, if we denounce the treaty, will have no sanction or security at all and be left wholly to the arbitrary action of Russia through her executive." Taft recognized, he told the Jewish leaders, that the establishment of equality was "our national principle and policy" which was "above and over every other consideration." Further, he would be quick to "sacrifice the interests that it certainly will sacrifice" by renouncing the treaty, if only he were not convinced that "instead of benefiting anybody . . . it would accomplish nothing at all." "In other words," Taft told the Jewish leaders, "the question is—must be—a balance of convenience and of comparative burden rather than a question of principle when what is proposed to be done is not going to accomplish any step toward that principle." The situation in Russia was deplorable, he admitted, but Ambassador Rockhill had left no doubt in his mind that "if we denounce the treaty we shall be no nearer the object that we all have in view, but that we shall imperil a good many interests which it is our duty to preserve." It could even result, he pointed out, in imperiling the flow of Russian immigrants to the United States. Taft concluded:

> A great many of you gentlemen do not agree with me, and I am sorry you do not; but I think perhaps that if I had the same justifiable pride of race that you have

and the same sense of outrageous justice that comes
home to a man of that race much more than it can to
a man who is not of the race, I should feel as you do.
But I am the President of the whole country, and I
feel that in exercising a responsibility affecting every-
body I have to try to look at the subject from all sides.
I have summoned you here to explain to you the
reasons for the conclusions I have reached.[56]

Taft left the American Jewish leaders little time for consultation on their response to his position since he was leaving for
an appointment, but Louis Marshall did rebut many of the
points which Taft had made in his presentation. In response
to the president's question whether Marshall, as a lawyer, believed that there was ample justification for the abrogation
of the treaty, Marshall replied that he "unquestionably" did.
As for the question of whether it would hinder the economic
relations between the two countries, Marshall told the president that "whatever the effect might be upon our commerce,
it was a negligible matter compared with the great and under-
lying question of the dignity of American citizenship."[57]
  After Marshall had responded to the president's presentation, Jacob Schiff, according to Simon Wolf's account:

protested that, as all of us had understood the invitation, the President desired to have a conference with
us to learn our views as to what should be done . . .
because of the unwillingness of the Russian Government to yield in the request our Government had made
to remove, or at least modify, the discrimination which
was being made against American Jews who desired to
enter Russia. Instead of this, what we had expected to
be a conference had resulted in a communication to us
by the President of foregone conclusions on his part,
that he had decided to do nothing whatsoever, without
even having given us an opportunity to state our own
views. Mr. Schiff continued: "Mr. President, you have
said that you are not prepared to permit the commer-

cial interests of ninety-eight million of the American people to suffer because two million feel that their rights as American citizens are being infringed upon. My own opinion has always been that it was the privilege of the head of this nation that, if only a single American citizen was made to suffer injury, the entire power of this great Government should be exercised to procure redress for such injury, and now you tell us because some special interests who are trading with Russia might suffer if the abrogation of the Treaty was carried into effect, you would not do anything to protect two million American citizens in the rights vouchsafed to them under our constitution and laws. We feel deeply mortified," Mr. Schiff continued, "that in this instance, Mr. President, you have failed us, and there is nothing left to us now but to put our case before the American people directly, who are certain to do us justice." Mr. Schiff added: "In 1861, a small but in some respects potent minority claimed that it would be better to permit the slave states to go out of the Union instead of risking a Civil War, but public opinion insisted that the slave must be free and the Union remain supreme at any cost; the war for the right was thereupon fought and won, even with all the sacrifice it necessitated. To this same public opinion, Mr. President, we shall now turn, and we have no fear of the results.[58]

Taft also apparently received the impression that Schiff was threatening him with "political destruction" and in addition was prepared to spend a million dollars to bring about the abrogation of the treaty.[59] After speaking, Schiff alone refused to shake the president's hand upon leaving.[60] As the Jewish leaders walked down the stairs from the meeting, Schiff told Marshall that the president's attitude meant "war," and he offered up to $25,000 for a fund to bring about the abrogation of the treaty.[61]

Schiff wrote to the president on February 20, making sub-

stantially the same points that had been made by the Jewish
leaders in their "conference" with Taft, and concluded: "Not-
withstanding the present discouragement we have received,
I have the unshakable belief that at some time public opinion
. . . will compel the Government to resent the continuous insult
to them which Russia has only too long been permitted to
inflict by the non-observance of its treaty obligations."[62] To
this Taft replied, once again making the points he had pressed
in his statement:

> I am very sorry to disappoint you, but I have considered
> this at great length and with every desire to secure a
> proper recognition of the American passport in Russia,
> but I differ with you as to the proper step to take to
> secure this object. I believe . . . that the present con-
> dition can be ameliorated by patient effort and constant
> attention to it, and this I shall continue to bring to bear
> on it no matter how severe your criticism and that of
> other gentlemen upon my course may be.[63]

Clearly, further discussions with the administration were pointless, and hereafter the issue would not rest upon attempts by
American Jewish leaders to persuade the president. Already
Representative Herbert Parsons (Republican from New York)
had introduced in the House of Representatives a joint resolution directing the president to give notice to the Russian
Government that the 1832 treaty would terminate after one
year. Hereafter, American Jewish efforts would be bent to
influencing the Congressional vote in favor of such a resolution.
    With the 1910 off-year elections ended and the resultant re-
organization of Congressional committees in the offing,
American Jewish leaders began to contemplate ways in which
friends of their cause might be induced to seek positions on the
important immigration and foreign relations committees in the
Senate.[64] In April 1911 the American Jewish Committee sought
to raise additional money, arguing: "With regard to the passport
question, the Committee believes that patience has ceased to
be a virtue and that diplomatic negotiations are valueless.

It proposes to have introduced in the next Congress, a bill abrogating the Treaty of 1832 with Russia. Our duty is to awaken the sentiment of the whole country in favor of the passage of this bill by intelligent and unremitting publicity."[65] A few days later Schiff wrote to Adolf Ochs, Jewish publisher of the *New York Times*, addressing himself to the arguments raised against abrogation and stating the beliefs of the supporters of abrogation that:

> public opinion in England, France and Germany would be largely influenced by our Government's action, as European nations, or at least some of them, would hardly be willing to remain in the position that the United States are doing more to protect the treaty rights of their citizens than their own respective governments, and . . . it will not be long after the United States have taken the initiative that Russia will be made to feel that the passport question may be settled.

As always, Schiff was candid in pointing out, however, that the real issue was not the few hundred American Jews who were denied the right to travel within Russia every year. The real point of the struggle was the Jewish population of Russia.[66] It does not seem to have occurred to the American Jewish leaders that the constant reiteration of the connection between the passport issue and the condition of Jews in Russia made it doubly unlikely that the Russian government would be willing to make concessions where the former was concerned.

Meantime, the American Jewish Committee (AJC) was concentrating its attention on the Senate, especially on the Senate Foreign Relations Committee which would have to approve the abrogation resolution before it could reach the floor of the Senate. Various states had already passed resolutions in their legislatures instructing their Congressional representatives to support abrogation, and the Committee on Foreign Affairs of the House of Representatives had passed unanimously a resolution for abrogation before Congress adjourned for the summer.[67] Washington attorney Fulton

Brylawski was liaison for the AJC with the Senate. He received assurances from members of the Senate committee that if the resolution were passed by the House of Representatives it would be supported by a majority of the Senate Foreign Relations Committee and would pass the Senate.[68]

To encourage the United States Congress to support abrogation the American Jewish Committee went forward with the formation of a publicity committee which, Schiff told Adolf Kraus of the B'nai B'rith, "is to take in hand the propaganda we will have to make for the next eighteen months in order that the American people shall become better acquainted with Russian conditions, and particularly with the insult which is being offered them by the Russian government." The publicity committee consisted of Louis Marshall as chairman, and Dr. Cyrus Adler, Samuel Straus, Leo Weil, Julius Rosenwald, and Schiff as members. Adolf Kraus also had been invited to participate, though not a member of the AJC, as well as such other members of the B'nai B'rith as he might designate in order to give the publicity effort a broad base.[69] Kraus, however, preferred to appoint a committee of the B'nai B'rith to cooperate with the committee of the AJC, which was acceptable to Schiff and the others.[70] By the time the executive committee of the American Jewish Committee met on March 19, 1911, more than 30,000 copies of Marshall's address to the convention of the Union of American Hebrew Congregations had already been distributed throughout the country, as well as 3,000 copies of a speech on the same topic delivered by Congressman Herbert Parsons in the House of Representatives. The legislatures of California, Montana, Washington, Arkansas, New York, and Connecticut had already passed resolutions of support for the abrogation effort.[71] Meanwhile, the executives of the American Jewish Committee, the B'nai B'rith, and the Union of American Hebrew Congregations, inaugurated a series of meetings with Senators and Representatives in their home districts to set before them the passport issue.[72]

When Congress reconvened in 1911, the favored resolutions calling for abrogation were introduced in the House of Representatives by Congressman William Sulzer (Democrat from New York) and in the Senate by Senator Charles Culberson (Democrat from Texas). Some opposition was expressed in the Senate Foreign Relations Committee, especially by Senator Henry Cabot Lodge (Republican from Massachusetts), that the Russian government was wholly within its rights under the existing treaty with the United States in refusing to visé the passports of Jews who were naturalized citizens of other countries. Senator Culberson, in his testimony before the committee, argued that Lodge's interpretation of the treaty was in error and his construction of that article of the treaty which he cited was inconsistent with the clear expression of intent contained elsewhere in the same treaty. Other senators questioned the precedent for such an act of abrogation. Culberson responded by citing the joint resolution of 1909, in which Congress had called for the renegotiation of the treaty in order to guarantee equal rights to all American citizens bearing U.S. passports, and pointed to the lack of progress which had been made by the State Department. The committee, however, sought additional information concerning the efforts of the State Department to renegotiate the treaty, and the hearings were held over until the next session of Congress.[73]

Pursuant to the committee's desire, Culberson wrote to the State Department inquiring "what efforts have been made to carry out this joint resolution [of March 4, 1909] and what the probabilities are with reference to the success of such negotiations."[74] In response, Culberson was told by Acting Secretary of State Huntington Wilson that the State Department had been unable to accomplish any definite progress in the negotiations with Russia, but that the Russians had shown "a spirit of friendliness" and it was hoped the question might be settled very shortly. There the matter rested until the next session of Congress met in the fall.[75]

To contribute to the build-up of public pressure for passage of the resolution in Congress a movement began in behalf of a mass meeting to be held in New York City to enlist support from all quarters of American life.[76] The motivating spirit was Henry Green, with help from Nissim Behar, and a typical

organizational letter was that to Senator Pierce Frye in which
Green wrote:

> After earnest discussion with several leading citizens,
> I have been asked to organize a mass meeting in this
> city to protest Russia's insult to American citizenship
> in refusing to honor American passports held by mem-
> bers of the clergy, Jews, and other classes of Americans.
> I am trying to make up a representative committee of
> influential Americans. It is understood, of course, that
> there are no politics in this; and while Jèws are the
> chief sufferers from Russia's discrimination, the mass
> meeting will be an expression of the resentment of all
> of the people of the United States. Will you tentative-
> ly, at least, express your consent to our using your
> name as a member of the committee under whose
> auspices the mass meeting will be held?[77]

While Green was the nominal organizer of the mass meeting,
Oscar Straus was the "guiding hand." Straus, while impressed
with the number of acceptances obtained by Green from such
distinguished Americans as Speaker of the House Champ Clark
and New Jersey Governor Woodrow Wilson, nevertheless
organized with Jacob Schiff a committee to "pick up the
matter in order to see that Mr. Green does not fall into any
serious errors."[78] The mass meeting ultimately came under the
sponsorship of the Citizens' Committee Protesting Against
Russia's Discrimination Against Classes of our Citizens in Violation of Treaty Obligations and Requesting our Government
no Longer to Delay Taking Suitable Action to put an end to
this Insult to American Citizens, or, as it was generally referred
to, the National Citizens' Committee. The first meeting of this
committee was held on October 10, 1911. The letter issuing
the call for the meeting was written on letterhead listing as
members of the National Committee a number of congressmen, senators, and governors as well as Clark and Wilson.[79]
In addition to such prominent Democrats as Wilson and Clark,
William Gibbs McAdoo also took a prominent role. In late

November of 1911 he was involved in sending a letter "in form of resolution to all of the churches of the country" enlisting their support behind the campaign for abrogation.[80] He also served as chairman of the mass meeting organized by the National Citizens' Committee and contributed $100 to the Committee, the same amount given by Jacob H. Schiff.[81]

After several protest meetings had been held throughout the country in late November and early December of 1911, the Carnegie Hall affair of the National Citizens' Committee was held on December 6. Champ Clark, Woodrow Wilson, and William Gibbs McAdoo were speakers, as were such prominent Republicans as Andrew D. White, Senator Boies Penrose, and Jacob Gould Schurman, president of Cornell University.[82] The *American Hebrew* editorialized:

> With the opening of Congress on Monday and the great non-sectarian demonstration at Carnegie Hall on Wednesday evening, the agitation for the abrogation of the treaty of 1832 received notable encouragement. It seems as if the last act in the drama is about to be played. The resolutions of Mr. Sulzer and Mr. Culberson are now before the legislators of the country backed by a demonstration of public opinion that extends from California to Maine among Jews and non-Jews. The question now is: having been given a convincing demonstration of the nation-wide sentiment behind the movement, what will President Taft do in the premises? Will he be content to let Congress force action on his part, or will he take the reins of government firmly in his hands in leading the sentiment of the nation and give notice to Russia of the termination of the treaty?[83]

A further bit of sensationalism helpful to the cause of abrogation was added in late November and early December. On December 17 a delegation of New York Jewish leaders—including Schiff, Daniel Guggenheim, Max J. Kohler, Louis Marshall, and Oscar Straus—met with New York's Senators Root and O'Gorman to ascertain their views on the abrogation question and to ask for their support of the resolutions before Congress. According to the *American Hebrew*'s account of the conference:

> Before the conference adjourned, Mr. Jacob H. Schiff arose and made the sensational and startling charge that while President Taft was assuring representative Jews here that Ambassador Rockhill was making every effort to obtain a change of attitude from Russia, in the matter of the passport, Mr. Rockhill in a public interview was saying that he considered the interests of American business superior to the passport question, which he considered of no importance. Mr. Schiff also charged that Russia in its endeavor to create favorable sentiment for its wrongful interpretation of the Treaty, had influenced Mr. John Hays Hammond to organize a syndicate of American capitalists to work in Russia, with the view of using Mr. Hammond's friendship with President Taft for its own ends.

Hammond responded that Schiff had "done more to accentuate the troubles of his co-religionists in Russia than any other one man because of his boastful statements that the money of Jewish bankers had made it possible for Japan to wage a successful war against Russia."[84] Schiff's charges against Rockhill, however, were substantiated by Jewish writer Herman Bernstein who described interviews he had held with Rockhill in May of 1911, in which Rockhill had told him of the folly of raising the passport question as an issue because of its effect on American commercial and financial relations with Russia. Rockhill also had discussed Hammond's projects in Russia, according to Bernstein.[85]

In December, American Jewish leaders testified before the House Committee on Foreign Affairs in behalf of the Sulzer resolution, and on December 15, 1911, the House of Representatives passed the resolution with but one dissenting vote. The following day Congressman Sulzer wrote Henry Green a "personal" letter:

The first thing Monday morning, I wish you and Mr.
McAdoo and all your friends on the [National Citizens']
Committee would send a telegram to Senator Cullom,
Senator Lodge, Senator Bacon, and the other mem-
bers on the Committee on Foreign Affairs [*sic*] in the
Senate, to report favorably without amendment, the
Sulzer resolution to terminate the Russian treaty and
pass it through the Senate before the holiday recess.
This is very important.[86]

In response to a letter of appreciation from Green, Sulzer wrote:
"We have won the fight, and it is a great victory for human
rights."[87] The fight in the Senate was anticlimactic. When it
became evident that the Senate would act in conformity with
the decision of the House, Senator Henry Cabot Lodge so informed President Taft and Taft took steps to provide, as of
December 31, 1911, notice of the termination of the treaty.
The president, however, sought to put a favorable face on the
whole affair for his administration, writing to Simon Wolf that
in giving notice of abrogation he had taken "the only course
that was open to me after the negotiations had exhausted every
resource of diplomacy."[88] Relations between Schiff and Taft,
which had become severely strained since the February meeting, now became somewhat more cordial. Schiff wrote Senator
Lodge on December 21: "I had an opportunity yesterday to
talk with the President on the position as it has now resulted,
and he appears to be entirely pleased and satisfied."[89]

Although Simon Wolf expressed disquietude over the abrogation of the 1832 treaty with Russia, most Jewish leaders were
jubilant. Marshall wrote to Wolf that he considered the abrogation "the most glorious victory that has ever been won in the
history of the world."[90] For Schiff the success in the treaty
fight was proof of the effectiveness of the American Jewish
Committee. As he wrote to his son-in-law Felix Warburg:

It has heretofore been frequently asked, what is the
reason for the existence of this committee. We think,
after the recent American Jewish passport episode,

the success of which is mainly due to the American
Jewish Committee, this query is answered—the committee, in short, represents and looks after, both na-
tionally and internationally, most of the matters
which concern the American citizen of Jewish extraction, and because of this every Hebrew irrespective of
his faith attachment, should cooperate with and aid
the Committee.[91]

To others, Schiff again reiterated his belief that the effect of
the abrogation would not be confined to American citizens of
Jewish extraction who sought to travel to Russia. As he wrote
to Israel Zangwill, he believed that now "better things are
likely to be in store for our hard-driven Russian coreligionists."
It was inconceivable to Schiff that the international publicity
which had been given to the whole abrogation affair in the
United States would not lead some of the European powers
to seek a similar removal of restrictions on the travel of their
Jewish subjects to Russia, and if so, "the Russian autocracy
will find it necessary to change its own attitude toward its unhappy Jewish subjects."[92] But this would require the application of pressure upon their governments by European Jews
equivalent to the successful campaign of American Jews. As
Schiff wrote a European coreligionist:

What . . . is now needed more than anything else to
make the action which our government has taken as
effective as we would wish it to become, is that the
government and people of England, of France, and of
Germany, all or either, follow the lead of the United
States and show to Russia that it can no longer treat
international public opinion as a negligible quantity.
I know conditions, especially political, are entirely
different in Europe from what they are here, but let
me remind you that even here, less than a year ago, it
appeared as though we were fighting for a forlorn hope,
and that a handful of men have brought about the
result which has now been so gloriously attained; and

> let me express the hope particularly at this time of
> the Maccabaean festival that there will be some
> Maccabaeans in Europe who will take up this fight and
> help to carry to a conclusion what we have here begun.[93]

As with the Rumanian matter, however, the expectations of the Americans that European Jews would be able to induce their governments to follow the American lead was a forlorn hope. Once again the full force of an American initiative was lost because European governments did not join in.

In the 1912 presidential election Woodrow Wilson, who had strongly supported the abrogation movement, was matched against the reelection bid of President Taft and the attempt by Theodore Roosevelt to recapture the presidency as a third party candidate on the Progressive Party ticket. The competing candidacies of Wilson and Roosevelt presented a difficult choice for American Jewish voters. Another difficult choice for them was between William Sulzer, who had done yeoman work in the abrogation movement as a congressman, and Oscar Straus for the governorship of New York. In the end Schiff supported both Wilson and Sulzer, the latter apparently because he feared that a strong showing by Straus (running with Roosevelt on the Progressive ticket) might affect Wilson's chances of carrying the state in the presidential election.[94]

Soon after the election American Jewish leaders were aroused anew by reports that, while the abrogation of the 1832 treaty would be effective with the end of 1912, the terms of the treaty would remain in force under an executive agreement until a new treaty could be negotiated. As Adolf Kraus of the B'nai B'rith put it:

> If it is true that the commercial treaty remains in force
> by executive agreement pending further negotiation,
> then there is going to be a howl from one end of the
> country to the other. The President will be accused of
> giving notice of the abrogation of the treaty for
> political purposes only, with the preconceived design
> to stop Congress from passing the resolution and fool-

ing the people, and our organization will be the laugh-
ing stock of the rest of the people for having believed
that the notice was given in good faith.[95]

Kraus asked Simon Wolf to seek an interview with President
Taft in order to ascertain the facts. Wolf, for his part, had no
doubt that a secret modus vivendi had been worked out between the Russians and Secretary of State Knox, whom Wolf
regarded as "cold-blooded and indifferent." Wolf wrote:

I have been very much aroused over the situation.
Marshall has written a very strong letter direct to the
President, and the President knows my feelings in the
matter. I should not be surprised if a resolution will
be offered in Congress for a categorical answer on the
part of the administration as to what they contemplate
doing in the matter, and to indicate by resolution that
no such modus vivendi will be established as spoken of
in the newspapers.[96]

Wolf wrote to the president that he had been inundated with
wires and letters asking him to see Taft concerning the press
reports of a modus vivendi under which trade relations were
continuing as before the abrogation of the treaty, "thus practically abrogating the abrogation and nullifying the wish of the
American people, who, by a unanimous [sic] vote of their
representatives in both houses of Congress, and by your own
act as executive of the nation, gave plain and unmistakable
notice to the Russian Government that the United States
would no longer tolerate any relations with Russia" unless the
Russians honored American passports in the hands of Jews.
Wolf concluded by saying he had received every assurance from
President-elect Wilson that the latter would resume no treaty
relations with Russia until and unless the passport question was
settled satisfactorily. Wolf now called upon Taft to make a
similar statement concerning the remaining months of his
presidency.[97]

Taft responded to Wolf's letter by writing that he expected
to make no agreements with Russia. What the administration
had been doing, he told Wolf, was to review the existing treaties,
statutes, and international laws applicable to the situation. Taft
told Wolf he did not "expect to change by any agreement or
so-called modus vivendi the status quo which the abrogation
of the treaty will leave on the first of January by ceasing to
have effect."[98] With this the fight for abrogation of the treaty
of 1832 was ended, and the new question became whether a
new treaty would be negotiated and, if so, what form it would
take.

While Schiff's Galveston movement was seeking to prevent
restrictive immigration policies by channeling the large
Russian Jewish immigration into the interior of the United
States, the struggle was going on at closer quarters in Washington, where American Jewish leaders including Marshall, Cyrus
Sulzberger, Max Kohler, Judge Leon Sanders, and Jacob Singer
fought against proposed restrictive immigration legislation.
American Jewish leaders opposed legislation that would provide
for the deportation of aliens who took advantage of their resi-
dence in the United States to conspire for the "violent overthrow of a foreign government recognized by the United
States," and also fought against the imposition of any literacy
requirement upon immigrants.[99]

American Jews also became concerned with the fate of Jews
living in the Balkan states during the wars in that troubled part
of Europe in 1912-1913. In January of 1913 the American
Jewish Committee urged the lame duck President Taft and his
secretary of state to "make representations to those concerned
in the war and to the European powers, in order that the status
and rights of the Jews who might be transferred from the jurisdiction of the Ottoman Empire to that of the several Balkan
States, might be protected."[100] In March representatives of the
American Jewish Committee conferred with President Wilson.
They requested the government to bring to the attention of
three influential groups—the delegates to the London Peace
Conference, the British Foreign Office, and ambassadors of the
European powers in London—the desire of the United States
that any peace treaty ending the Balkan Wars should include

a provision securing to all peoples of every race and religion protection for their lives, liberty, and property, as well as equality of citizenship and freedom of religion.[101] The State Department later informed the committee that instructions had been sent to the American ambassador in London to express to the British Foreign Office "that the United States would regard with satisfaction the inclusion in any agreement that might ultimately be concluded in regard to the settlement of the affairs in the Balkan Peninsula of a provision assuring the full enjoyment of civil and religious liberty to the inhabitants of the territory in question, without question of race or creed." The American ministers to the Balkan governments had similarly been instructed to inform those countries of the American interest in such stipulations. The Balkan states asserted, however, that such legal protection already existed in each nation concerned and to make further stipulations in the peace treaty would be "superfluous." Louis Marshall, president of the American Jewish Committee, found "the action of our Government is most gratifying, resulting in the assurances of the conferees, that the Jewish citizens of the annexed territories are to be accorded the same consideration as that which other citizens residing therein are to receive."[102]

This was considerably more hopeful than the American Jewish Committee had any right to be from the replies of the Balkan states, and it did not quiet demands among other American Jews that those rights be stipulated in the peace treaty.[103] Others believed that the State Department had blundered in taking such an initiative and inviting the obvious reply. The *American Hebrew*, however, defended the unsuccessful initiative as "up to the best American tradition" and according to the model set by Secretary of State Hay in 1902. The newspaper found it "to the credit of our Government that it is willing to make tactical mistakes rather than to prove untrue" to its humanitarian ideals.[104] Less than six years later Europe would be the site of another peace conference, in which the United States would be a participant, and from which American and other Jews would obtain more satisfactory results.

NOTES

1. Schiff to Adler, March 27, 1907, Cyrus Adler Papers, American Jewish Historical Society Library.

2. *American Hebrew*, March 29, 1907.

3. Ibid., April 5, 1907.

4. Ibid., April 26, 1907.

5. Zosa Szajkowski, "Paul Nathan, Lucien Wolf, Jacob H. Schiff and the Jewish Revolutionary Movements in Eastern Europe, 1903-1917," 2 pts. *Jewish Social Studies* 29 (January 1967), 2: 20-21.

6. Montagu to Sulzberger, March 20, 1908, National Committee for the Relief of Sufferers of Russian Massacres Papers (hereafter cited as NCRSRM), American Jewish Historical Library.

7. Jacob to Sulzberger, April 13, 1908, and Stettauer to Schiff, July 10, 1908, NCRSRM.

8. "Minutes of the American Jewish Committee, meeting of the executive committee, May 29, 1907," in Louis Marshall Papers, American Jewish Archives.

9. Quoted in Lauterbach to Straus, January 20, 1908, Oscar S. Straus Papers.

10. Straus to Lauterbach, January 22, 1908, Straus Papers.

11. Straus to Lauterbach, January 25, 1908, Straus Papers.

12. Naomi Cohen, "The Abrogation of the Russo-American Treaty of 1832," *Jewish Social Studies* 35 (January 1963): 6.

13. Schiff to Wise, November 17, 1910, Jacob H. Schiff Papers.

14. Sulzberger to Roosevelt, May 18, 1908, *Records of the Department of State Relating to Internal Affairs of Russia and the Soviet Union, 1910-1929*, National Archives Microfilm Publication M316, reel 93 (hereafter cited as DS M316/93).

15. "MH" to Bacon, June 1, 1908, memorandum in *Numerical and Minor Files of the Department of State, 1906-1910*, National Archives Microfilm Publication M862, reel 115 (hereafter cited as DS M862/115).

16. Root to Sulzberger, June 4, 1908, copy in Straus Papers.

17. Sulzberger to Root, June 17, 1908, copy in Straus Papers.

18. Schiff to Taft, July 24, 1908, Schiff Papers.

19. Schiff to Taft, August 3, 1908, Schiff Papers.

20. Wolf to Cowen, September 24, 1908, Philip H. Cowen Papers.

21. Schiff to Root, September 23, 1908, Schiff Papers.

22. Letter from Bryan of October 8, 1908, printed in *American Hebrew*, October 16, 1908.

23. Root to Schiff, October 19, 1908, Schiff Papers.

24. Schiff to Adler, October 21, 1908, Schiff Papers.

25. *American Hebrew*, October 23, 1908.

26. Ibid.

27. Schiff to Cassel, November 11, 1908, Schiff Papers.

28. Friedenwald to Straus [December 1908], and Friedenwald to Straus, December 9, 1908, Straus Papers.

29. *American Hebrew*, March 5, 1909.

30. Ibid., March 12, 1909.

31. Sarasohn and Son (*Jewish Daily News*) to Taft, February 9, 1910, DS M316/93.

32. Cohen, "Abrogation," pp. 9-10; Sulzberger to Taft, February 24, 1910, DS M316/93.

33. Knox to Taft, February 26, 1910, DS M316/93.

34. Knox to Rockhill, March 3, 1910, DS M316/93.

35. Rockhill to Knox, March 7, 1910, DS M316/93.

36. Rockhill to Knox, March 9, 1910, DS M316/93.

37. Schiff to Sulzberger, March 31, 1910, Schiff Papers.

38. Cohen, "Abrogation," makes no mention of the president's invitation or of any meeting.

39. Rockhill to Knox, April 20, 1910, DS M316/93.

40. Cohen, "Abrogation," pp. 12-13.

41. Adee to Young, July 13, 1910, DS M316/93.

42. Schiff to Taft, October 20, 1910, Schiff Papers.

43. Schiff to Wise, November 17, 1910, Schiff Papers.

44. Schiff to Feinberg, December 2, 1910, Schiff Papers.

45. Schiff to Greer, October 7, 1910, Schiff Papers.

46. Schiff to Feinberg, December 2, 1910, Schiff Papers.

47. Friedenwald to Sulzberger, December 20, 1910, Marshall Papers.

48. Cohen, "Abrogation," p. 14.

49. Ibid.

50. Reprinted in *American Hebrew*, January 20, 1911.

51. Quoted in Cohen, "Abrogation," pp. 19-20.

52. Scott to Knox, February 1, 1911, DS M316/93.

53. Schiff to Adler, January 27, 1911, Schiff Papers.

54. Simon Wolf, *The Presidents I Have Known* (Washington, D.C., 1918), p. 293.

55. Charles Reznikoff, *Louis Marshall: Champion of Liberty* (Philadelphia, 1957), 2: 77.

56. Wolf, *Presidents*, pp. 294-304.

57. Reznikoff, *Marshall*, 2: 84-85.

58. The account is in a memorandum corrected by Schiff, enclosed with Schiff to Wolf, October 16, 1916, Simon Wolf Papers, and published in Wolf, *Presidents*, pp. 309-10.

59. Taft to Bannard, June 17, 1911, Schiff Papers.

60. Reznikoff, *Marshall*, 2: 86; Schiff asked Wolf to leave this out of his published account. See Schiff to Wolf, October 16, 1916, Wolf Papers.

61. Reznikoff, *Marshall*, 2: 86; Wolf, *Presidents*, pp. 309-10.

62. Schiff to Taft, February 20, 1911, in Cyrus M. Adler, *Jacob H. Schiff: His Life and Letters*, 2 vols. (Garden City, N.Y., 1928), 2: 147-49.

63. Taft to Schiff, February 23, 1911, copy in Wolf Papers.

64. Friedenwald to Marshall, March 8, 1911, Marshall Papers.

65. Sulzberger to Kahn, April 25, 1911, Otto Kahn Papers, Princeton University.

66. Schiff to Ochs, April 28, 1911, Schiff Papers.

67. Schiff to Nathan, March 10, 1911, Schiff Papers.

68. Brylawski to Friedenwald, May 22 and July 6, 1911, Marshall Papers.

69. Schiff to Kraus, March 24, 1911, Schiff Papers.

70. Kraus to Schiff, April 3, 1911, Schiff Papers.

71. *American Hebrew*, March 31, 1911.

72. Wolf, *Presidents*, p. 317.

73. Brylawski to Friedenwald, July 27, 1911, Marshall Papers.

74. Culberson to Knox, July 26, 1911, copy in Marshall Papers.

75. Brylawski to Sulzberger, August 3, 1911, copy in Marshall Papers.

76. See material in Box 1, National Citizens' Committee Papers (hereafter cited as NCC), American Jewish Historical Society Library.

77. Green to Frye, September 21, 1911, ibid.

78. Friedenwald to Sulzberger, February 28, 1911, copy in Marshall Papers.

79. Green to McAdoo, October 6, 1911, NCC.

80. McAdoo to Marshall, November 18, 1911, NCC.

81. Green to Robinson, November 21, 1911, NCC.

82. Ibid.

83. *American Hebrew*, December 8, 1911.

84. Ibid., November 24, 1911.

85. Ibid., December 1, 1911.

86. Sulzer to Green, December 16, 1911, NCC.

87. Sulzer to Green, December 19, 1911, NCC.

88. Adler, *Schiff*, 2: 151; Taft to Wolf, December 21, 1911, Wolf Papers.

89. Schiff to Lodge, December 21, 1911, in Adler, *Schiff*, 2: 151.

90. Marshall to Wolf, December 19, 1911, in Reznikoff, *Marshall*, 2: 102.

91. Schiff to Warburg, December 29, 1911, Warburg Papers.

92. Schiff to Zangwill, January 2, 1912, Schiff Papers.

93. Schiff to Nathan, December 21, 1911, Schiff Papers.

94. Brisbane (*New York Evening Journal*) to Lewis Straus, October 24, 1912, Straus Papers.

95. Kraus to Wolf, November 21, 1912, Wolf Papers.

96. Wolf to Kraus, November 22, 1912, Wolf Papers.

97. Wolf to Taft, November 12, 1912, Wolf Papers.

98. Taft to Wolf, November 26, 1912, Wolf Papers.

99. Hourwich to Marshall, April 30, 1912, Marshall Papers; Schiff to Kohler, May 2, 1912, Kohler Papers.

100. Marshall statement in *American Hebrew*, August 22, 1913.

101. Ibid. See also *American Jewish Yearbook, 1913-1914*, p. 240.

102. *New York Evening Post* editorial quoted in *American Hebrew*, August 8, 1913.

103. *American Jewish Yearbook, 1913-1914*, p. 240.

104. *American Hebrew*, August 8, 1913.

Epilogue

The outbreak of war in Europe in 1914 created new problems
for American Jewish leaders. Straus, Schiff, and Wolf had all
been born in Germany. Schiff, especially, retained strong business and familial relationships in that country, although he also
had friendships and family members in the Allied countries as
well. One of Schiff's first acts after the outbreak of the war
was to use his influential contacts in Japan in an effort to avert
a Japanese declaration of war against Germany despite Japan's
obligations under its alliance with Great Britain. His effort
was unsuccessful.[1] However, as Zosa Szajkowski has pointed
out, Schiff's attitude toward the belligerents was conditioned
less by his sympathies for one or the other side than by his
undying animosity toward the foremost enemy of international
Jewry, the Russian Empire. As Schiff had sympathized with
Japan in its war with Russia a decade earlier in the hope that a
Russian defeat would bring about the overthrow of the czarist
regime, so he now hoped that a similar result might be obtained
through German military successes on the eastern front. But
instead of wedding himself to the German cause against Russia,
Schiff sought to use the gambit of financial aid to Russia in her
extremity as a device to bring about the final granting of complete civil rights to Russian Jews.[2]

The disruptions caused by the war, meanwhile, had reduced
the flow of immigration to the United States from Europe to
a trickle. American Jewish leaders were now taxed less by the
effort to accommodate new arrivals than by their efforts to
insure that the door would be kept open for immigration once
the war had ended. The passage by Congress of an immigration
bill containing a literacy test meant that, if signed into law by
the president, the first real obstacle would be posed to such
immigration. The bill had passed Congress by a decisive vote,
and Schiff and other American Jewish leaders recognized that
it would be difficult for President Wilson to veto it.[3] Thus
Schiff wrote Wilson to urge him not to sign the bill into law.
He was sure, he told the president, that Wilson opposed the
bill, especially the literacy test which to Schiff was "the most
obnoxious part of the measure which should never be placed
upon the statute books of this country." The enactment of
such a measure, he argued, would bar from the United States
large numbers of the very class of people who had done the
most to build the United States "into the great and strong
nation it now is," and if the traditional policy of the United
States were now changed it would have unfortunate implica-
tions for the nation's future.[4]

Two weeks later President Wilson vetoed the immigration
act, but there was strong pressure within Congress to override
the veto.[5] American Jewish leaders worked to rally opposition
in Congress to such an action since, as Louis Marshall put it,
"The bill is fathered by those who frankly admit that they are
opposed to all immigration. It is a know-nothing measure,
and I have reason to know that it is largely anti-Catholic and
anti-Jewish in its object."[6] Wilson's veto was narrowly sustained, but in 1917 a similar provision was again presented,
and this time the President's veto was overridden. The first significant step had been taken in the direction of restricting
immigration into the United States, and the way was opened
to even more restrictive legislation which would become law
in 1921 and 1924.

Fighting desperately on the immigration front, American
Jewish leaders were all the more sensitive to any prospects that

their past efforts might be undone on another. When rumors persisted that the Wilson administration had decided to enter into a new commercial treaty with Russia, Schiff and Simon Wolf quickly protested against any such action. Schiff reminded the President that he had been "a powerful factor among the forces who compelled" the abrogation of the 1832 treaty, and he therefore found it impossible to believe that Wilson would now enter into a new treaty with the Russians that would not correct the passport issue. Even if the administration proceeded with such a treaty, Schiff told the president that he would be unsuccessful in getting the support of the Senate for ratification. What was more, Schiff said, such an action by Wilson's administration would almost certainly "alienate from the Democratic Party an important part of our citizenship, which would not consent without the most vigorous protest, that American citizens of the Jewish faith be placed in a separate class as far as our relations with Russia, or any other foreign power are concerned."[7] Wilson quickly responded that he was "anxious to enter into and conclude such a treaty, but you may be sure that it will not be done without a satisfactory adjustment of the great question to which you allude."[8] No treaty was negotiated with the Russians.

The suffering of European Jewry under the wartime conditions, especially on the eastern front where the German-Russian conflict raged over their lands, led to relief efforts by American Jews beginning late in 1914.[9] But despite the suffering American Jews were hopeful that improved conditions would result from Jewish sacrifices during the war. They looked to the revealed weakness of the Russian Empire in its conflict with Germany and to the new conditions likely to be forged at the peace conference at the conclusion of the war. As Schiff observed in September 1915, he derived "sincere pleasure" from the prospect that Germany and Austria appeared "to be succeeding in putting an end to wretched tsarism and I hope and pray that the Russian autocracy will now be given its real death blow."[10] Louis Marshall, too, was optimistic that the situation of Russian Jews would be improved after the war, although he confessed he had no real grounds for his belief.[11] Simon Wolf was hopeful that Wilson's leadership at the peace conference would contribute to this end. He told the president that at no time in the history of the world had there been such an opportunity "to secure equal rights for the Jews in Russia as at the time when terms of peace shall be agreed upon by the belligerent powers." With Wilson's "wise and sane statesmanship" the United States could be "a dominating factor in the solution of this great and important question." The solution to the problems of European Jewry would not only "be conducive to the welfare and prosperity of the people in question," he told Wilson, "but aid very materially the citizens of the United States." He therefore urged the president to give "due consideration" to the problem in preparing for the peace conference which would come once the guns had been stilled.[12]

As one of the leading investment bankers in the United States, Schiff continued during the early war years to refuse to participate in any loans of which all or a portion of the proceeds were destined for Imperial Russia. According to his biographer, Cyrus Adler, Schiff protested to the president and to members of the Senate the granting of any credits to that country.[13] Throughout 1915 Schiff opposed the flotation of any Allied loan in the United States in which Russia participated and withdrew his opposition only when Russia pulled out of the loan.[14] Even then Schiff refused to allow Kuhn, Loeb and Company to participate in the floating of the loan.[15] In November he wrote to Max Warburg in Germany:

> Recently Russia has tried to obtain a large acceptance credit here through our banks—there is talk of sixty million dollars. However, I got wind of it very early and have succeeded thus far in getting a considerable number of Trust Companies and bankers to decline participation. That I shall be able to frustrate the endeavor completely is not likely; but I shall not refrain, if an opportunity arises, from coming out publicly against Russian financing—even for Russian banks. This I have avoided thus far in order not to arouse too

much ill will, particularly on the part of Morgan's and
the City Bank, who are the chief offenders.[16]

When, in late February of 1916, Schiff learned that the negotiations for a Russian loan virtually had been concluded, he
did come out publicly against such financing, calling it "one
of the most insidious pieces of financing ever done in this
country." Whoever participated in such a transaction, he warned,
would "have no cause to be proud of the help it is going to
give the Russian Government." He added:

> If brutality and inhumanity have ever run riot, certain-
> ly the Russian Government has to bear the charge that
> it has been the master tyrant in this respect. That such
> a Government should be helped by American bankers
> is truly a reason for the American people to bow their
> heads in shame and mortification. I feel quite convinced
> that at some time those who shall become responsible
> for this financing will have cause to regret it.[17]

Schiff received "quite a number of letters and personal expressions of approbation" for his public utterances in opposition
to the Russian credit, but he was convinced that the loan
would go through despite his opposition, "for the commissions
Russia is willing to pay are no doubt too tempting."[18] Schiff
would not, however, give up the struggle. He still believed in
"constant agitation in the press throughout the country" in
opposition to loans to Russia, and even if this did not keep
bankers from underwriting such loans, he said, "it may have
the consequence of keeping the public from eventually taking
the loan off the hands of the contractors, who would then get
stuck with it, which would be good."[19] In June of 1916, shortly
before a Russian loan was to be floated, Schiff sought to have
a letter printed in the *New York Times* over his signature
"going into the merits or rather demerits of the loan, and into
the dangers of opening the New York market to Russian securities," but the publisher, his coreligionist Adolph Ochs, refused

to print it.[20] Schiff, however, obtained some consolation from the belief that the loan "has not been at all successful, although the issuing banks claim differently, but I have thus far not found anyone down here who showed the least interest in the loan."[21]

The interest of American Jewish leaders like Schiff and Straus in the form the post-war world would take also led them to participate in the League to Enforce Peace. The League, one of dozens of such societies throughout the world, was an organization of Americans who sought the creation of an international organization that would promote peace and justice in the world. The possibilities of such a supranational organization as a device for promoting the human rights of Jews in eastern Europe and elsewhere were obvious. Throughout the war years the League to Enforce Peace, in cooperation with similar societies in Europe, kept proposals for such a "league of nations" before the American people. Both Schiff and Straus played prominent roles in the League to Enforce Peace. When the League sought in May of 1916 to raise a fund to finance the promotion of the organization and the task of national organization, Schiff and Straus were members of the fund raising committee and Schiff's personal contribution was $10,000.[22] Schiff, however, differed from most others in the organization in seeking a role for the League in bringing about peace as soon as possible. In a speech of November 24, 1916, Schiff suggested that rather than waiting for the war to be fought to its bloody end before seeking to attain its ends, the League should work to bring the war to an early conclusion.[23] Schiff's speech brought attacks from Great Britain accusing him of "intriguing for peace for Germany's benefit."[24]

Such controversy was created by Schiff's position that the Board of Management of the League met late in the month and issued a statement pointing out that the League was not a "stop the war movement," and that it was not committed to the views expressed by its individual members. The president of the League to Enforce Peace, former president William Howard Taft, said additionally:

> Mr. Schiff who is prominent in the league, is strongly
> in favor of steps being taken to bring about peace in
> Europe, but those are his individual views and not those
> of the league. . . . From the beginning we have been
> careful to limit this movement to one the purpose of
> which is to bring about an agreement among the na-
> tions after the present war which we hope will make
> impossible other wars in the future. As to Mr. Schiff,
> he is one of the strongest and most valuable members,
> and the resolution in no wise reflects upon him.[25]

Schiff, meanwhile, had become active in yet another organiza-
tion, one which came closer to sharing his views. On November
25, 1916, Schiff with approximately fifty others—including
Oswald Garrison Villard, Hamilton Holt, David Starr Jordan,
Rabbi Stephen S. Wise, Amos Pinchot, Scott Nearing, Theodore
Marburg, and Lillian Wald—met to form the New York branch
of the American Neutral Conference Committee, the purpose
of which was "to carry into effect many of the plans of the
American Neutral Conference Committee for arousing the
American public to a sense of what it may contribute toward
stopping the war." Contemplated were the employment of
speakers to preach peace from city to city and the formulation of a petition to the president, asking him to take steps to
mediate an end to the war in Europe.[26]

Diverse American Jewish organizations began to discuss the
question of what position international Jewry should take at
the peace conference after the war. Pressure for the convening
of a congress of American Jewish organizations grew in part
from this desire but also from the dissatisfaction of many
American Jewish groups, especially those representative of the
more recent immigrants from eastern Europe, with the leading
role which the American Jewish Committee had assumed for
itself in speaking for American Jewry. The established American Jewish leaders like Schiff, Straus, and Wolf responded
predictably in opposing such a congress as premature at best.
As Oscar Straus put it, "emphatically and strongly," he regarded it "as the height of folly to insist on holding" such a

congress for as long as the war continued.[27] Simon Wolf felt
such a conference would "do more injury than possible good,"
since "shooting off our powder now leaves us with blank car-
tridges when the time for action shall come" at the peace conference. "We must," Wolf counseled, "handle this whole subject
diplomatically with great forbearance, and yet affirmative
vigilance, pushing the other fellow forward as an advocate for
human rights and subordinating our own feelings to win out."
Wolf's primary concern was with the question of securing
equality for Jews in Russia and Rumania.[28]

Schiff, a fervent anti-Zionist, opposed the idea of a congress
in large part because the principal agitation for it seemed to
him to emanate from members of the Zionist organization.[29]
In Schiff's view, the holding of such a congress could lead
only to "the coming of political anti-Zionism into this land,"
since there was in his opinion "no room in the United States
for any other Congress upon national lines, except the American Congress." He feared such a congress as the Zionists sought
to organize would lead Americans to regard the Jews amongst
them "as an entirely separate class, whose interests are different from those" of other Americans and who were "Jews first
and Americans second."[30] The American Jewish Committee,
however, was led steadily in the direction of a compromise
with the Zionist and other elements until American entry into
the war provided an opportunity for the older American Jewish
leaders to delay the holding of any congress until after the war
was ended. Simon Wolf solicited the support of President Wilson
for such a delay, writing to him on June 11, 1917:

> I would like very much indeed to have your opinion—
> confidentially if you choose, otherwise for publica-
> tion—as to the feasibility and practicability of American
> citizens of Jewish faith holding a congress at this
> present juncture. Personally, I am utterly opposed to
> it. I think it is bound to embarrass the government and
> thwart the very objects for which the congress is to be
> convened. . . . Besides this, the reckless utterances of
> some of the delegates to this congress might seriously

affect the situation and instead of helping the Jews
or the United States, might have the reverse effect.[31]

Wilson agreed with Wolf and the congress was postponed once
again.[32] An accommodation was reached among American
Jewish leaders, however, and the American Jewish Congress
was finally convened with the support of Schiff and Straus
after the war had ended, in mid-December 1918.[33] The American Jewish Congress was represented at the Paris Peace Conference by a delegation headed by Julian Mack and Louis
Marshall.[34] At Schiff's insistence the American Jewish Committee was represented separately at the peace conference by
Dr. Cyrus Adler who, in Schiff's words, was there to aid "the
Jews of Eastern Europe in presenting their claims to the
Peace Conference."[35]

In the meantime, however, events in Russia had brought
both hope and despair to American Jewish leaders. The March
1917 revolution in that country brought instant support from
American Jews. Jacob Schiff, who throughout his years of
banking had consistently refused to handle Russian financing,
now moved quickly to make his firm's resources available to
the Allied powers, including the new government in Russia.
After the Provisional government had been established he
wrote to a banker in Russia:

> May I say to you that nothing would give me greater
> satisfaction than to be of advantage to new Russia in
> all or any opportunities that may present themselves.
> . . . Meantime, in order to practically demonstrate my
> own warm interest, I have decided to make a subscrip-
> tion to the "Liberty Loan" just issued by the new
> Russian Government, and I am cabling you to sub-
> scribe for me Rbls. 1,000,000 par value to this loan,
> which I understand is being issued at the price of 85
> per cent.[36]

Schiff, Straus, Marshall, and Henry Morgenthau also conferred
with the secretary of state in early May of 1917 concerning a

possible appeal for large scale subscriptions to the Russian liberty loan but apparently received no encouragement in that quarter.[37] Schiff rejoiced at the news that the new Provisional government had removed all disabilities from the Jews in Russia, writing to Lillian Wald that it was

> like a miracle, and I never expected that during my own
> life so complete and bloodless a revolution could occur
> in the dominion of the Romanoffs, nor that this . . .
> dynasty could be so suddenly and so completely ended.
> I am a bit anxious that all may not go as smoothly as
> we hope, and that there may be some upheaval yet in
> Russia, but the old order of things will never return,
> no matter what may happen.[38]

Prophetic words, indeed!

Schiff also was active with Louis Marshall in a Russian Jewish Emancipation Banquet held in May 1917 under the auspices of the American Jewish Friends of Free Russia and the American Committee for the Encouragement of Democratic Government in Russia.[39] When a delegation representing the new Russian government visited New York City, Schiff consented to serve as a member of the official welcoming committee arranged by the mayor.[40] A reception was held for the Russian delegation at Lillian Wald's Henry Street settlement, of which Schiff wrote afterward to Miss Wald:

> When I came home on Monday evening I said to Mrs.
> Schiff that I had seldom seen so happy and gratified
> an expression on your face as on Monday afternoon,
> and that it looked to me you felt that the reception
> to the ambassador of New Russia was a heavenly re-
> ward to you for years of unselfish efforts in imbuing
> with courage and confidence for better things to come
> those who were so sacrificingly struggling in Russian
> darkness in order to reach the light. I am sure every-
> body who was at the unique gathering at the house in
> Henry Street—the ambassador, the members of the

commission, your guests, and the throng outside—
caught the spirit of this remarkable occasion, of which
sometime I hope a permanent record may be made in
a new addition of the "House in Henry Street."[41]

Such was the enthusiasm of American Jews for the Provisional
government. But the November revolution of the Bolsheviks
was not greeted with approval by Schiff. His enthusiasm for
the investment in Russian liberty bonds quickly evaporated
and he was glad when his agent in Russia was able to strike
the subscription from the books. He still had hope for the
course of the revolution, however, writing his banker friend
there that Americans were intensely interested in the struggle
through which Russia was passing, and "we hope with you
that when the present fury has spent itself, Russia will emerge
stronger and healthier than before—a country of liberty and
democracy."[42]

Throughout the war years American Jewish leaders remained
concerned with the suffering of Jews in the European war zones,
primarily in Poland. To provide relief for their coreligionists in
Europe, American Jews launched fund raising efforts in which
President Wilson and members of Congress were invited to
participate. American Jewish leaders, with the end of the war
in sight and an independent Polish nation clearly to be
established, bent their efforts to assuring Polish Jews equal
rights under the new Polish government.[43] It was Straus, who
was in Paris representing the League to Enforce Peace, who
"formulated the conditions which we shall insist upon as part
of the condition of the new Poland." American Jewish leaders
were equally concerned that minority rights also should be
incorporated in any treaties with the other new states being
created in Europe, as well as in the enlarged territories of existing states.[44] As Adolf Kraus of the B'nai B'rith put it to President Wilson:

> While the war was pending, I received requests from
> leading Jews of those countries to appeal when the
> war should cease, and the peace conference meet, to

you who have taken such a broad and humane view of
the European situation, not only to aid in securing the
small nations the right of self-government, but also
secure to all inhabitants of those lands equal rights
regardless of their religious belief and that should such
a tribunal of nations be established, power to enforce
such rights be granted to such tribunal. I have hesitated,
Mr. President, to submit such an appeal to you, because I felt sure that you would, on your own initiative,
insist that justice be done to all of the people. My
apology for addressing you at this time . . . is that I
owe it as a duty to those for whom I speak. I am confident that it is unnecessary for me to submit facts
showing how essential it is for the future safety and
happiness of my co-religionists that the allied powers
consider their situation.[45]

The authority possessed by the peace conference could also
be used, as Louis Marshall perceived, to calm the anti-Semitism
which was now reasserting itself in the unstable conditions of
armistice Europe. Writing Wilson of his fears of pogroms in
Poland and Rumania, Marshall told the president that he
recognized the difficulties created by the "extraordinary conditions" existing in the eastern European countries, but that
he felt if Wilson would give expression publicly to his "abhor-
rence of these outbreaks of religious and racial prejudice," it
would "go far to thwart the plans of those who may seek to
profit politically or otherwise by these wanton attacks on the
Jews." Poland and Rumania, he pointed out, looked to the
peace conference for their political independence and for
the expansion of their boundaries. The goodwill of the United
States was important to them. Thus a public expression by
Wilson warning those countries that "persistence in anti-
Semitic activity will be regarded as creating an obstacle to the
giving of the recognition desired cannot fail to make a deep
impression." Marshall recounted for the president the course
of talks which were being held between American Jewish representatives and Polish leaders. The Poles had made no favorable

response despite the attempts of American Jewish leaders to bring about the termination of an anti-Jewish boycott in that country. Now Marshall sought to enlist the support of the United States government in bringing the Polish leaders to heel. He suggested that the Polish leaders be made to recognize that "their aspirations for a new Poland cannot receive sympathetic consideration until they first give evidence that they are possessed with that spirit of justice and righteousness which is essential to the establishment of a free and independent government."[46]

Simon Wolf also pressed, by a letter of the same date, for action by Wilson to eliminate the persecution of Jews in Poland and Rumania.[47] The president concluded, however, that such a public pronouncement as Marshall, Wolf, and others sought from him would be "unwise." He did not believe that he should attempt "leadership in too many ways," he told the American Jewish leaders, and preferred to wait until there were opportunities "to impress upon the peace council the serious aspects of the very great and appealing problem on which you dwell, and I shall deem it a privilege to exercise such influence as I can."[48]

American Jewish leaders, of course, had counted on the postwar peace conference to be the tribunal for bringing Russia to the bar of justice for its treatment of Jews and for ensuring their civil rights in that country after the war. The events of 1917 in Russia, however, thwarted their plans. The overthrow of the Romanov dynasty in the March revolution eliminated what American Jews had regarded as the principal source of Jewish oppression in Russia. The institution of a moderately liberal government, fighting in league with the United States against Germany, was greeted with hope by American Jewish leaders. The Bolshevik revolution—which overthrew the moderate Kerensky government and made a separate peace with Germany—meant that the older Jewish leaders like Schiff, Straus, and Wolf were now confronted with a government which, however much it might appeal to the radical elements within American Jewry, was anathema to them. What was worse, from the standpoint of international protection of

Russian Jewish rights, was the fact that the Bolshevik government was not a participant in the Paris Peace Conference and therefore could not be required by the international agreements reached there to extend full civil rights without regard to race or religion.

Still, the traditional Jewish disabilities in Rumania and in Russia's former Polish domains were now under the jurisdiction of the peace conference. The new "succession" states to be carved from the former territories of the Russian and Austro-Hungarian empires also might be forced to include provisions in treaties or in their constitutions to outlaw religious and racial persecution. Moreover, American Jewish leaders, as they viewed the civil wars raging in Russia between the Bolsheviks and counter-revolutionary forces, could not but view the Bolsheviks as at least a more acceptable alternative to the rightist forces, since it was in the areas controlled by the latter that anti-Semitic outrages were most pronounced.[49] In addition to pressing the peace conference for actions favorable to international Jewry, however, Straus and other American Jewish leaders in Paris were also monitoring the day-to-day situation in central and eastern Europe and bringing pressure to bear on the governments there whenever evidence of anti-Semitic actions surfaced.[50] These efforts were supported by Jewish leaders in the United States, including Jacob Schiff. On May 21, 1919, for example, a mass meeting was held in New York's Madison Square Garden to protest the atrocities against Jews in Poland. Schiff not only participated in the protest but also sent a cablegram of nearly 2,000 words to President Wilson in Paris which described American outrage at the incidents in Poland and the Ukraine.[51] One of Wilson's top campaign aides, Gavin McNab of California, was sufficiently concerned that he asked Wilson if he could not by some direct action rebuke the Poles for their behavior.[52]

The efforts of American Jewish leaders like Louis Marshall, Judge Julian Mack, Felix Frankfurter, Oscar Straus, and others were rewarded at Paris by the inclusion of what they regarded as satisfactory provisions in the treaties approved there. As Marshall reported the fruits of their efforts:

About the time this letter reaches you, the news of
the Polish treaty will have reached you. We are all de-
lighted. There is not one dissenting voice among the
members of our committee. . . . I would not take a
million dollars for the satisfaction. We had anxious
days. It was a fight down to the last minute. Poland,
Rumania, Greece, Czechoslovakia, and Yugoslavia
combined on the theory that the treaties would constitute an invasion of their sovereign rights. I was in
constant communication with the President and was
informed through several sources that he said that
there was no occasion for anxiety. . . . The other
treaties will follow the Polish without question. The
only changes required will be in the definition of
citizenship, and the Rumanian treaty which will be
in good shape.[53]

Late in July of 1919 Simon Wolf expressed to the president
his own gratitude over the results that had been achieved at
Paris:

Personally and officially, as the representative of the
Independent Order of B'nai B'rith, and as chairman of
the Board of Delegates of the Union of American Hebrew
Congregations, I take great pleasure in thanking and
congratulating you for the outcome, as reported, in
securing equal rights for the peoples of such countries
as have heretofore been denied. During your entire
administration you have promptly answered every
appeal to use your good offices at the Peace Conference. Your repeated assurances made to me, as evidenced
in the published correspondence, have been redeemed,
and the dawn of a better day has at last been ushered
in for my long-suffering coreligionists. This is doubly
gratifying to have an American and a Christian work
for the accomplishment so essential to the happiness
of all peoples.[54]

By the end of the summer of 1919, then, most of what American Jewish leaders had sought to achieve between 1890 and 1914 seemed accomplished. Despite the continued civil war raging in Russia, and the presence of anti-Semitic atrocities in the Ukraine and other areas under the control of rightists, the hated Romanov dynasty had been deposed, and in Bolshevik-ruled areas of Russia there were few signs of overt anti-Semitism. The removal of all discriminations against Jews in Russia on the basis of ethnic, religious, or social grounds by the Provisional government after the March revolution had been confirmed by the Bolsheviks in November with the promulgation of the Declaration of Rights of Peoples, which formally abolished "all national and national-religious privileges and restrictions," and similar guarantees were contained in the Russian and other Soviet republic constitutions.[55] International treaties had been signed also, guaranteeing Jewish rights in heretofore troublesome areas of Europe such as Rumania and Poland.

In retrospect, however, it is clear that American Jewish leaders put too much trust in international agreements to protect their coreligionists in Europe. Rumania's willingness to ignore her treaty obligations during the period under study ought to have cautioned American Jewish leaders in their optimism as to the results that could be expected from forcing new treaty obligations on an unwilling Rumania and on other states in which similar anti-Semitic sentiments persisted. But in their defense, American Jews had good reason to believe that the creation of an international organization, the League of Nations—in which they expected the United States, under their stimulus, would exert a strong influence in support of human rights—would make the new treaties more effective than those of the past. Ironically, the capstone on those achievements was not added because the United States Senate voted down the peace treaty and its provisions for American participation in the League of Nations on two occasions, in 1919 and 1920, while President Wilson steadfastly refused to compromise with Senate opponents on conditions under which the treaty might have passed. The failure of the United States to participate in the League of Nations is rightly viewed as a tragedy from the standpoint of the preservation of peace in the world. Certainly it must also be viewed as a tragedy from the standpoint of the human rights of Jews and other minorities in central and eastern Europe, since it denied them the support they almost certainly would have received from American participation in the League of Nations, when anti-Semitic repression intensified in the 1930s culminating in the holocaust.

In the summer of 1919, too, American Jewish leaders could not help but be aware of the growth of restrictionist sentiment in the United States under the stimulus of the war. The immigration restrictions imposed by legislation in 1921 and 1924 would virtually close to oppressed minorities the American haven which had welcomed others in their situation for centuries. It would be only with difficulty that American Jewish leaders would be able to induce the United States government to provide a haven for tragically small numbers of Jews fleeing the repression in Nazi Germany in the 1930s.

After 1914, at any rate, the earlier generation of American Jewish leaders was giving up, often reluctantly, the baton of leadership to new hands. After 1914 the American Jewish Committee began to exert an influence discrete from that represented by American Jewish leaders like Schiff and Straus who, within or outside the committee, were the most effective spokesmen for their coreligionists until World War I. Increasingly under attack for their elitism and their self-appointed role as spokesmen for American Jewry, and in opposition to the vocal Zionist movement in the United States, the earlier generation of American Jewish leaders gradually gave way to new leaders more able and willing to cooperate with the Zionists and other elements, at least in the pursuit of certain common goals. At the same time, Zionists and others became more numerous and more articulate in their own activities, diffusing the leadership of the American Jewish community. But while the success of the Jewish lobby at Paris was primarily an organizational effort, and one in which diverse American Jewish movements cooperated, the older generation of American Jewish leaders like Schiff, Straus, and Wolf continued to play a role.

The earlier generation of leaders did not survive for very long after the apparent successes of American Jewry at the Paris Peace Conference, however. Jacob Schiff died in 1920, Simon Wolf and Mayer Sulzberger in 1923, Oscar Straus in 1926, and Louis Marshall in 1929. They and their compatriots left behind a distinguished record of achievement in their efforts to free the Jews of eastern Europe and established a tradition of intervention by the United States in behalf of human rights in the world.

NOTES

1. Schiff cabled Takahashi Korekiyo but the cable is not in the Jacob H. Schiff Papers (American Jewish Archives), nor is it printed in Cyrus M. Adler, *Jacob H. Schiff: His Life and Letters*, 2 vols. (Garden City, N.Y., 1928). However, see Takahashi cable to Schiff, August 17, 1914, and Wakatsuki cable to Schiff, August 22, 1914, Schiff Papers.

2. Zosa Szajkowski, "Paul Nathan, Lucien Wolf, Jacob Schiff and the Jewish Revolutionary Movements in Eastern Europe, 1903-1917," 2 parts, *Jewish Social Studies* 29 (April 1967), 2: 79.

3. Schiff to Kohler, January 4, 1915, Max J. Kohler Papers.

4. Schiff to Wilson, January 15, 1915, Woodrow Wilson Papers, Library of Congress.

5. Schiff to Wilson, January 29, 1915, Woodrow Wilson Papers.

6. Marshall to Glynn, February 1, 1915, Louis Marshall Papers.

7. Schiff to Wilson, March 25, 1915, Schiff Papers.

8. Wilson to Schiff, April 1, 1915, Schiff Papers. See also Wilson to Wolf, April 12, 1915, Wilson Papers and Naomi Cohen, *A Duel Heritage* (Philadelphia, 1969), p. 245.

9. See Schiff to Kahn, December 22, 1914, and Schiff and Lewisohn to Kahn, December 21, 1914, Otto M. Kahn Papers.

10. Schiff to Warburg, September 22, 1915, Schiff Papers.

11. Marshall to Mortimer Schiff, March 15, 1915, Schiff Papers.

12. Wolf to Wilson, February 9, 1915, Simon Wolf Papers.

13. Adler note in Schiff Papers.

14. *New York Times*, September 29, 1915.

15. Ibid., October 2, 1915.

16. Schiff to Warburg, November 23, 1915, Schiff Papers.

17. *New York Times*, February 29, 1916.

18. Schiff to Bernstein, March 1, 1916, Schiff Papers.

19. Schiff to Hass, March 8, 1916, Schiff Papers.

20. Schiff to Marshall, June 21, 1916, Schiff Papers.

21. Schiff to Adler, June 23, 1916, Schiff Papers.

22. *New York Times*, May 28, 1916.

23. Ibid., November 25, 1916.

24. Ibid., November 30, 1916.

25. Ibid.

26. Ibid., November 26, 1916.

27. Quoted in Cohen, *A Dual Heritage*, p. 246.

28. Wolf to Kraus, January 24, 1916, Wolf Papers.

29. Adler, *Schiff*, 2: 297.

30. Quoted in Melvin Urofsky, *American Zionism from Herzl to the Holocaust* (Garden City, N.Y., 1976), p. 161.

31. Wolf to Wilson, June 11, 1917, Wilson Papers.

32. See Wilson's note, Landman to Tumulty, July 1, 1917, and Wise to Forster, July 2, 1917, all in Wilson Papers.

33. Adler, *Schiff*, 2: 304-6.

34. Cohen, *A Dual Heritage*, p. 265.

35. Adler, *Schiff*, 2: 305.

36. Ibid., 2: 255.

37. Schiff to Asch, May 8, 1917, Schiff Papers.

38. Quoted in Adler, *Schiff*, 2: 257.

39. Bernstein to Kahn, April 18, 1917, Kahn Papers; Charles R. Flint, *Memories of an Active Life* (New York and London, 1923), pp. 232-33.

40. Schiff to Rousseau, July 5, 1917, Schiff Papers.

41. Schiff to Wald, July 11, 1917, Schiff Papers.

42. Schiff to Kamenka, December 27, 1917, Schiff Papers.

43. See "The New Polish Nation and Jewish Liberty, November 11, 1918," describing a conference between Louis Marshall of the American Jewish Committee and Judge Julian W. Mack, president of the American Zionists, with Polish leaders, Straus Papers.

44. Straus to Marshall, November 14, 1918, Straus Papers. See also Cohen, *A Dual Heritage*, p. 266.

45. Kraus to Wilson, November 14, 1918, Wilson Papers.

46. Marshall to Wilson, November 16, 1918, Wilson Papers.

47. Wolf to Wilson, November 16, 1918, Wilson Papers.

48. Wilson to Marshall, November 20, 1918, Wilson Papers.

49. See, for example, *The Massacres and Other Atrocities Committed Against the Jews in Southern Russia*, pamphlet issued by the American Jewish Congress in cooperation with the Committee on Protest Against the Massacres of Jews in Ukrainia and Other Lands, New York, 1920.

50. See, for example, "Paris Mission, January to June, 1919," entries for March 25 and April 8, Straus Papers.

51. Adler note in Schiff Papers.

52. McNab to Wilson, June 12, 1919, Wilson Papers.

53. Marshall to Kohler, June 30, 1919, Kohler Papers.

54. Wolf to Wilson, July 24, 1919, Wilson Papers.

55. William Korev, "The Legal Position of Soviet Jewry: A Historical Enquiry," in *The Jews in Soviet Russia Since 1917*, ed. Lionel Kochan, 3rd edition (Oxford, 1978), pp. 90-91.

Bibliography

MANUSCRIPT COLLECTIONS

American Jewish Archives, Hebrew Union College, Cincinnati, Ohio

Rabbi Henry Cohen Papers
Louis Marshall Papers
Jacob H. Schiff Papers
Felix Warburg Papers

American Jewish Historical Society, Brandeis University, Waltham, Mass.

Cyrus M. Adler Papers
Philip H. Cowen Papers
Galveston Immigration Plan Papers
Industrial Removal Office Papers
Max J. Kohler Papers
Louis Marshall Papers
National Citizens' Committee Papers
National Committee for the Relief of Sufferers from Russian Massacres
    Papers
Simon Wolf Papers

Library of Congress, Washington, D.C.

Grover A. Cleveland Papers
Benjamin H. Harrison Papers
John Hay Papers
George Kennan Papers
Theodore Roosevelt Papers
Oscar S. Straus Papers
Woodrow Wilson Papers

Princeton University, Princeton, N.J.

Otto M. Kahn Papers

GOVERNMENT SOURCES:

U.S. Congress. *Letter From the Secretary of the Treasury Transmitting a Report of the Commissioners of Immigration Upon the Causes Which Incite Immigration to the United States.* 2 vols, 52d Cong., 1st sess., House Executive Document 235 (Washington, D.C.: Government Printing Office, 1892).

U.S. Department of State. *Diplomatic Instructions of the Department of State, 1801-1906, Russia.* National Archives Microfilm Publication M77, Washington, D.C.

——. *Despatches from United States Ministers to Russia, 1808-1906.* National Archives Micofilm Publication M35, Washington, D.C.

——. *Numerical and Minor Files of the Department of State, 1906-1910.* National Archives Microfilm Publication M862, Washington, D.C.

——. *Records of the Department of State Relating to Internal Affairs of Russia and the Soviet Union, 1910-1929.* National Archives Microfilm Publication M316, Washington, D.C.

——. *Papers Relating to the Foreign Relations of the United States.* Volumes for 1890-1914. Washington, D.C.: Government Printing Office, 1891-1922.

U.S. Department of the Treasury. Record Group 85, File 52779/29, National Archives, Washington, D.C.

PERIODICALS:

American Hebrew, 1890-1914. Klau Library, Hebrew Union College, Cincinnati, Ohio.

American Israelite, 1890-1914. Klau Library, Hebrew Union College, Cincinnati, Ohio.

Free Russia, 1890-1905. Hoover Institution on War, Revolution and Peace, Stanford University, Stanford, Calif.

New York Times. 1890-1914, New York.

BOOKS:

Adler, Cyrus M. *Jacob H. Schiff: His Life and Letters.* 2 vols. Garden City, N.Y.: Doubleday, Doran, 1928.

———. *The Voice of America on Kishinev.* Philadelphia: Jewish Publication Society, 1904.

———, and Aaron W. Margalith. *American Intercession on Behalf of the Jews in the Diplomatic Correspondence of the United States, 1840-1938.* New York: American Jewish Historical Society, 1943.

———. *With Firmness in the Right.* New York: American Jewish Committee, 1946.

Bailey, Thomas A. *America Faces Russia.* Ithaca, N.Y.: Cornell University Press, 1950.

Bentwich, Norman D. *For Zion's Sake.* Philadelphia: Jewish Publication Society, 1954.

Clymer, Kenton J. *John Hay.* Ann Arbor, Mich.: Xerox University Microfilms, 1975.

Cohen, Naomi W. *A Dual Heritage.* Philadelphia: Jewish Publication Society, 1969.

———. *Not Free to Desist.* Philadelphia: Jewish Publication Society, 1972.

———. *American Jews and the Zionist Idea.* New York, Ktav Publishing House, 1975.

Cowen, Philip H. *Memories of an American Jew.* New York: International Press, 1932.

Dennett, Tyler. *John Hay.* New York: Dodd, Mead & Co., 1934.

Dubnow, S. M. *History of the Jews in Russia and Poland.* 3 vols. Philadelphia: Jewish Publication Society, 1918.

Flint, Charles R. *Memories of an Active Life.* New York and London: G. P. Putnam's Sons, 1923.

Foster, John W. *Diplomatic Memoirs.* 2 vols. Boston and New York: Houghton-Mifflin, 1909.

Fulbright, J. William. *The Crippled Giant.* New York: Random House, 1972.

Grusd, Edward R. *B'nai B'rith: The Story of a Covenant.* New York: Appleton-Century, 1966.

Jessup, Philip C. *Elihu Root,* 2 vols. New York: Dodd, Mead & Co., 1938.

Jones, Maldwyn A. *American Immigration.* Chicago and London: University of Chicago Press, 1960.

Joseph, Samuel. *History of the Baron De Hirsch Fund.* Philadelphia: Jewish Publication Society, 1935.

——. *Jewish Immigration to the United States from 1881 to 1910.* New York: The Author, 1941.

Kraus, Adolf. *Reminiscences and Comments.* Chicago: Toby Rubovits, Inc., 1925.

Morison, Elting E., ed. *The Letters of Theodore Roosevelt.* 8 vols. Cambridge, Mass.: Harvard University Press, 1951-1954.

Reznikoff, Charles. *Louis Marshall: Champion of Liberty.* 2 vols. Philadelphia: Jewish Publication Society, 1957.

Richardson, James D., ed. *A Compilation of the Messages and Papers of the Presidents.* Vol. 13. Washington, D.C.: Bureau of National Literature and Art, 1909.

Rischin, Moses. *The Promised City: New York's Jews, 1870-1914.* New York: Corinth Books, 1964.

Rosenstock, Norton. *Louis Marshall: Defender of Jewish Rights.* Detroit: Wayne State University Press, 1965.

Schachner, Nathan. *The Price of Liberty: A History of the American Jewish Committee.* New York: American Jewish Committee, 1948.

Singer, Isidore. *Russia at the Bar of the American People.* New York and London: Funk & Wagnalls, 1904.

Straus, Oscar S. *Under Four Administrations.* Boston: Houghton Mifflin, 1922.

Szajkowski, Zosa. *Jews, Wars and Communism.* 2 vols. New York: Ktav Publishing House, 1972.

Urofsky, Melvin. *American Zionism from Herzl to the Holocaust.* Garden City, N.Y.: Anchor Press, 1976.

Wischnitzer, Mark. *To Dwell in Safety.* Philadelphia: Jewish Publication Society, 1948.

Witte, Sergei. *The Memoirs of Count Witte.* Garden City, N.Y.: Doubleday, Page & Co., 1921.

Wolf, Lucien. *Notes on the Diplomatic History of the Jewish Question.*
London: Spottiswoode, Ballentyne & Co., 1919.
Wolf, Simon. *The Presidents I Have Known.* Washington, D.C.: Adams,
1918.

ARTICLES:

Adler, Selig. "The Palestine Question in the Wilson Era." *Jewish Social
Studies* 10 (October 1948): 303-34.
Aronsfeld, C. C. "Jewish Bankers and the Tsar." *Jewish Social Studies*
35 (April 1973): 87-104.
Best, Gary Dean. "Financing a Foreign War: Jacob H. Schiff and Japan,
1904-05." *American Jewish Historical Quarterly* 61 (June 1972):
313-24.
——. "Jacob H. Schiff's Galveston Movement: An Experiment in Immi-
grant Deflection, 1907-1914." *American Jewish Archives* 30 (April
1978): 43-79.
——. "The Jewish 'Center of Gravity' and Secretary Hay's Roumanian
Notes." *American Jewish Archives* 32 (April 1980): 23-34.
Cohen, Naomi W. "The Reaction of Reform Judaism to Political Zionism
(1897-1922)." *American Jewish Historical Quarterly* 40 (1950): 361-
94.
——. "The Abrogation of the Russo-American Treaty of 1832." *Jewish
Social Studies* 35 (January 1963): 3-41.
Egan, Clifford L. "Pressure Groups, the Department of State, and the
Abrogation of the Russian-American Treaty of 1832." *American
Philosophical Society Proceedings* 115 (August 1971): 328-34.
Fein, Isaac M. "Israel Zangwill and American Jewry: A Documentary
Study." *American Jewish Historical Quarterly* 60 (September 1970):
12-36.
Glanz, Rudolf. "Jewish Social Conditions as Seen by the Muckrakers."
Yivo Annual of Jewish Social Science 9 (1954): 308-31.
Kennan, George. "How Russian Soldiers Were Enlightened in Japan."
Outlook, March 17, 1915, pp. 622-26.
Korev, William. "The Legal Position of Soviet Jewry: A Historical En-
quiry." In *The Jews in Soviet Russia Since 1917,* 3rd ed., edited by
Lionel Kochan. Oxford: Oxford University Press, 1978.
Rischin, Moses. "The Early Attitude of the American Jewish Committee
to Zionism, 1906-1922." *Publications of the American Jewish Histori-
cal Society* 49 (1959): 188-201.

Schoenberg, Ernest. "The American Reaction to the Kishinev Pogrom of 1903." *American Jewish Historical Quarterly* 61 (June 1972): 262-83.

Stults, Taylor. "Roosevelt, Russian Persecution of Jews, and American Public Opinion." *Jewish Social Studies* 30 (January 1971): 13-22.

Szajkowski, Zosa. "The Alliance Israelite Universelle in the United States, 1860-1949." *Publications of the American Jewish Historical Society* 39 (June 1950): 389-443.

——. "The Attitude of American Jews to East European Jewish Immigration (1881-1893)." *Publications of the American Jewish Historical Society* 40 (March 1951): 221-80.

——. "The European Aspect of the American-Russian Passport Question." *Publications of the American Jewish Historical Society* 41 (1951): 86-100.

——. "Jewish Diplomacy," *Jewish Social Studies* 22 (July 1960): 131-58.

——. "Paul Nathan, Lucien Wolf, Jacob H. Schiff and the Jewish Revolutionary Movements in Eastern Europe, 1903-1917," 2 pts. *Jewish Social Studies* 29 (January 1967): 3-26, and (April 1967): 75-91.

——. "The *Yahudi* and the Immigrant: A Reappraisal." *American Jewish Historical Quarterly* 63 (September 1973): 13-44.

UNPUBLISHED SOURCES:

Berman, Myron. "The Attitude of American Jewry Towards East European Jewish Immigration, 1881-1914." Ph.D. diss., Columbia University, 1963.

Goldstein, Judith. "The Politics of Ethnic Pressure: The American Jewish Committee as Lobbyist, 1906-1917." Ph.D. diss., Columbia University, 1972.

Marinbach, Bernard. "The Galveston Movement." Ph.D. diss., The Jewish Theological Seminary of America, 1977.

Neuringer, Sheldon M. "American Jewry and United States Immigration Policy, 1881-1953." Ph.D. diss., University of Wisconsin, 1969.

Yodfat, Aryeh. "The Jewish Question in American-Russian Relations (1875-1917)." Ph.D. diss., American University, 1963.

Index

About the Author

GARY DEAN BEST is Associate Professor of History at the University of Hawaii at Hilo. He is the author of *The Politics of American Individualism: Herbert Hoover in Transition* (Greenwood Press, 1975).